Ibn Taymiyyah's Essay on
Servitude

Translated by
Abu Safwan Farid Ibn Abdulwahid Ibn Haibatan

ISBN 1 898649 36 7

British Library Cataloguing in Publication Data.
A catalogue record for this book is available from the British Library.

First Edition, 1420 AH/1999 CE

Typeset by: Al-Hidaayah Publishing and Distribution

Published by: Al-Hidaayah Publishing and Distribution
                   P.O. Box 3332
                   Birmingham
                   United Kingdom
                   B10 9AW

                   Tel: 0121 753 1889
                   Fax: 0121 753 2422
                   E-Mail: ahpd@hidaayah.demon.co.uk
                   Internet: www.al-hidaayah.co.uk

Printed by: The Alden Group, Oxford, United Kingdom

Contents

Transliteration Table

Consonants

ء	'		ض	d
ب	b		ط	t
ت	t		ظ	dh
ث	th		ع	'
ج	j		غ	gh
ح	h		ف	f
خ	kh		ق	q
د	d		ك	k
ذ	dh		ل	l
ر	r		م	m
ز	z		ن	n
س	s		ه	h
ش	sh		و	w
ص	s		ي	y

Vowels

َ	a		اَ	aa
ُ	u		وُ	oo
ِ	i		يِ	ee

Translator's Introduction

All praise is for Allaah. We praise Him and seek His help and forgiveness. We seek refuge in Allaah from the evil of our own selves and the wickedness of our own deeds. Whomsoever Allaah guides, cannot be lead astray and whomsoever Allaah misguides, none can guide him.

I bear witness that none has the right to be worshipped except Allaah, alone without any partner, who proclaims in His Book:

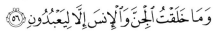

"And I have not created the *jinn* and mankind except that they should worship Me (Alone)."

Soorah adh-Dhaariyaat (51): 56

I also bear witness that Muḥammad is His slave and Messenger, who has declared: *"I was sent with the sword just before the Hour so that Allaah is worshipped, with no partner."*[1]

The discussion before you is of tremendous standing and great importance. It focuses on answering specific questions posed to the author, which deservedly, gives rise to great praise for the questioner. Since, not all questions - or the very thoughts themselves, which lead on to questions - warrant a status, as do these particular ones.

Shaykhul-Islaam Ibn Qayyim al-Jawziyyah, one of the great students of the author, writes: "The best of thoughts are those regarding

(1) The welfare of one's Hereafter.
(2) The ways of achieving such welfare.
(3) The repulsion of the evils of the Hereafter.
(4) The ways of avoiding such evils.

These are four (types of) thoughts, which are the most sublime of all thoughts. They are followed by four (other types of thoughts):

---

[1] Refer to p.93 for its *takhreej*.

5

(1) Thoughts about the welfare of one's worldly existence.
(2) The ways of acquiring such welfare.
(3) The evils of the world.
(4) The methods of protecting one's self from such evils.

It is on these eight categories that the thoughts of the sane centre."[2]
Hence, questions that lead to clarification of matters dealing with
the first category are the most important of all. One can only truly
attain happiness if he or she is able to answer three questions that
remain lodged within the bosoms of all people:

1. Who brought me here?
2. Why have I been brought here?
3. To where is my destination?

The Muslim – and all praise is for Allaah - not only possesses the
general answers to these questions, but he also has, by way of protection from Allaah, the means to acquire the detailed specifics that
spring off from these questions. These need to be comprehended
and implemented for the true attainment of happiness in this life
and success in the Hereafter.

After having understood the answer to the second question, which
is that one has been created for worship of Allaah, one's logical
thought process then generates a next question: '*What is worship?*'

It is this question and others related to it that forms the basis of this
treatise.

Points to note:

- The version of *al-'Uboodiyyah* adopted for translation is the
  one published by Daar al-Asaalah, Jordan.[3] It surpasses the other
  versions available by the greater concentration paid to it by its

---

[2] *Al-Fawaa'id*, pg. 255, fifth print 1404H, published by Daar an-Nafaa'is, Beirut.
[3] *Al-'Uboodiyyah*, slight commentary and *takhreej* by 'Alee Hasan al-Halabee al-Atharee,
first print 1412H, Daar al-'Asaalah, Jordan.

checker, Shaykh 'Alee Hasan al-Halabee, may Allaah preserve him. In his introduction, Shaykh 'Alee points out a number of examples of inaccuracies and omissions found in other existing versions.

* I have relied solely on Shaykh 'Alee's verification of the *hadeeths* and as a result, the following system has been adopted for the footnotes:
Any footnote terminated with a [t] is from the translator.
Any footnote terminated with a [s] is from the commentary given by Shaykh 'Abdul-'Azeez ar-Raajihee.[4]
Any footnote that is not terminated by one of the previous signs is that of Shaykh 'Alee Hasan, as his footnotes form the majority.

* This book does not contain a complete compilation of the commentaries given by Shaykh 'Abdul-'Azeez and Shaykh 'Alee as I have only taken a selection of them.

* Chapter headings are not from the pen of Ibn Taymiyyah but have been taken from Shaykh 'Alee's version of *al-'Uboodiyyah.*

* Translation of the Qur'aan is based on 'The Noble Qur'an' by Dr. Muhammad Taqi-ud-Din al-Hilali and Dr. Muhammad Muhsin Khan with slight modification where necessary.

* Certain Arabic words have been transliterated and their meanings can be found in the glossary.

---

[4] *Sharh al-'Uboodiyyah* of Shaykh 'Abdul-'Azeez Ibn 'Abdullaah ar-Raajihee, first print 1319H, Daar al-Fadeelah, Riyadh.

- I have included the following short biography of Shaykhul-Islaam Ibn Taymiyyah, which has been mainly benefited from a modern day biography written by D. 'Abdur-Rahmaan Ibn Saalih al-Mahmood in his thesis *Mawqif Ibn Taymiyyah min Al-Ashaa'irah*, vol. 1. I have cited his references to source books within this brief discussion on Ibn Taymiyyah for further benefit to the reader.

- May Allaah reward all those who have helped in this translation and with Him lies all success. May He make our actions sincerely for His Face and not let anyone have a share in them.

Ibn Taymiyyah (رحمه الله)

As for the author, his calibre and prestige goes without saying. He is the great scholar, Shaykhul-Islaam Ibn Taymiyyah, may Allaah have mercy upon him. Scholars of Islaam acknowledge his astonishing excellence in all fields of knowledge – and Allaah favours whom He chooses.

His name is Ahmad Ibn 'Abdul-Haleem Ibn 'Abdis-Salaam. His *kunyah* is Aboo al-'Abbaas and he is also referred to as Taqiyy ad-Deen. As for his most common appellation: *Ibn Taymiyyah*, scholars give different accounts for why he was referred to by this term. Some say that one of his ancestors performed *hajj* through the route of Taymaa and he saw a maid (there) who had came out of a tent, when he returned (to his homeland) he found that his wife had given birth to a daughter and they raised her up to him, whereupon he said: "O Taymiyyah, O Taymiyyah" i.e., she resembled the maid he had seen at Taymaa. It is also said that the mother of his grandfather Muhammad, was named Taymiyyah and thus he came to be ascribed to her.[4] He was born in Harraan, an old city within the Arabian Peninsula between Shaam[5] and Iraq, on the tenth or the twelfth of the month Rabee' al-Awwal in the year 661H. He later fled at a young age with his family to Damascus because of the terrible conditions of his homeland and those surrounding it as a result of the occupation by the Tartars.

His family was renowned for its knowledge and stature; both his father and grandfather were people of scholarly repute. Three of his brothers were also known for their knowledge and excellence: 'Abdur-Rahmaan, 'Abdullaah and his half-brother, Muhammad.

---

[4] Refer to *Al-'Uqood ad-Durriyyah min Manaaqib Shaykhul-Islaam Ahmad Ibn Taymiyyah* of Ibn 'Abdil-Haadee, pg. 2, *tahqeeq* of Muhammad Haamid al-Faqee, 1356H print, Matba'ah Hijaazee, Cairo and *Siyar 'Alaam an-Nubalaa* of adh-Dhahabee, 22/289, *tahqeeq* by a number of researchers, *takhreej* and supervision by Shu'ayb al-Arna'oot, *Mu'assasah ar-Risaalah*, Beirut.

[5] An old name that represents the areas of Syria, Jordan, Palestine and Lebanon.

1. His Early Life

Ibn Taymiyyah was brought up, cared for and nurtured by his father. He obtained knowledge from him and the other *shaykhs* of his era. He did not confine himself to the knowledge of those around him but also directed his attention to the works of the scholars before his time by way of perusal and memorisation.

The following observations can be drawn from his early life:

1. The strength of his memory and speed of his comprehension.[6]
2. His strict observance of time from an early age,[7] which later led the rest of his life to be filled with actions such as *jihaad*, teaching, commanding the good, forbidding the evil, writing books and letters and refuting opponents.
3. The scope and strength of his effect and arguments. A Jew accepted Islaam at his hands whilst he was still very young.[8]
4. He started issuing legal verdicts at the age of nineteen[9] and started teaching in *Daar al-Hadeeth as-Sukriyyah* when he was approximately 22 years of age.[10]
5. His initial sources of knowledge centred around diverse sciences like: *Tafseer*; Sciences of the Qur'aan; the *Sunnah*; the

---

[6] Refer to *al-'Uqood ad-Durriyyah*, pg. 4, and *al-Kawaakib ad-Durriyyah Fee Manaaqib al-Mujtahid Ibn Taymiyyah* by al-Karmee al-Hanbalee, pg.80, *tahqeeq* of Najm 'Abdur-Rahmaan Khalaf, 1406H print, Daar al-Gharb al-Islaamee, Beirut.

[7] Refer to *ar-Radd al-Waafir 'alaa man za'ama bi anna man sammaa Ibn Taymiyyah Shaykhul-Islaam Kaafir* by Ibn Naasir ad-Deen ad-Dimashqee, pg. 218, *tahqeeq* of Zuhayr ash-Shaaweesh, first edition, 1400H, al-Maktab al-Islaamee, Beirut, and *A'yaan al-'Asr 'an Shaykhul-Islaam Ibn Taymiyyah, Seeratuh wa Akhbaaruh 'inda al-Mu'arrikheen* by al-Munajjid, pg. 49.

[8] Refer to *al-A'laam al-'Aliyyah Fee Manaaqib Shaykhul-Islaam Ibn Taymiyyah* by al-Bazzaar, *tahqeeq* of Zuhayr Shaaweesh, 3rd edition, 1400H, al-Maktab al-Islaamee, Beirut.

[9] Sharaf ad-Deen al-Maqdasee (d. 694H) gave him permission to deliver legal verdicts. He later used to take pride in this, saying, 'I gave him the permission to give legal verdicts." See *al-Bidaayah wan-Nihaayah* by Ibn Katheer, 13/341, first edition 1966, Maktabah al-Ma'aarif, Beirut, and *al-'Uqood ad-Durriyyah*, pg. 4.

[10] Refer to *al-'Uqood ad-Durriyyah*, pg. 5; *al-Bidaayah wan-Nihaayah*, 13/303; *ar-Radd al-Waafir*, pg. 146 and *adh-Dhayl 'alaa Tabaqaat al-Hanaabilah* of Ibn Rajab, 2/388, *tahqeeq* Muhammad Haamid al-Faqee, 1972 print, Matba'ah as-Sunnah al-Muhammadiyyah, Cairo.

Six books; *Musnad Imaam Ahmad*; *Sunan ad-Daarimee*; *Mu'jam at-Tabaraanee*; Sciences of *Hadeeth* and narrators; *Fiqh* and it's *Usool*; *Usool ad-Deen* and sects; language; writing; mathematics; history and other subjects like astronomy, medicine and engineering. This is quite evident from examining the works he later authored; any topic he tackled and wrote about leaves the reader thinking that Ibn Taymiyyah was a specialist in that particular field.

2. His Teachers[11]

He took his knowledge from a great number of scholars and he himself mentioned a number of them as related by adh-Dhahabee directly from him.[12] This particular chronicle of *shaykhs* includes forty male scholars and four female scholars. The total number of scholars whom he took knowledge from exceeds two hundred.[13]

The following is a selection of some of his teachers:
* Aboo al-'Abbaas Ahmad Ibn 'Abdud-Daa'im al-Maqdasee
* Aboo Nasr 'Abdul-'Azeez Ibn 'Abdul-Mun'im
* Aboo Muhammad Ismaa'eel Ibn Ibraaheem at-Tanookhee
* al-Manjaa Ibn 'Uthmaan at-Tanookhee ad-Dimashqee
* Aboo al-'Abbaas al-Mu'ammil Ibn Muhammad al-Baalisee
* Aboo 'Abdullaah Muhammad Ibn Abee Bakr Ibn Sulaymaan al-'Aamiree
* Aboo al-Faraj 'Abdur-Rahmaan Ibn Sulaymaan al-Baghdaadee
* Sharaf ad-Deen al-Maqdasee, Ahmad Ibn Ahmad ash-Shaafi'ee

---

[11] Refer to *Majmoo' Fataawa Shaykhul-Islaam*, 18/76-121, compilation and arrangement of 'Abdur-Rahmaan Ibn Muhammad Ibn Qaasim and his son Muhammad, first print 1381H, Mataabi' ar-Riyaadh; *Dhayl Ibn Rajab* (2/387); *al-Bidaayah wan-Nihaayah* (14/136-137); *al-Waafee bee al-Wafayaat* by as-Safadee (7/16); *Tadhkirah al-Huffaadh* of adh-Dhahabee (3/1496), fourth edition 1388H, Daa'irah al-Ma'aarif al-'Uthmaaniyah, India; *ad-Durar al-Kaaminah fee 'Ayaan al-Mi'ah ath-Thaaminah* (1/154) of Ibn Hajar al-'Asqalaanee, second edition 1395H, Daa'irah al-Ma'aarif al-'Uthmaaniyah, India and others.

[12] It is recorded in *Majmoo' al-Fataawa* 18/76-121.

[13] *al-'Uqood ad-Durriyyah*, pg. 3 and *al-Kawaakib ad-Durriyyah*, pg. 52.

11

- Muhammad Ibn 'Abdul-Qawee al-Maqdasee
- Taqee ad-Deen al-Waasitee, Ibraaheem Ibn 'Alee as-Saalihee al-Hanbalee
- His paternal aunt, Sitt ad-Daar bint 'Abdus-Salaam Ibn Taymiyyah

3. The *Jihaad* and Actions of Ibn Taymiyyah

The life of Ibn Taymiyyah was distinguished with the tremendous qualities of ordering the good, forbidding the evil and performing *jihaad* for the cause of Allaah. He combined his roles of teaching, issuing legal verdicts and writing with actions of the highest magnitude. His whole life was in fact filled with *jihaad*. With a very brief examination of his life in this area we can point out at a number of incidents:

I. ORDERING THE GOOD AND FORBIDDING THE EVIL

a. His destruction of idols and places[14] that were worshipped besides Allaah and prevention of people from visiting such places:[15] This practical aspect was preceded by two stages: the first, by explaining the reality of these shrines in that many of them were fabricated and that many of the graves that were glorified and journeyed to were in fact not even those of whom they were attributed to.[16] The second, by way of intellectual discourse through direct debates, books and letters and explaining the *shirk* and innovations

---

[14] Read for example his destruction of a pillar, at *Masjid at-Taareekh* in Damascus, which people used to seek blessing from. *Nahiyaah min Shaykhul-Islaam Ibn Taymiyyah*, pg. 10-11; *al-Bidaayah wa an-Nihaayah*, 13/34; *as-Sulook lee Ma'rifah Duwal al-Mulook* of al-Miqreezee, *tahqeeq* Mustafaa Ziyaadah, second print 1957, Matba'ah Lajnah at-Ta'leef wa at-Tarjamah, Cairo and *Badaa'i az-Zuhoor fee Waqaa'i' ad-Duhoor* of Muhammad Ibn Ahmad Ibn 'Iyaas al-Hanafee, *tahqeeq* Muhammad Mustafaa, second print 1402H, al-Hay'ah al-Misriyyah al-'Aamah lee al-Kitaab, Cairo.

[15] See examples of this in *Naahiyah min Hayaat Shaykh Al-Islaam Ibn Taymiyyah* by his attendant, Ibraaheem Ibn Ahmad al-Ghayaathee, pg. 6-24, *tahqeeq* of Muhibb ad-Deen al-Khateeb, third edition 1396H, al-Matba'ah as-Salafiyyah, Cairo.

[16] Refer to *Ra's al-Husayn* of Ibn Taymiyyah recorded in *Majmoo' al-Fataawa*, Vol. 27 and also 17/500, 27/173 and 27/61 on the topic of Nooh's grave.

connected to such acts and also through presenting the opinions of opponents and refuting their arguments.

b. His stance against the Christians:
He wrote a letter to the then Christian King of Cyprus inviting him to Islaam and exposing the lies and corruption being committed by the priests and monks whilst they knew fully well that they were upon falsehood. After mentioning the devoutness of the King, his love for knowledge and good conduct towards the people, Ibn Taymiyyah then invited him to embrace Islaam and adopt the correct belief. He did this in a gentle and exemplary manner addressing his intellect, and entrusted him to behave benevolently towards the Muslims in Cyprus, not to strive to change the religion of a single one of them.[17]

He also engaged in debates with Christians, some of which he himself referred to in his book *al-Jawaab as-Saheeh*.[18]

c. He took many stances against the *Soofiyyah*. A famous one was against the *Bataa'ihiyyah*.[19] He refuted them and exposed their satanic behaviour such as entering into fire and emerging unharmed and claiming that this was an indication of their miraculous nature. He explained that even if they did this or flew in the air it would not be an evidence that could be used to declare their violations of the *Sharee'ah* to be correct.[20] He challenged them by proposing to also enter into the fire with them on the condition that they first wash

---

[17] *Risaalah al-Qubrussiyah* of Ibn Taymiyyah, within *Majmoo' al-Fataawa*, Vol. 28. This is available translated along with a number of Ibn Taymiyyah's letters: *Ibn Taymiyyah's Letters from Prison*, published by Message of Islam, U.K.

[18] *Al-Jawaab as-Saheeh lee man Baddala Deen al-Maseeh* of Ibn Taymiyyah, 2/172, printed under the supervision of 'Alee as-Subh al-Madanee, Matba'ah al-Madanee, Cairo.

[19] They are referred to as *al-Ahmadiyyah* and *ar-Rafaa'iyyah* in attribution to their founder Ahmad ar-Rafaa'ee, originally from one of the villages of al-Bataa'ih.

[20] Imaam ash-Shaafi'ee, may Allaah have mercy upon him, said: "If you see someone walking on water or flying through the air, then do not believe him until you ascertain his conformity to the *Sunnah*."

themselves with vinegar and hot water. Ultimately, they were exposed and defeated and they agreed to a complete adherence to the Book and *Sunnah*.[21]

d. In the year 699H, he and a number of his companions rose against some taverns; they broke their utensils, spilt their wine and chastised a number of them, which caused the people to come out and rejoice at this[22].[23]

e. As for his stances against the rulers, they were famous. One of the well-known ones was his stance against Qaazaan, the ruler of the Tartars. At a time when the Tartars commanded awe and authority, he spoke to the ruler with strong words concerning their actions, spread of corruption and infringement of the sanctities of the Muslims whilst they themselves claimed to be Muslims.[24] Likewise, his strong words with Sultan an-Naasir, convinced the Sultan to refrain from pursuing a course of action which was impermissible.[25]

f. Ibn Taymiyyah also had an effect in causing the rulers to assume their role of commanding the good and forbidding the evil. An example of this is when bribery became widespread and became an influencing factor in holding offices and even in abolishing capital punishment in the year 712H. An official decree was sent to Damascus, from the Sultan, citing that no one should be granted a post

---

[21] See *Majmoo' al-Fataawa*, 11/456-457, *al-'Uqood ad-Durriyyah*, pg. 194 and *al-Bidaayah wa an-Nihaayah* 14/36.

[22] *Al-Bidaayah wa an-Nihaayah*, 14/122-123.

[23] Such incidents that the Shaykh performed are of course done within the guidelines and principles pertaining to commanding the good and forbidding the evil. Ibn Taymiyyah himself discusses such guidelines in his treatise *al-Amr bi al-Ma'roof wa an-Nahy 'an al-Munkar.*

[24] *Al-Bidaayah wa an-Nihaayah*, 14/89; *al-'Alaam al-'Aliyyah*, pg.69; *al-Kawaakib ad-Durriyyah*, pg. 93 and *Dawlah Banee Qalaawoon fee Misr*, pg. 178 of Muhammad Jamaal ad-Deen Suroor, Daar al-Fikr al-'Arabee, Cairo.

[25] *Al-'Uqood ad-Durriyyah*, pg. 281; *al-Bidaayah wa an-Nihaayah*, 14/54; *al-Kawaakib ad-Durriyyah*, pg. 138 and *Husn al-Muhaadarah fee Taareekh Misr wa al-Qaahirah* of as-Suyootee, *tahqeeq* Muhammad Aboo al-Fadl Ibraaheem, first print 1967, Daar Ihyaa' al-Kutub al-'Arabiyyah.

or office through money or bribery and that the killer is to be punished by the law of the *Sharee'ah*; this decree emanated through the advice and consultation of Ibn Taymiyyah.[26]

These are some examples that demonstrate the efforts of Ibn Taymiyyah, may Allaah have mercy upon him, in ordering the good and forbidding the evil.

One also notices when reading his biography that Ibn Taymiyyah had the assistance of a number of companions in carrying out such tasks.

II.   HIS JIHAAD AGAINST THE TARTARS

Ibn Taymiyyah played a great role in establishing *jihaad* against the Tartars. He clarified the reality of their condition and showed that it was an obligation to fight them, firstly, because of the consensus of the scholars on the obligation of fighting any group that openly rejects and resists the laws of Islaam and secondly, explaining that this ruling is applicable to the Tartars because of their condition.

He elucidated the causes for victory and explained that it was not impossible or difficult to achieve victory over them if the Muslims adopted the causes that achieve victory such as judging by the *Sharee'ah,* putting an end to oppression, spreading justice and being sincere in one's intention when performing *jihaad* in Allaah's cause.

We find Ibn Taymiyyah ordering the people in the battle of *Shaqhab*, which took place in the month of *Ramadaan*, to break fast in emulation of the guidance of the Prophet (ﷺ). Again, when Ibn Taymiyyah encouraged the Sultan to perform *jihaad*, the Sultaan asked him to take position by his side to which Ibn Taymiyyah replied: "The *Sunnah* is for each man to stand behind the flag of his people and we are from Shaam so we will only stand with them."[27]

---

[26] See *al-Bidaayah wa an-Nihaayah*, 14/66.

[27] See *al-Bidaayah wa an-Nihaayah*, 14/26.

After performing *jihaad* against the Tartars and defeating them, we see Ibn Taymiyyah analysing the battles, expounding upon the beneficial lessons that can be derived from them and illustrating the areas of similarity between these battles against the Tartars and the battles of the Prophet (ﷺ).[28]

III. HIS JIHAAD AGAINST THE CHRISTIANS AND THE RAAFIDAH

The majority of references do not make mention of Ibn Taymiyyah's role in *jihaad* against the Christians before their final expulsion from Shaam. Al-Bazzaar however, does mention the following when discussing the bravery and strength of heart of Ibn Taymiyyah: "They relate that they saw of him at the conquest of 'Akkah, such a display of bravery that was beyond description. They say that he was a reason behind it's seizure by the Muslims because of his deeds, advice and sharp perception."[29]

As for the *Raafidah*, they fortified themselves in the mountains of al-Jard and al-Kasrawaaniyyeen. Ibn Taymiyyah headed for them in the year 704H with a group of his companions and requested a number of them to repent and they enjoined the laws of Islaam upon them. In the beginning of the year 705H, Ibn Taymiyyah went to battle with a brigade and the deputy Sultan of Shaam and Allaah aided them over the *Raafidah*.[30]

These are examples of the *jihaad* of Ibn Taymiyyah, may Allaah have mercy upon him, and his unification of knowledge with action.

IV. THE STATUS AND RANK OF IBN TAYMIYYAH

Shaykhul-Islaam Ibn Taymiyyah held a lofty status amongst the scholars of his time. This was for a number of reasons, such as his

---

[28] *Al-'Uqood ad-Durriyyah*, pg. 121.

[29] *Al-'Alaam al-'Aliyyah*, pg. 68.

[30] Refer to *al-'Uqood ad-Durriyyah*, pg. 179-194, *al-Bidaayah wa an-Nihaayah*, 14/35 and *as-Sulook*, 12/2. Read another incident of his *jihaad* in *Majmoo' al-Fataawa*, 11/474.

ability to clarify matters that were vague to the other scholars of his time, such as the issue of fighting the Tartars and the issue of the wealth obtained from some of the sects of the *Raafidah*;[31] Ibn Taymiyyah expounded upon these matters and clarified them to the people.

In the year 701H, a Jew came from Khaybar alleging that he had a letter from the Messenger of Allaah (ﷺ), which abrogated the *Jizyah* that the Jews had to pay to the Muslims. Ibn Taymiyyah exposed his lies and critically scrutinised and invalidated the letter from a *hadeeth* point of view and relying upon historical knowledge.[32]

Whilst Ibn Taymiyyah was in prison in Cairo, Ibn Katheer mentions: "Difficult legal questions used to be sent to him from governors and specific people, which the Jurists could not deal with, and he would respond from the Book and *Sunnah* in a way that would bewilder the minds."[33]

Another reason was his role in *jihaad*; he was not only a brave soldier but also an instructor and leader. He was sought after for advice and military strategy.

Most importantly, one of the greatest causes behind his exalted rank amidst the scholars and common folk alike was his comprehensive knowledge. When he gave a lecture; delivered a sermon; gave a legal ruling; wrote a letter or authored a book in any field, he would produce a level of knowledge that far excelled the other scholars of his time. This is why Ibn Taymiyyah became a reference point amongst the people. Whenever two people fell into dispute over a matter – and they could be from the people of knowledge and students alike as noticed from some questions - his opinion would be the deciding factor.

---

[31] *Al-Bidaayah wa an-Nihaayah*, 14/78.

[32] *Al-Bidaayah wa an-Nihaayah*, 14/19.

[33] *Al-Bidaayah wa an-Nihaayah*, 14/46.

Al-Haafidh adh-Dhahabee said: "He is far greater than the likes of me to inform on his qualities. If I were made to swear (by Allaah) by the corner (of the Ka'bah) and the place (of Ibraaheem), I would swear that I have not seen with my two eyes the like of him and by Allaah, he himself has not seen his own like in knowledge."[34]

Al-Haafidh al-Mizzee said: "I have not seen the like of him and nor has he seen the like of himself. I have not seen one more knowledgeable of the Book of Allaah and the *Sunnah* of His Messenger and more compliant to it than him."[35]

Al-Imaam Ibn Daqeeq al-'Eed said: "When I met Ibn Taymiyyah, I saw a person who had all the types of knowledge between his eyes; he would take of it what he desired and leave of it what he desired."[36]

Al-Haafidh Ibn Hajar al-'Asqalaanee, may Allaah have mercy upon him, mentioned in the context of refuting the one who opposed that Ibn Taymiyyah be termed 'Shaykhul-Islaam': "The acclaim of Taqiyy ad-Deen is more renown than that of the Sun and titling him Shaykhul-Islaam of his era remains until our time upon the virtuous tongues. It will continue tomorrow just as it was yesterday. No one refutes this but a person who is ignorant of his prestige or one who turns away from equity."[37]

---

[34] *Ar-Radd al-Waafir*, pg. 35. The edition of *Ar-Radd al-Waafir* under this section is also the first edition but its year of print is 1393H.

[35] *Ar-Radd al-Waafir*, pg. 128.

[36] *Ar-Radd al-Waafir*, pg. 59.

[37] *Ar-Radd al-Waafir*, pg. 144. This statement of Ibn Hajar, may Allaah have mercy upon him, is included towards the end of the book *Ar-Radd al-Waafir*. Ibn Hajar was one of the scholars who wrote an approval of the book *Ar-Radd al-Waafir* by Ibn Naasir ad-Deen ad-Dimashqee (d. 842), which contains scholarly praise and accounts of Ibn Taymiyyah by more than 80 scholars. It was written in refutation of the unjust, partisan, oppressive and ignorant statement *'Whoever refers to Ibn Taymiyyah as Shaykhul-Islam is a Kaafir'*!

Shaykh Kamaal ad-Deen Ibn az-Zamlakaanee, who debated with Ibn Taymiyyah on more than one occasion, said: "Whenever he was questioned on a particular field of knowledge, the one who wit nessed and heard (the answer) concluded that he had no knowledge of any other field and that no one possessed such as his knowledge. The jurists of all groups, whenever they sat with him, they would benefit from him regarding their own schools of thought in areas they previously were unaware of. It is not known that he debated anyone whereby the discussion came to a standstill or that whenever he spoke on about a particular field of knowledge - whether it be related to the sciences of the *Sharee'ah* or else - that he would not then excel the specialists of that field and those who are affiliated to it."[38]

He also said: "The prerequisites of *ijtihaad* were combined within him in the way they should be. He was very proficient in authoring very well and in excelling in expression, arrangement, classification and explanation."[39]

Al-Haafidh Ibn Katheer said "…It was rare for him to he hear something and not memorise it and he occupied himself with the sciences. He was intelligent and had committed much to memory and thus, became an Imaam in *tafseer* and what pertained to it. He had (comprehensive) knowledge of *fiqh*; it was said that he had more knowledgeable of the *fiqh* of the *madhabs* then the followers of those very same *madhabs* in his time and other times. He was fully aware of the different opinions of the scholars. He was a scholar in *Usool,* the branches of the religion, grammar, the language and other textual and intellectual sciences. He was never overcome in a sitting and no noble (scholar) would speak to him on a particular science except that he thought that this science was the speciality of Ibn Taymiyyah and he would see him as being well-versed in it and

---

[38] *Ar-Radd al-Waafir*, pg. 58.
[39] *Ar-Radd al-Waafir*, pg. 58.

having perfected it.. As for _hadeeth_ then he was the carrier of its flag, a _haafidh_ in _hadeeth_, and able to distinguish the weak from the strong, fully acquainted with the narrators and being proficient in this..."[40]

Abu Hayyaan al-Andalusee said: "By Allaah, my two eyes have never seen the like of Ibn Taymiyyah."[41]

Al-_Haafidh_ Badr ad-Deen al-'Aynee al-_Hanafee said: "He is the Imaam, the noble, the masterful, the pious, the pure, the devout, the proficient in the two sciences of _hadeeth_ and _tafseer_, _fiqh_ and the two fundamentals (i.e., the Book and _Sunnah_) with determination and precision. He is the sharp sword against the innovators, the authority, who established the matters of the religion and the great commander of the good and forbidder of evil. He possessed (noble) concern, bravery and embarked upon that which frightened and deterred. He was of much remembrance, fasting, prayer and worship."[42]

VI. THE ORDEALS AND IMPRISONMENT OF IBN TAYMIYYAH

Ibn Taymiyyah was put through many trials throughout his life and it is extremely difficult to deal with them and present them properly in this brief discussion on him so I will merely list the more famous ones.

- His ordeal because of his treatise _al-Hamawiyyah_ in the year 698H.
- His ordeal and debates because of his treatise _al-Waasitiyyah_ in the year 705H.
- His ordeal, summons to Egypt and imprisonment there in the year 705H for 18 months.
- His ordeal with the _Soofiyyah_ in Egypt after his release.

---

[40] _Al-Bidaayah wa an-Nihaayah_ of Ibn Katheer, 14/157, _tahqeeq Maktab Tahqeeq at-Turaath_, 1413H, _Daar Ihyaa at-Turaath al-Islaamee_, Beirut.
[41] _Ar-Radd al-Waafir_, pg. 63.
[42] _Ar-Radd al-Waafir_, pg. 159.

- His deportation to Alexandria in the year 709H and imprisonment there for 8 months.
- His ordeal because of specific verdicts related to divorce and resultant imprisonment in the year 720H, for five months.
- His ordeal because of his legal verdict banning the undertaking of journeys specifically to visit graves and resultant imprisonment in the year 726H until he passed away, may Allaah have mercy upon him, in the year 728H.

Ibn Taymiyyah's response to these ordeals was always a positive one which turned these trials and tribulations – by the favour of Allaah - into great opportunities for increasing *eemaan* and reacting positively in knowledge and action. His summons to Egypt, for example, led him to debate and thoroughly deal with the innovators who had spread their beliefs throughout the region. His role in prison was another manifestation of this blessing, such as his efforts in educating the prisoners and nurturing them to the extent that the dissemination of knowledge and religion within the prison excelled certain institutions outside the prison. This happened in both Egypt and Alexandria. His decision to remain in Egypt after being released, was as he mentioned in a letter[43] to his mother, because of matters necessary to religion and the world. This brought about much goodness in aiding the *Sunnah* and suppressing innovations. One of the greatest positive results was the books and papers he wrote and authored within prison. He also pardoned those who oppressed him, even when Ibn Taymiyyah had the opportunity to exact revenge. One of his opponents, Ibn al-Makhloof, the Maalikee Judge said: "We did not see the likes of Ibn Taymiyyah; we incited against him but were not able to overpower him, when he was able to overpower us, he instead pardoned us and pleaded on our behalf."[44]

Another positive outcome was that these ordeals in themselves were a reason for the widespread circulation of Ibn Taymiyyah's works.[45]

[43] Read the English translation of this heart-stirring letter in *Ibn Taymiyyah's letters from Prison*. [t]
[44] *Al-Bidaayah wa an-Nihaayah*, 14/54.
[45] *Al-'Uqood ad-Durriyyah*, pg. 283.

He had many students and those that were affected by him are countless, some of his students were:

- Ibn Qayyim al-Jawziyyah, Muhammad Ibn Abee Bakr, (d. 751H).
- adh-Dhahabee, Muhammad Ibn Ahmad, (d.748H).
- al-Mizzee, Yoosuf Ibn 'Abdur-Rahmaan, (d. 742H).
- Ibn Katheer, Ismaa'eel Ibn 'Umar, (d. 774).
- Ibn 'Abdil-Haadee, Muhammad Ibn Ahmad, (d. 744H).
- al-Bazzaar, 'Umar Ibn 'Alee, (d. 749).
- Ibn Qaadee al-Jabal, Ahmad Ibn Hasan, (d. 771H).
- Ibn Fadlillaah al-'Amree, Ahmad Ibn Yahyaa, (d. 749H).
- Muhammad Ibn al-Manjaa Ibn 'Uthmaan at-Tanookhee, (d. 724).
- Yoosuf Ibn 'Abdul-Mahmood Ibn 'Abdis-Salaam al-Battee, (d. 728).

VIII. His Works

The existing works of Ibn Taymiyyah are great in number, despite the fact that a proportion of his works have perished.

He was a very quick writer. His brother 'Abdullaah said: "Allaah blessed him with the ability to write quickly and he used to write from memory without copying."[47] Ibn Taymiyyah had a scribe who used to make copies of his work because of the fact that he used to write so fast. There was a person known as 'Abdullaah ibn Rasheeq al-Maghrabee who used to write the works of the Shaykh; Ibn Katheer says of him: "He could make out the handwriting of the Shaykh better than the Shaykh himself."[48] He used to take a lot of time out to review his works as he did when he came out of prison

---

[46] See for example *ar-Radd al-Waafir* and *ash-Shahaadah az-Zakkiyyah fee Thanaa' al-'A'immah 'alaa Ibn Taymiyyah* of al-Karmee al-Hanbalee, *tahqeeq* of Najm 'Abdur-Rahmaan Khalaf, first print 1404H, Mu'assisah ar-Risaalah, Beirut.

[47] *Al-'Uqood ad-Durriyyah*, pg. 64.

[48] *Al-Bidaayah wa an-Nihaayah*, 14/229.

–because of the issue of divorce - in the year 721H.[49] After his return to Shaam in the year 712H, he dedicated a lot of time to authoring
lengthy works.[50] He would pay great attention to the writings that
used to be attributed to him;[51] it seems that the constant fabrication
about him by his enemies and the twisting of his words was a reason for this.

He would not delay in answering questions that came to him and he
authored and wrote from his memory while in prison.[52]

Some of his works are:
- *Minhaaj as-Sunnah an-Nabawiyyah*
- *Dar Ta'aarud al-'Aql wa an-Naql*
- *al-Istiqaamah*
- *Iqtidaa' as-Siraat al-Mustaqeem Li Mukhaalafah As-haab al-Jaheem*
- *Naqd Maraatib al-Ijmaa'*
- *as-Saarim al-Maslool 'alaa Shaatim ar-Rasool*
- *al-Jawaab as-Saheeh li man baddala Deen al-Maseeh*
- *ar-Radd 'alaa al-Mantiqiyyeen*
- *ar-Radd 'alaa al-'Akhnaa'ee*
- *Naqd at-Ta'sees*
- *an-Nuboowaat*

There are so many other works that have been included in *Majmoo'
al-Fataawa*, which is a compilation of his writings and verdicts put
together by Ibn Qaasim and his son. These include:
- *Qaa'idah fee Tawheed al-Uloohiyyah*
- *al-Waasitah bayna al-Haqq wa al-Khalq*
- *Qaa'idah Jaleelah fee at-Tawassul wa al-Waseelah*

---

[49] *Al-'Uqood ad-Durriyyah*, pg. 327.
[50] *Al-Bidaayah wa an-Nihaayah*, 14/67.
[51] See *Majmoo' al-Fataawa*, 27/315.
[52] *Al-'Alaam al-'Aliyyah*, pg. 22, *al-Kawaakib ad-Durriyyah*, pg. 81 and *ad-Durar al-Kaaminah*, 1/163.

- *ar-Radd al-Aqwam 'alaa maa fee Fusoos al-Hikam*
- *ar-Risaalah at-Tadmuriyyah*
- *al-'Aqeedah al-Waasitiyyah*
- *al-Wasiyyah al-Kubraa*
- *al-Hamawiyyah al-Kubraa*
- *Sharh Hadeeth an-Nuzool*
- *Kitaab al-Eemaan*
- *Amraad al-Quloob wa Shifaa' uhaa*
- *al-'Uboodiyyah*[53]
- *al-Wasiyyah as-Sughraa*
- *al-Furqaan bayna Awliyaa' ar-Rahmaan wa Awliyaa' ash-Shaytaan.*
- *al-Furqaan bayna al-Haqq wa al-Baatil*
- *Muqaddimah fee Usool at-Tafseer*
- *Tafseer Soorah al-Ikhlaas*
- *Raf' al-Malaam 'an al-A'immah al-A'laam*
- *al-Hisbah*
- *al-Amr bi al-Ma'roof wa an-Nahy 'an al-Munkar*
- *as-Siyaasah ash-Shar'iyyah*
- *al-Madhaalim al-Mushtarakah.*

IX. A DISCUSSION ON HIS PERSONAL STATE AND WORSHIP OF HIS LORD

It is appropriate here to discuss this aspect of Ibn Taymiyyah's life, mainly to exhibit that the discussion he presents in this book does not emanate from one who is void of enacting such descriptions found within this discourse and that it does not merely derive from his academic knowledge and excellence.

In fact, one who reads his biography will realise that Ibn Taymiyyah had a great attachment to his Lord which manifested in his worship and strong reliance on Him, this is how we deem him to be and we do not put anyone's commendation in front of Allaah's.

---

[53] The translation of which, is the book before you. It is located in volume 10, pages 149-236 of *Majmoo' al-Fataawa*.

Those who wrote his biography discussed the worship, asceticism, piety, selflessness, humility and generosity he was famous for.[54]

Ibn al-Qayyim says of Ibn Taymiyyah's remembrance of his Lord: "I heard Shaykhul-Islaam Ibn Taymiyyah, may Allaah (ﷻ) sanctify his soul, say, 'Remembrance to the heart is like water to fish. What will be the state of the fish if it becomes separated from water?...I once attended *fajr* prayer with Shaykhul-Islaam Ibn Taymiyyah, he then sat and remembered Allaah (ﷻ) until it was nearly midday. He then turned round to me and said, 'This is my early morning meal, If I do not take this breakfast, my strength will drop'."[55]

A great manifestation of his worship was in his genuine reliance upon his Lord and his belief in the decree of Allaah. At times when he was subjected to the severest forms of treatment, he had the greatest reliance upon his Lord. When the news of his expulsion to Alexandria came to him and it was said to him: "They are plotting to kill you, expel or imprison you." He replied: "If they kill me it will be a *shahaadah* for me. If they expel me, it will be a *hijrah* for me; if they expel me to Cyprus, I will call its people to Allaah so that they answer me. If they imprison me, it will be a place of worship for me."[56]

Ibn al-Qayyim also says: "He used to say frequently in prostration when imprisoned, 'O Allaah, assist me to remember you, to be grateful to you and to worship you properly.' and he said to me once, 'The one who is (truly) imprisoned is the one whose heart is imprisoned from Allaah and the captivated one is the one whose desires have enslaved him.'"[57]

---

[54] See *al-A'laam al-'Aliyyah*, pg. 36-41, 42, 48 & 63 and *al-Kawaakib ad-Durriyyah*, pg. 83-88.

[55] *Al-Waabil as-Sayyib* of Ibn al-Qayyim, pg. 60, Daar al-Bayaan.

[56] *Naahiyah min Hayaah Shaykhul-Islaam*, pg. 30.

[57] *Al-Waabil as-Sayyib*, pg. 61.

When he was ultimately banned from having any books, papers and pens during the latter stage of his final imprisonment, Ibn Taymiyyah devoted all of his time to worship and reciting the Qur'aan. He remained in this state for a short period until he passed away on the twentieth of Dhu al-Qa'dah of the year 728H. He fell sick for the few days that led to his death.

This came as a great shock to the people and they turned out in enormous numbers.

Historians regard this as one of those rare funerals and they compare it to the funeral of Imaam Ahmad Ibn Hanbal, may Allaah have mercy upon him.

Ibn Taymiyyah died at a time when he was imprisoned, with resentment from the Sultaan and when many of the jurists and *Soofiyyah* were mentioning many things about him. However, despite that, his funeral was one that was witnessed by many and was famous.

Al-Bazzaar says: "Once the people had heard of his death, not a single person in Damascus who was able to attend the prayer and wanted to, remained until he appeared and took time out for it. As a result, the markets in Damascus were closed and all transactions of livelihood were stopped. Governors, heads, scholars, jurists came out. They say that none of the majority of the people failed to turn up, according to my knowledge - except three individuals; they were well known for their enmity for Ibn Taymiyyah and thus, hid away from the people out of fear for their lives."[58]

Ibn Katheer mentions that the deputy Sultaan was absent and the State was perplexed as to what it should do. Then the deputy of the prison came to give his condolences and sat by Ibn Taymiyyah. He

---

[58] *Al-A'laam al-'Aliyyah*, pg. 82-83.

opened the entrance for those of his close companions and beloved people to enter upon him. They sat by him, cried and praised him.[59] "Then they started to wash the Shaykh... they only let those who helped in the washing to remain by him. Amongst them was our Shaykh al-Haafidh al-Mizzee and a group of the senior righteous and good people; people of knowledge and *eemaan*... then they proceeded with him to the *Jaami' al-Umawee*. There was so many people in front of his *janaazah*, behind it, to it's right and to it's left. None but Allaah could enumerate them, then one shouted out 'This is how the *janaazahs* of the *Imaams* of the *Sunnah* are to be!" At that, the people, started to cry... when the *adhaan* of *dhuhr* was given they prayed after it straight away against the usual norm. Once they finished prayer, the deputy *khateeb* came out – as the main *khateeb* was absent and in Egypt - and he led the prayer over Ibn Taymiyyah... Then the people poured out from everywhere and all the doors of the *Jaam'i*... and they assembled at al-Khayl market."[60]

On open land, his *janaazah* was placed down and his brother, 'Abdur-Rahmaan, led prayer over him. Then his *janaazah* was taken to his grave and he was buried in the *Soofiyyah* graveyard by the side of his brother, 'Abdullaah, may Allaah have mercy upon them all.

People then arrived praying over him at his grave, those who had not yet managed to pray previously. Whenever news of his death reached a region, the people would gather in the main mosques and pray over him, especially in Shaam, Egypt, Iraq, Tibreez and Basra.[61]

May Allaah reward Shaykhul-Islaam Ibn Taymiyyah with goodness and grant him *al-Firdaws al-A'laa* and may He cause those after him to benefit from his knowledge.

---

[59] *Al-Bidaayah wa an-Nihaayah*, 14/138.
[60] *Al-Bidaayah wa an-Nihaayah*, 14/138.
[61] Refer to *al-'Alaam al-'Aliyyah*, pg. 85.

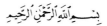

Ibn Taymiyyah's Essay on Servitude

All praise is for Allaah. We praise Him and seek His help and forgiveness. We seek refuge in Allaah from the evil of our selves and the wickedness of our own deeds. Whomsoever Allaah guides, cannot be lead astray and whomsoever Allaah misguides, none can guide him. I bear witness that none has the right to be worshipped except Allaah, alone without any partner and I bear witness that Muhammad is His slave and Messenger.

Shaykhul-Islaam, the famous of the famous, protector of the *Sunnah* and suppresser of innovation, Ahmad ibn 'Abdul-Haleem ibn Taymiyyah, may Allaah have mercy upon him, was questioned on the saying of Allaah (ﷻ):

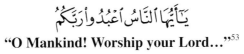

"O Mankind! Worship your Lord..."[53]

What is 'Ibaadah (worship)?
What are its branches?
Is the whole of the Deen embodied within it?
What is the reality of 'uboodiyyah (servitude)?
Is it the highest (attainable) station in this world and in the Hereafter, or are there other stations above it?

Please elaborate for us on all of this.

Thus, Ibn Taymiyyah, may Allaah have mercy upon him, replied:

---

[53] Soorah al-Baqarah (2): 21.

Introduction

'*Ibaadah* is a comprehensive term that encompasses everything that Allaah loves and is pleased with, of both statements and actions, (both) the apparent and hidden.[54]

Hence, prayer; *zakaah*; fasting; *hajj*; being truthful in speech; fulfilling one's trust; kindness towards parents; maintaining relations with kin; fulfilling pledges; commanding the good; forbidding the evil; *jihaad* against the disbelievers and the hypocrites; being beneficent towards the neighbour, the orphan, the poor person, the traveller and the owned human or animal; supplication; remembrance (of Allaah); recitation (of the Qur'aan) and the like of such, are all types of worship.

Likewise is the case with love of Allaah and His Messenger; reverence of Allaah; turning to Allaah in repentance; sincerity of *Deen* for Him; patience with His judgement; gratitude for His favours; contentment with His decree; *tawakkul* upon Him; hope for His Mercy; fear of His Punishment and the like of such, all are forms of worship of Allaah.

This is so because worship of Allaah is the end objective that is beloved to Him and it is what pleases Him. It is the purpose for which He created the creation, as Allaah (ﷻ) has said:

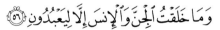

"And I have not created the *jinn* and mankind except that they should worship Me (Alone)."[55]

---

[54] Al-Miqreezee states in *Tajreed at-Tawheed al-Mufeed*, pg. 82 with my checking: "And know that '*ibaadah* (worship) is four principles, they are: ascertainment of what Allaah and His Messenger love and are pleased with, and the enactment of that in the heart, upon the tongue and limbs. Thus, '*uboodiyyah* is a term that embodies these four levels and the people of worship in truth are the people of these (four principles)."

[55] Soorah adh-Dhaariyaat (51):56.

He sent all the Messengers with this worship, as when Noo<u>h</u> said to his people:

$$\text{اعْبُدُوا اللَّهَ مَا لَكُم مِّنْ إِلَٰهٍ غَيْرُهُ}$$

"Worship Allaah, you have no other deity but Him."[56]

Likewise, Hood, <u>S</u>aali<u>h</u>, Shu'ayb and others, said the same to their people.[57] Allaah (ﷻ) says:

$$\text{وَلَقَدْ بَعَثْنَا فِي كُلِّ أُمَّةٍ رَّسُولًا أَنِ اعْبُدُوا اللَّهَ}$$
$$\text{وَاجْتَنِبُوا الطَّاغُوتَ ۖ فَمِنْهُم مَّنْ هَدَى اللَّهُ وَمِنْهُم مَّنْ}$$
$$\text{حَقَّتْ عَلَيْهِ الضَّلَالَةُ}$$

"And verily We have sent amongst every nation a messenger (saying), 'Worship Allaah (Alone) and avoid all false deities'. Then of them were some whom Allaah guided and of them were some upon whom the straying was justified."[58]

Allaah (ﷻ) says:

$$\text{وَمَا أَرْسَلْنَا مِن قَبْلِكَ مِن رَّسُولٍ إِلَّا نُوحِي إِلَيْهِ أَنَّهُ لَا إِلَٰهَ}$$
$$\text{إِلَّا أَنَا فَاعْبُدُونِ ﴿٢٥﴾}$$

"And We did not send any messenger before you (O Mu<u>h</u>ammad) but We revealed unto him that none has the right to be worshipped but I (Allaah), so worship Me (Alone)."[59]

---

[56] Soorah al-A'raaf (7):59.
[57] As in Soorah al-A'raaf (7):50-84.
[58] Soorah an-Na<u>h</u>l (16):36.
[59] Soorah al-Anbiyaa (21):25.

Allaah (ﷻ) says:

$$\text{إِنَّ هَـٰذِهِۦٓ أُمَّتُكُمۡ أُمَّةً وَٰحِدَةً وَأَنَا۠ رَبُّكُمۡ فَٱعۡبُدُونِ ﴿٩٢﴾}$$

"Verily, this *ummah* of yours is one *ummah* and I am your Lord, therefore worship Me (Alone)."[60]

Allaah also says in another *aayah*:

$$\text{يَـٰٓأَيُّهَا ٱلرُّسُلُ كُلُوا۟ مِنَ ٱلطَّيِّبَـٰتِ وَٱعۡمَلُوا۟ صَـٰلِحًا إِنِّي بِمَا تَعۡمَلُونَ عَلِيمٌ ﴿٥١﴾ وَإِنَّ هَـٰذِهِۦٓ أُمَّتُكُمۡ أُمَّةً وَٰحِدَةً وَأَنَا۠ رَبُّكُمۡ فَٱتَّقُونِ ﴿٥٢﴾}$$

"O Messengers! Eat of the good things and perform righteous deeds; verily I am well acquainted with all that you do. And verily, this *ummah* of yours is one *ummah* and I am your Lord, therefore have *taqwaa* of Me."[61]

Allaah made this (worship) binding upon His Messenger until death, as He (ﷻ) says:

$$\text{وَٱعۡبُدۡ رَبَّكَ حَتَّىٰ يَأۡتِيَكَ ٱلۡيَقِينُ ﴿٩٩﴾}$$

"And worship your Lord (O Mu<u>h</u>ammad) until there comes unto you the *yaqeen* (i.e., the hour that is certain: death)."[62]

With this (depiction of worship), He describes His Angels and Prophets; He (ﷻ) said:

---

[60] Soorah al-Anbiyaa (21):92.

[61] Soorah Al Mu'minoon (23):51-52.

[62] Soorah al-<u>H</u>ijr (15):99.

وَلَهُۥ مَن فِى ٱلسَّمَٰوَٰتِ وَٱلْأَرْضِ وَمَنْ عِندَهُۥ لَا يَسْتَكْبِرُونَ عَنْ عِبَادَتِهِۦ وَلَا يَسْتَحْسِرُونَ ﴿١٩﴾ يُسَبِّحُونَ ٱلَّيْلَ وَٱلنَّهَارَ لَا يَفْتُرُونَ ﴿٢٠﴾

"To Him belongs whoever is in the heavens and the earth. And those who are with Him (i.e., the Angels) do not disdain to worship Him and they never become weary. They exalt Him night and day, never slackening."[63]

Allaah (ﷻ) says:

إِنَّ ٱلَّذِينَ عِندَ رَبِّكَ لَا يَسْتَكْبِرُونَ عَنْ عِبَادَتِهِۦ وَيُسَبِّحُونَهُۥ وَلَهُۥ يَسْجُدُونَ ﴿٢٠٦﴾

"Surely those who are with your Lord do not disdain to worship Him. They exalt Him and prostrate before Him."[64]

Allaah censured those who are too haughty and proud to worship Him in His (ﷻ) saying:

وَقَالَ رَبُّكُمُ ٱدْعُونِىٓ أَسْتَجِبْ لَكُمْ إِنَّ ٱلَّذِينَ يَسْتَكْبِرُونَ عَنْ عِبَادَتِى سَيَدْخُلُونَ جَهَنَّمَ دَاخِرِينَ

"And your Lord said, 'Invoke Me, I will respond to your (invocation)'. Verily, those who scorn My worship, will enter Hell in humiliation!"[65]

---

[63] Soorah al-Anbiyaa (21):19-20.

[64] Soorah al-A'raaf (7):206.

[65] Soorah al-Ghaafir (40):60.

He also described the finest of His creatures[66] with servitude to Him; Allaah (ﷻ) said:

$$عَيْنًا يَشْرَبُ بِهَا عِبَادُ ٱللَّهِ يُفَجِّرُونَهَا تَفْجِيرًا ٦$$

"A fountain where the *'Ibaad* (i.e., worshippers) of Allaah will drink, making it gush forth in abundance."[67]

He (ﷻ) also said:

$$وَعِبَادُ ٱلرَّحْمَٰنِ ٱلَّذِينَ يَمْشُونَ عَلَى ٱلْأَرْضِ هَوْنًا وَإِذَا خَاطَبَهُمُ ٱلْجَٰهِلُونَ قَالُوا سَلَٰمًا ٦٣$$

"And the *'Ibaad* of ar-Rahmaan are those who walk upon the earth in humility, and when the foolish address them, they reply with words of gentleness."[68]

Furthermore, when *Shaytaan* said:

$$رَبِّ بِمَا أَغْوَيْتَنِي لَأُزَيِّنَنَّ لَهُمْ فِي ٱلْأَرْضِ وَلَأُغْوِيَنَّهُمْ أَجْمَعِينَ ٣٩ إِلَّا عِبَادَكَ مِنْهُمُ ٱلْمُخْلَصِينَ ٤٠$$

"O my Lord! Because You misled me I shall indeed adorn (the path of error) for them (i.e., mankind) on earth and I shall mislead them all; save Your chosen, guided *'Ibaad* amongst them."[69]

Allaah (ﷻ) replied:

$$إِنَّ عِبَادِي لَيْسَ لَكَ عَلَيْهِمْ سُلْطَٰنٌ إِلَّا مَنِ ٱتَّبَعَكَ مِنَ ٱلْغَاوِينَ ٤٢$$

"Certainly, you have no authority over My *'Ibaad*, except those who follow you of the errant."[70]

---

[66] They are the righteous ones, who establish His command.

[67] Soorah al-Insaan (76):6.

[68] Soorah al-Furqaan (25):63.

[69] Soorah al-Hijr (15):39-40.

[70] Soorah al-Hijr (15):42.

Furthermore, Allaah (ﷻ) said in connection to describing the Angels with this (servitude):

وَقَالُوا۟ ٱتَّخَذَ ٱلرَّحْمَـٰنُ وَلَدًا سُبْحَـٰنَهُۥ

بَلْ عِبَادٌ مُّكْرَمُونَ ﴿٢٦﴾ لَا يَسْبِقُونَهُۥ بِٱلْقَوْلِ وَهُم

بِأَمْرِهِۦ يَعْمَلُونَ ﴿٢٧﴾ يَعْلَمُ مَا بَيْنَ أَيْدِيهِمْ وَمَا خَلْفَهُمْ

وَلَا يَشْفَعُونَ إِلَّا لِمَنِ ٱرْتَضَىٰ وَهُم مِّنْ خَشْيَتِهِۦ مُشْفِقُونَ

**"And they say, 'ar-Rahmaan has begotten children.'
How perfect He is! They are but honoured 'Ibaad.
They do not speak until He has spoken and they act
by His Command. He knows what is before them
and what is behind them. They cannot intercede
except for one whom He (Himself) is pleased with,
and they stand in awe for fear of Him."[71]**

Allaah (ﷻ) also says:

وَقَالُوا۟ ٱتَّخَذَ ٱلرَّحْمَـٰنُ وَلَدًا ﴿٨٨﴾ لَّقَدْ

جِئْتُمْ شَيْـًٔا إِدًّا ﴿٨٩﴾ تَكَادُ ٱلسَّمَـٰوَٰتُ يَتَفَطَّرْنَ مِنْهُ

وَتَنشَقُّ ٱلْأَرْضُ وَتَخِرُّ ٱلْجِبَالُ هَدًّا ﴿٩٠﴾ أَن دَعَوْا۟ لِلرَّحْمَـٰنِ وَلَدًا

﴿٩١﴾ وَمَا يَنۢبَغِى لِلرَّحْمَـٰنِ أَن يَتَّخِذَ وَلَدًا ﴿٩٢﴾ إِن كُلُّ مَن فِى

ٱلسَّمَـٰوَٰتِ وَٱلْأَرْضِ إِلَّا ءَاتِى ٱلرَّحْمَـٰنِ عَبْدًا ﴿٩٣﴾ لَّقَدْ أَحْصَىٰهُمْ

وَعَدَّهُمْ عَدًّا ﴿٩٤﴾ وَكُلُّهُمْ ءَاتِيهِ يَوْمَ ٱلْقِيَـٰمَةِ فَرْدًا ﴿٩٥﴾

**"And they say, 'ar-Rahmaan has begotten children.'
Indeed, you have brought forth a terrible evil thing.
The heavens are about to rip apart, the earth to split
asunder and the mountains to fall in ruins; in that,
they ascribed children to ar-Rahmaan. It is not be-**

---

[71] Soorah al-Anbiyaa (21):26-28.

fitting (the Majesty) of ar-Rahmaan that He should beget children. There is none in the heavens and the earth but comes unto ar-Rahmaan as an 'abd. Verily He knows their number and has enumerated them most definitely and precisely. Every one of them will come to Him on the Day of Resurrection, alone."[72]

Allaah (ﷻ) says regarding al-Maseeh (i.e., Prophet 'Eesaa (عليه السلام)) to whom divinity[73] and son-ship (to Allaah) were alleged:

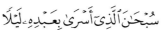

إِنْ هُوَ إِلَّا عَبْدٌ أَنْعَمْنَا عَلَيْهِ وَجَعَلْنَاهُ مَثَلًا لِّبَنِي إِسْرَءِيلَ

"He (i.e., 'Eesaa) was no more than an 'abd. We favoured him and made him an example for the Children of Israa'eel."[74]

This is why the Prophet (ﷺ) said as in the authentic *hadeeth:*[75] "*Do not praise me as the Christians have praised 'Eesaa, son of Maryam; for I am only an 'abd, so say, ' 'abdullaah (i.e., the 'abd of Allaah) and his Messenger.'*"

Furthermore, Allaah described the Messenger with *'uboodiyyah* in his most perfect states. He (ﷺ) said in reference to *al-Israa* (i.e., the Night Journey):

سُبْحَانَ ٱلَّذِي أَسْرَىٰ بِعَبْدِهِ لَيْلًا

"Exalted is He (i.e., Allaah), Who took His 'abd (i.e., Muhammad (ﷺ)) for a journey by night..."[76]

---

[72] Soorah Maryam (19):88-95.

[73] As alleged by the Christians, who distorted 'Eesaa's book and wreaked havoc upon their beliefs. I have elaborated on this general summation in my book *Diraasah wa Tahleel Li Usool an-Nasraaniyyah wa al-Anaajeel*; may Allaah facilitate its completion.

[74] Soorah az-Zukhruf (43):59.

[75] Related by al-Bukhaaree (3445); ad-Daarimee (2/320); Ahmad (1/23, 24 & 55); at-Tayaalisee (2424); al-Baghawee in both *Sharh as-Sunnah* (13/246) and *al-Anwaar* (420); at-Tirmidhee in *ash-Shamaa'il* (284); Ma'mar in his *Jaami'* (20524); al-Humaydee (1/16/27) and al-Bayhaqee in *Dalaa'il an-Nuboowwah* (5/498) from 'Umar Ibn al-Khattaab.

[76] Soorah al-Israa' (17):1.

He (ﷺ) said in reference to (receiving) revelation:

فَأَوْحَىٰٓ إِلَىٰ عَبْدِهِۦ مَآ أَوْحَىٰ ﴿١٠﴾

"So did Allaah reveal to His *'abd* what he revealed (through the Angel Jibraa'eel)."[77]

In reference to (the station of) *Da'wah*, He (ﷺ) said:

وَأَنَّهُۥ لَمَّا قَامَ عَبْدُ ٱللَّهِ يَدْعُوهُ كَادُواْ يَكُونُونَ عَلَيْهِ لِبَدًا ﴿١٩﴾

"And when *'abdullaah* (i.e., the *'abd* of Allaah, Muhammad (ﷺ)) stood up, calling unto Him (i.e., Allaah) they gathered against him and almost suppressed him."[78]

Allaah (ﷺ) said in reference to the challenge (of producing anything like the Qur'aan):

وَإِن كُنتُمْ فِى رَيْبٍ مِّمَّا نَزَّلْنَا عَلَىٰ عَبْدِنَا
فَأْتُواْ بِسُورَةٍ مِّن مِّثْلِهِۦ

"And if you are in doubt concerning that which We have sent down to Our *'abd* (i.e., Muhammad (ﷺ)) then produce a *Soorah* of its like."[79]

Hence, the *Deen* in its entirety is embodied within *'Ibaadah*.[80]

It has been established in the <u>Saheeh</u>[81] that when Jibreel (عليه السلام) came to the Prophet (ﷺ) in the appearance of a Bedouin and questioned

---

[77] Soorah an-Najm (53):10.

[78] Soorah al-Jinn (72):19.

[79] Soorah al-Baqarah (2):23.

[80] This is a very important statement and it is the answer to one of the questions directed to the author. [s]

[81] *Saheeh Muslim* (No. 8). Also related by an-Nasaa'ee (8/97); at-Tirmidhee (2738); Aboo Daawood (4695); Ibn Maajah (64) and Ahmad (1/27, 28, 52 & 53) from 'Umar. It has been related by al-Bukhaaree (1/106); Muslim (9 & 10); Ibn Maajah (64) and Ahmad (2/426) from Aboo Hurayrah. It has been related by Ahmad (1/319) from Ibn 'Abbaas. It has been related by an-Nasaa'ee (8/101) and Aboo Daawood (4698) from Aboo Dharr and Aboo Hurayrah.

him about Islaam, he answered: *"Islaam is that you testify that none has the right to be worshipped except Allaah and that Mu<u>h</u>ammad is the Messenger of Allaah; that you establish prayer; give zakaah; fast (the month of) Rama<u>d</u>aan and you perform the pilgrimage to the House, if you are able to do so."*

Jibreel (then) asked: *"And what is eemaan?"* He replied: *"That you have eemaan in Allaah, His Angels, His Books, His Messengers, in the Resurrection after death and that you have eemaan in al-Qadar, it's good and bad."*

Jibreel (then) questioned: *"And what is I<u>h</u>saan?"* He answered: *"That you worship Allaah as if you can see Him, and if you are not able to see Him, then He indeed sees you."*

The Prophet stated at the end of the <u>h</u>adeeth: *"That was Jibreel; he came to teach you your Deen."* Thus, he made all of this part of the *Deen.*

(The term) *ad-Deen* embodies the meanings of lowliness, submission and humility. It is said, '*dintuhu*[82] *fadaana*' i.e., '*I subdued him so he humbled*'. It is also said, '*yadeenu Allaaha*' or '*yadeenu lillaahi*' i.e., '*he worships Allaah, obeys Him and submits to Him*'. Thus '*Deen of Allaah*' is worship, obedience and submission to Him.

As for '*Ibaadah*, its original meaning also denotes lowliness and submission. One says, 'a pathway that is *mu'abbad*' i.e., it has become smoothed out because of being treaded upon.

However, the '*Ibaadah* that has been enjoined (upon us) encompasses the meaning of submission along with the meaning of love. It embodies the utmost degree of submission to Allaah (ﷻ) through the utmost degree of love of Him.

---

[82] *Al-Qaamoos al-Mu<u>h</u>eet* (1546), *Mukhtaar a<u>s</u>-<u>S</u>i<u>h</u>aa<u>h</u>* (217) and *al-Mi<u>s</u>baa<u>h</u> al-Muneer* (205).

37

The final level of love[83] is *at-Tatayyum* (i.e., enslavement, infatuation, captivation and adoration). Its initial level is *al-'Alaaqah* (i.e., connection) because of the hearts connection to the beloved. Thereafter, comes the level of *as-Sabaabah* (i.e., craving, longing and desire) as the heart starts to crave for the beloved. Next is the level of *al-Gharaam* (i.e., love, passion and fondness), which is the love that is inseparable from the heart. Thereafter, *al-'Ishq*[84] (i.e., ardent and passionate love) and its final level is *at-Tatayyum*. One says, '*taym* of Allaah' i.e., the '*abd* of Allaah. Thus, the *mutayyam* is the *mu'abbad* of his beloved.

One who submits to a person whilst possessing hatred for him is not an '*aabid* (i.e., worshipper) of him and (in contrast) if he was to love someone and at the same time does not submit to him, he is likewise not an '*aabid* of him, as is the case of a man who loves his child and friend.

Consequently, only one of the two (qualities) is not sufficient as far as the '*ibaadah* of Allaah (ﷻ) is concerned. Rather, it is necessary that Allaah be the most beloved above all else to the '*abd* and that he holds Allaah to be the greatest of all. Indeed, None other than Allaah deserves total love and submission.

Moreover, anything that is loved for other than Allaah; love of such a thing is unsound and anything that is glorified without the order of Allaah; glorification of such a thing is false. Allaah (ﷻ) says:

---

[83] Refer to these levels in detail with the Author's student, the great scholar Ibn Qayyim al-Jawziyyah, in *Rawdah al-Muhibbeen* (pg. 16) and *'Ighaathah al-Lahfaan* (pg. 103 –*Mawaarid al-Amaan* –my work).

[84] Allaah is not described with this particular category [s]. This category connotes a sexual love that Allaah is exalted above. Ibn Taymiyyah here is mentioning the levels of love in a general manner and not for Allaah specifically. A number of scholars have discussed this issue, such as Ibn Taymiyyah himself in his other works, Ibn Qayyim al-Jawziyyah and Aboo al-Faraj Ibn al-Jawzee, may Allaah have mercy upon them. [t]

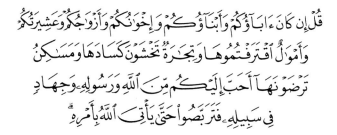

"Say, 'If your fathers; your sons; your brothers; your wives; your kindred; the wealth that you have gained; the commerce in which you fear a decline and the dwellings in which you delight, are dearer to you than Allaah and His Messenger and striving hard and Fighting in His Cause, then wait until Allaah brings about His Decision (torment).'"[85]

Thus, the genus of love should be for Allaah and His Messenger, as in the case of obedience; obedience is for Allaah and His Messenger and pleasing is for Allaah and His Messenger:

وَٱللَّهُ وَرَسُولُهُۥ أَحَقُّ أَن يُرۡضُوهُ

"…But it is more fitting that they should please Allaah and His Messenger…"[86]

The issue of bestowal also belongs to Allaah and His Messenger:

وَلَوۡ أَنَّهُمۡ رَضُوا۟ مَآ ءَاتَىٰهُمُ ٱللَّهُ وَرَسُولُهُۥ

"If only they had been contented with what Allaah and His Messenger gave them."[87]

---

[85] Soorah at-Tawbah (9):24.
[86] Soorah at-Tawbah (9):62.
[87] Soorah at-Tawbah (9):59.

As for 'Ibaadah and that which relates to it, such as *tawakkul*, fear and their like, these are for none other than Allaah alone,[88] as He (ﷻ) has said:

قُل يَـٰٓأَهَلَ ٱلۡكِتَـٰبِ تَعَالَوۡاْ إِلَىٰ كَلِمَةٍ سَوَآءِۭ بَيۡنَنَا وَبَيۡنَكُمۡ أَلَّا نَعۡبُدَ إِلَّا ٱللَّهَ وَلَا نُشۡرِكَ بِهِۦ شَيۡـًٔا وَلَا يَتَّخِذَ بَعۡضُنَا بَعۡضًا أَرۡبَابًا مِّن دُونِ ٱللَّهِۚ فَإِن تَوَلَّوۡاْ فَقُولُواْ ٱشۡهَدُواْ بِأَنَّا مُسۡلِمُونَ ﴿٦٤﴾

"Say, 'O people of the Book! Come to a word that is just to you and us; that we worship none but Allaah, that we associate nothing in worship with Him and that none of us shall take others as lords besides Allaah'. Then, if they turn away, say, 'Bear witness that we are Muslims'."[89]

Allaah (ﷻ) also said:

وَلَوۡ أَنَّهُمۡ رَضُواْ مَآ ءَاتَىٰهُمُ ٱللَّهُ وَرَسُولُهُۥ وَقَالُواْ حَسۡبُنَا ٱللَّهُ سَيُؤۡتِينَا ٱللَّهُ مِن فَضۡلِهِۦ وَرَسُولُهُۥٓ إِنَّآ إِلَى ٱللَّهِ رَٰغِبُونَ ﴿٥٩﴾

"If only they had been contented with what Allaah and His Messenger gave them and had said, 'Allaah is sufficient for us. Allaah and His Messenger will give us of His Bounty. It is Allaah that we implore (to enrich us)'."[90]

Hence, (the issue of) bestowal belongs to Allaah and His Messenger, as He (ﷻ) has said:

---

[88] This is an explanation of the specific unique rights that belong to Allaah as well as the common rights that belong to both Allaah and the Messenger. [s]

[89] Soorah Aal-'Imraan (3):64.

[90] Soorah at-Tawbah (9):59.

وَمَآ ءَاتَىٰكُمُ ٱلرَّسُولُ فَخُذُوهُ وَمَا نَهَىٰكُمْ عَنْهُ فَٱنتَهُواْ

"...and whatsoever the Messenger gives you, take it, and whatsoever he forbids you from, abstain (from it)..."[91]

As for al-Hasb, which is what suffices, it is Allaah alone, as Allaah (ﷻ) has said:

ٱلَّذِينَ قَالَ لَهُمُ ٱلنَّاسُ إِنَّ ٱلنَّاسَ قَدْ جَمَعُواْ لَكُمْ فَٱخْشَوْهُمْ فَزَادَهُمْ إِيمَٰنًا وَقَالُواْ حَسْبُنَا ٱللَّهُ وَنِعْمَ ٱلْوَكِيلُ ﴿١٧٣﴾

"Those (i.e., the believers) unto whom the people (i.e., the hypocrites) said, 'Verily, the people have gathered against you (in the form of a great army), so fear them'. However, it (only) increased them in eemaan and they said, 'Our Hasb (i.e., one who suffices us) is Allaah and How fine a trustee (He is)'."[92]

Allaah (ﷻ) also says:

يَٰٓأَيُّهَا ٱلنَّبِيُّ حَسْبُكَ ٱللَّهُ وَمَنِ ٱتَّبَعَكَ مِنَ ٱلْمُؤْمِنِينَ ﴿٦٤﴾

"O Prophet! Your Hasb (i.e., one who suffices) as well as those who follow you of the believers, is Allaah."[93]

i.e., Allaah is the one who suffices you and the believers who follow you. As for the one who presumes the meaning to be *'the one who suffices you (O Muhammad) is Allaah and the believers together'*, then he has committed an atrocious error, as we have already clarified this in a different place.[94]

---

[91] Soorah al-Hashr (57):7.

[92] Soorah Aal-'Imraan (3):173.

[93] Soorah al-Anfaal (8):64.

[94] The author, may Allaah have mercy upon him, said when explaining this *aayah* correctly in *Minhaaj as-Sunnah* (7/201): "Its meaning is that Allaah is sufficient for you (i.e., Muhammad ﷺ). Thus, He alone is sufficient for you and sufficient for the believers that follow you. =

He (ﷻ) also said:

أَلَيْسَ ٱللَّهُ بِكَافٍ عَبْدَهُ

"Is not Allaah sufficient for His *'abd?...*"[95]

The clarification of this is that the term *'abd* refers to the *mu'abbad*, whom Allaah has subjugated, so Allaah subdues, governs and administers him.

From this perspective, all creatures are the *'Ibaad* of Allaah; the righteous as well as the immoral, the believers, the unbelievers, the inhabitants of Paradise and the inhabitants of the Fire. Since, Allaah is the Lord and Owner of them all. None can escape His will, omnipotence and His perfect words, which no righteous or unrighteous person can transgress.[96] Whatever He has willed, will come to be even if they have not willed it, and whatever they will, will not come to be if He does not will it, as Allaah (ﷻ) says:

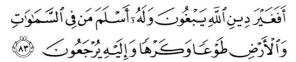

أَفَغَيْرَ دِينِ ٱللَّهِ يَبْغُونَ وَلَهُۥٓ أَسْلَمَ مَن فِى ٱلسَّمَٰوَٰتِ وَٱلْأَرْضِ طَوْعًا وَكَرْهًا وَإِلَيْهِ يُرْجَعُونَ ٨٣

= This (particular style of construction of words) is (in the same style) as (when) the Arabs say, *'Sufficient for you and Zayd is a dirham'*. Another example is the saying of a poet:

So sufficient for you and ad-Dahhaak is a sharp sword."

Ibn Taymiyyah then went to lengths in affirming this. Also refer to (2/32) and (8/487) of *Minhaaj as-Sunnah.*

[95] Soorah az-Zumar (39):36.

[96] This contains a reference to the statement that has been established from the Prophet (ﷺ): *"Jibreel came to me and said, 'Recite' I said, 'And what should I recite?' He replied, 'Say, "I take refuge within Allaah's perfect words, which no righteous or unrighteous person can transgress, from the evil of what he has created..."."* It has been related by Ahmad (3/19); Ibn as-Sunnee (631); al-Uzdee in *al-Makhzoon* (122); al-Bukhaaree in *at-Taareekh* (3/1/248); ad-Daaruqutnee in *al-Mu'talif* (2/697) and others from 'Abdur-Rahmaan Ibn Khanbash with a chain of narration that is *hasan*. As-Suyootee mentioned it in *Jaami' al-Jawaami'* (No. 5018 – his own numbering) and he added that it is also related by Ibn Abee Shaybah, al-Bazzaar, al-Hasan Ibn Sufyaan, Aboo Zur'ah, Ibn Mandah and Aboo Na'eem in *ad-Dalaa'il*. He also mentioned (3980) from the *mursal* of Makhool from Ibn Abee Shaybah. See *Ta'jeel al-Manfa'ah* (pg. 249) and *al-'Isaabah* (4/300-301).

"Do they then seek other than the *Deen* of Allaah? While all that is in the heavens and the earth have submitted to Him willingly or unwillingly. And to Him they shall all be returned."[97]

Thus, He (سبحانه) is the Lord of the worlds; their Creator; their Provider; the One Who bestows life upon them and causes their death; the One who fluctuates their hearts and the One who disposes of their affairs. They do not have any other lord; they do not have any other king and owner and they do not have any other creator, irrespective of whether they admit to it or deny it, and whether they are aware of it or are ignorant of it.

However, the people of *eemaan* know of it and believe in it, in contrast to the one who is ignorant of it or rejects it, being arrogant towards his Lord, not acknowledging or submitting to it, with the (full) knowledge that Allaah is his Lord and Creator.

Whenever knowledge of the truth is accompanied with arrogance towards accepting it and its denial, it will be a (reason for) punishment for its possessor, as Allaah (ﷻ) said:

$$وَجَحَدُواْ بِهَا وَٱسۡتَيۡقَنَتۡهَآ أَنفُسُهُمۡ ظُلۡمٗا وَعُلُوّٗاۚ فَٱنظُرۡ كَيۡفَ كَانَ عَٰقِبَةُ ٱلۡمُفۡسِدِينَ ﴿١٤﴾$$

"And they denied them (i.e., Allaah's signs) unjustly and arrogantly, though their own selves were convinced of them. So, see what was the end of the *mufsidoon*."[98]

Allaah (ﷻ) also says:

$$ٱلَّذِينَ ءَاتَيۡنَٰهُمُ ٱلۡكِتَٰبَ يَعۡرِفُونَهُۥ كَمَا يَعۡرِفُونَ أَبۡنَآءَهُمۡۖ وَإِنَّ فَرِيقٗا مِّنۡهُمۡ لَيَكۡتُمُونَ ٱلۡحَقَّ وَهُمۡ يَعۡلَمُونَ ﴿١٤٦﴾$$

---

[97] Soorah Aal-'Imraan (3):83.
[98] Soorah an-Naml (27):14.

"Those to whom We gave the Scripture (i.e., the Jews and Christians) recognise him (i.e., Muhammad (ﷺ)) as they recognise their own sons. However, a party of them indeed, conceal the truth whilst they know it (i.e., in reference to the descriptions of Muhammad (ﷺ), which are written in the *Tawraat* and the *Injeel*)."[99]

Allaah (ﷻ) also says:

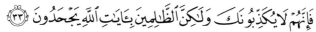

"Indeed, It is not you (i.e., Muhammad (ﷺ)) that they deny, but it is the Signs (i.e., the *aayaat* of the Qur'aan) of Allaah that the *dhaalimoon* deny."[100]

Therefore, if the *'abd* knows that Allaah is his Lord and Creator, and that he is in need of Him, then he is aware of the *'uboodiyyah* that is related to the Lordship of Allaah.[101]

This *'abd* asks of his Lord, beseeches Him and relies upon Him. However, he may obey His Command or he might disobey it. He may also worship Him and he may worship *Shaytaan* and idols.

This category of *'uboodiyyah* does not distinguish the people of Paradise from the people of the Fire, nor does a person become a Muslim on account of it, as Allaah (ﷻ) says:

وَمَا يُؤْمِنُ أَكْثَرُهُم بِٱللَّهِ إِلَّا وَهُم مُّشْرِكُونَ ١٠٦

"And most of them believe not in Allaah except that they attribute partners (unto Him)."[102]

---

[99] Soorah al-Baqarah (2):146.

[100] Soorah al-An'aam (6):33.

[101] Thus, the general *'uboodiyyah* pertains to the Lordship of Allaah and that Allaah is the *Rabb* of everything. As for the specific *'uboodiyyah*, it pertains to worship of Him, His *tawheed*, being sincere to him alone through submission, one's choice and out of love and fear of Him. [s]

[102] Soorah Yoosuf (12):106.

In fact, the *mushrikoon* (at the time of the Prophet (ﷺ)) used to acknowledge that Allaah is their Creator, and with that, they used to worship other than Him. Allaah (ﷻ) said:

$$\text{وَلَئِن سَأَلْتَهُم مَّنْ خَلَقَ ٱلسَّمَـٰوَٰتِ وَٱلْأَرْضَ لَيَقُولُنَّ ٱللَّهُ}$$

"And verily, if you ask them, 'Who created the heavens and the earth?' They will surely reply, 'Allaah'..."[103]

Allaah (ﷻ) says:

$$\text{قُل لِّمَنِ ٱلْأَرْضُ وَمَن فِيهَا إِن كُنتُمْ تَعْلَمُونَ ۝ سَيَقُولُونَ لِلَّهِ قُلْ أَفَلَا تَذَكَّرُونَ ۝ قُلْ مَن رَّبُّ ٱلسَّمَـٰوَٰتِ ٱلسَّبْعِ وَرَبُّ ٱلْعَرْشِ ٱلْعَظِيمِ ۝ سَيَقُولُونَ لِلَّهِ قُلْ أَفَلَا تَتَّقُونَ ۝ قُلْ مَنۢ بِيَدِهِۦ مَلَكُوتُ كُلِّ شَىْءٍ وَهُوَ يُجِيرُ وَلَا يُجَارُ عَلَيْهِ إِن كُنتُمْ تَعْلَمُونَ ۝ سَيَقُولُونَ لِلَّهِ قُلْ فَأَنَّىٰ تُسْحَرُونَ ۝}$$

"Say, 'To who does the earth and whosoever is within it belong to? If you truly know!' They will reply, 'To *Allaah*!' Say, 'Will you not then remember?' Say, 'Who is the Lord of the seven heavens and the Lord of the Great Throne?' They will reply, '(That belongs) to *Allaah*.' Say, 'Will you not then fear Allaah'. Say, 'In Whose Hand is the sovereignty of everything and He protects (all), whilst against Him, there is no protector, if indeed you know?' They will reply, '(It belongs) to *Allaah*'. Say, 'Then how is it that you are deceived (and averse from the truth)?"[104]

---

[103] Soorah az-Zumar (39):38.
[104] Soorah al-Mu'minoon (23):84-89.

Many of those who speak about this truth[105] and consequently bear witness to it, do not witness except this very truth. It is the universal truth, of which, its truth, witness of it and knowledge of it are common to the believer, the disbeliever, the righteous, and the unrighteous. Indeed, even *Iblees* and the people of the Fire admit to this truth. *Iblees* said:

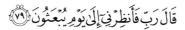

"*My Lord*! Give me then respite till the Day they (i.e., the dead) are resurrected."[106]

He also said:

قَالَ رَبِّ بِمَآ
أَغْوَيْتَنِى لَأُزَيِّنَنَّ لَهُمْ فِى ٱلْأَرْضِ وَلَأُغْوِيَنَّهُمْ أَجْمَعِينَ ﴿٣٩﴾

"*O my Lord*! Because You misled me I shall indeed adorn the path of error for them (i.e., mankind) on earth and I shall indeed mislead them all."[107]

He also said:

قَالَ فَبِعِزَّتِكَ لَأُغْوِيَنَّهُمْ أَجْمَعِينَ ﴿٨٢﴾

"Then *by Your Might*, I will surely mislead them all."[108]

Iblees also said:

قَالَ أَرَءَيْتَكَ هَٰذَا ٱلَّذِى كَرَّمْتَ عَلَىَّ لَئِنْ أَخَّرْتَنِ
إِلَىٰ يَوْمِ ٱلْقِيَٰمَةِ لَأَحْتَنِكَنَّ ذُرِّيَّتَهُۥ إِلَّا قَلِيلًا ﴿٦٢﴾

---

[105] i.e., the reality of *Ruboobiyyah* (i.e., Lordship) and the existence of Allaah (ﷻ) , like the *Soofiyyah* and their likes!

[106] Soorah Saad (38):79.

[107] Soorah al-Hijr (15):39.

[108] Soorah Saad (38):82.

"Do You see this one whom You have honoured above me, *if You grant me* respite (i.e., keep me alive) to the Day of Resurrection, I will surely cut the roots of his offspring (by sending them astray), all but a few!"[109]

There are other instances of such an address where *Iblees* acknowledges that Allaah is his Lord and Creator and the Creator of all others. Similarly, the people of the Fire said:

قَالُوا۟ رَبَّنَا غَلَبَتْ عَلَيْنَا شِقْوَتُنَا وَكُنَّا قَوْمًا ضَآلِّينَ ﴿١٠٦﴾

"They will say, 'Our Lord! Our wretchedness overwhelmed us and we were an erring people'."[110]

Allaah (ﷻ) says concerning them:

وَلَوْ تَرَىٰ إِذْ وُقِفُوا۟ عَلَىٰ رَبِّهِمْ قَالَ أَلَيْسَ هَٰذَا بِالْحَقِّ قَالُوا۟ بَلَىٰ وَرَبِّنَا

"If you could but see when they will be detained in front of their Lord! He will say, 'Is not this (Resurrection and the taking of the accounts) the truth?' They will reply, 'Yes indeed, *by our Lord!* ...'"[111]

Thus, whoever halts at this reality[112] and at (merely) acknowledging it, but does not establish the *religious* truth that Allaah has commanded him with, which is the worship of Him that pertains to his *uloohiyyah*, obedience of His command and His Messenger's, will be of the same genre as Iblees and the people of the Fire.

Moreover, if such a person presumes himself to be amongst the elite of Allaah's *awliyaa'*, the people of *ma'rifah* and *ithbaat*, who are absolved of any religious commands and prohibitions, he will be of the worst people of *kufr* and *ilhaad*.[113]

---

[109] Soorah al-Israa (17):62.

[110] Soorah al-Mu'minoon (23):106.

[111] Soorah al-An'aam (6):30.

[112] i.e., regarding Allaah's Lordship.

[113] Compare this with what Imaam Ibn al-Jawzee wrote in his amazing book *Talbees Iblees*, pg. 456 (my edition *al-Muntaqaa an-Nafees*)

Whosoever imagined that al-Khadir[114] and others besides him were not answerable to the Command because *they had witnessed the Will* or something similar to that, such a person's profession is one of the most evil utterances of the disbelievers in Allaah and His Messenger, until he enters into the second type of meaning of *al-'Abd*. This is the connotation of *al-'Abd* as *al-'Aabid* (the worshipper).

Hence, he should be a worshipper of Allaah, not worshipping anything but Him, therefore obeying His command and that of His Messenger, having allegiance with the *awliyaa'* of Allaah, the believers and the pious ones and holding animosity towards His enemies.

This *'ibaadah* pertains to the *ilaahiyyah* of Allaah (ﷻ) and this is why the epitome of *tawheed* was لا إله إلا الله *'None has the right to be worshipped but Allaah'* in contrast to the one who acknowledges the Lordship of Allaah but does not worship Him or one who worships alongside him another deity.

Thus, the *ilaah* (الإله) is what the heart defies with total love, glorification, reverence, grandeur, fear, hope and such matters.

This is the *'Ibaadah* that Allaah loves and is pleased with. With it, He depicted the chosen of His slaves and with it, He sent the Messengers.

As for the connotation of *al-'Abd* as being the subdued one, irrespective of whether he maintains it or rejects it, this meaning is common to both the believer and disbeliever.

---

[114] The author, may Allaah have mercy upon him, has a lengthy discussion on al-Khadir (عليه السلام) and he refuted many false beliefs surrounding him, which have been mentioned by the *Soofiyyah* and other deviant people. Refer to *Majmoo' al-Fataawa* (4/337-341, 10/434, 11/430, 13/266, 27/100-102) and other places.

Through the disparity between these two types, one can distinguish the difference between the religious (*deeniyyah*) realities that pertain to the worship of Allaah, His religion and His Legislative Command, which He loves, is pleased with, offers *walaa'* to its people and honours them with His garden, and between the universal (*kawniyyah*) realities that are common to both the believer and disbeliever, and the righteous and unrighteous.

Whoever limits himself to the universal realities and does not accede to the religious realities, is of the followers of the accursed *Iblees* and of the disbelievers in the Lord of the Worlds.

As for the one who limits himself to some of these matters (i.e., religious realities) and forgoes others, or in only certain standings or circumstances, his *eemaan* and *wilaayah* with Allaah decreases according to the decrement that is present of the religious realities.

This is a tremendous area in which the errant ones were mistaken and in which confusion increased upon the travellers (to Allaah) to the extent that the number of senior *shaykhs* who alleged that they were people of *tahqeeq*, *tawheed* and *'irfaan*, but who slipped (in this regard) cannot be enumerated except by Allaah, Who knows the secret and the revealed.

Shaykh 'Abdul-Qaadir[115] pointed out this very thing, as is mentioned of him.[116] He explained that: "When many people arrive at

---

[115] He is al-Jeelaanee, an ascetic scholar. He is the author of the book *al-Ghunyah* and he passed away in the year 561H. Adh-Dhahabee gave a biographical account of him in *Siyar al-'Alaam an-Nubalaa'* (20/451). He concluded his biography with the words: "In summary, Shaykh 'Abdul-Qaadir is of great standing. He has some statements and claims that are objectionable and disapproved of and with Allaah is his appointment. Some of these (statements) are falsely attributed to him."

[116] Note that the author attributed the statement to him in an unasserted manner.

(the topic of) *al-Qadaa* and *al-Qadar*, they refrain,[117] but not me. As a window has been opened in it for me and I contend the decrees of the truth, with the truth, for the truth.[118] Moreover, a (real) man is one who contends with *al-Qadar*, not one who sanctions it."

What has been mentioned by the *Shaykh*, may Allaah have mercy upon him, is what Allaah and His Messenger have commanded.

However, many people have erred in this regard. They may witness the disobedience and sins that have been ordained upon one of them or another person, or even indeed if it is *kufr*. They witness that this is occurring by the Will of Allaah and by His *al-Qadaa* and *al-Qadar* and as being included within the command of His Lordship and the dictates of His Will. Hence, they believe that acceptance of this, agreement of it and contentment of it and so on, is part of the *Deen*, the way and worship. In such circumstances, they resemble the *Mushrikoon* who said:

لَوۡ شَآءَ ٱللَّهُ مَآ أَشۡرَكۡنَا وَلَآ ءَابَآؤُنَا وَلَا حَرَّمۡنَا مِن شَيۡءٍ

"If Allaah had willed, we would not have taken partners (in worship with Him) nor would our fathers, and we would not have forbidden anything (against His Will)."[119]

They also said:

أَنُطۡعِمُ مَن لَّوۡ يَشَآءُ ٱللَّهُ أَطۡعَمَهُۥٓ

"Shall we feed those whom, if Allaah willed, He (Himself) would have fed?"[120]

---

[117] This is what is correct. Since, one should not indulge excessively into the issues of *al-Qadar* as has been established from the Prophet (ﷺ) that he said: *"When al-Qadr is mentioned, then refrain."* Refer to the discussion on the grade and sources of it's chain of narration in *as-Saheehah* (34).

[118] i.e., 'I do not stop at *al-Qadar* and say disobedience had been decreed on me. Thus if Allaah decrees obedience, I do not stop but instead I turn in repentance to Allaah and repel this *Qadar* (of disobedience) with *Qadar* (of obedience).' [s]

[119] Soorah al-An'aam (6):148.

[120] Soorah Yaa Seen (36):47.

50

They said:

لَوۡ شَآءَ ٱلرَّحۡمَٰنُ مَا عَبَدۡنَٰهُمۡ

"If it had been the Will of the Most Beneficent (Allaah), we should not have worshipped them."[121]

If they had been rightly guided, they would have understood that we have been ordered to be content with *al-Qadar* and to be patient with its injunctions in the calamities that afflict us, such as poverty, sickness, and fear. Allaah (ﷻ) said:

مَآ أَصَابَ مِن مُّصِيبَةٍ إِلَّا بِإِذۡنِ ٱللَّهِۗ وَمَن يُؤۡمِنۢ بِٱللَّهِ يَهۡدِ قَلۡبَهُۥ

"No calamity befalls, but by the permission of Allaah, and whosoever believes in Allaah, He guides his heart."[122]

Some of the *Salaf*[123] have said: "This is in reference to the person who is afflicted with a calamity, but he knows that it is from Allaah and therefore is content with it and submits to it." Allaah (ﷻ) also says:

مَآ أَصَابَ مِن مُّصِيبَةٍ فِي ٱلۡأَرۡضِ وَلَا فِيٓ أَنفُسِكُمۡ إِلَّا فِي كِتَٰبٍ مِّن قَبۡلِ أَن نَّبۡرَأَهَآۚ إِنَّ ذَٰلِكَ عَلَى ٱللَّهِ يَسِيرٌ ۝ لِّكَيۡلَا تَأۡسَوۡاْ عَلَىٰ مَا فَاتَكُمۡ وَلَا تَفۡرَحُواْ بِمَآ ءَاتَىٰكُمۡ

"No calamity befalls on earth or in yourselves but it is (recorded) in a Book, before We bring it (i.e., the calamity) into existence. Verily, that is easy for Allaah. In order that you may not be sad over matters that you fail to gain, nor rejoice at that which has been given to you."[124]

---

[121] Soorah az-Zukhruf (43):20.

[122] Soorah at-Taghaabun (64):11.

[123] He is 'Alqamah as related from him by 'Abd Ibn Humayd, Ibn al-Mundhir and al-Bayhaqee in *Shu'ab al-Eemaan* as mentioned in *ad-Durr al-Manthoor* (8/183 – 2nd print).

[124] Soorah al-Hadeed (57):22-23.

It is reported in the *Saheehayn*[125] that the Prophet (ﷺ) said: "*Aadam and Moosa had an argument. Moosa said, 'You are Aadam, whom Allaah created with His Hand, into whom He breathed the soul He created (for you), to whom He made the Angels prostrate and whom He taught the names of everything. So why have you expelled us and yourself from Paradise?' Aadam replied, 'You are Moosa, whom Allaah favoured with His Message and His Speech. Have you not found that this had been written upon me before I was even created?' Moosa replied, 'Yes'.*" Then he (i.e., the Messenger (ﷺ)) remarked: "*Thus, Aadam got the better of Moosa in the argument.*"

Note that Aadam did not prove his argument over Moosa by means of *al-Qadar*, thinking that the sinner can use *al-Qadar* as an argument. Therefore, this is not asserted by any Muslim, nor any sane person. If this had been an excuse, it would have (equally) been one for Iblees, the people of Nooh, the people of Hood and every disbeliever.

Likewise, Moosa did not censure Aadam over the sin itself, as Aadam had repented to His Lord and His Lord then chose Him and guided him. Moosa, however, censured him over the resultant calamity that befell them because of the sin. This is why Moosa asked, 'So why have you expelled us and yourself from Paradise?' and Aadam answered, 'This is what had been recorded upon me before I was created.'[126]

Hence, the action and the resultant calamity upon him were ordained. The calamities that are ordained must be submitted to, as this is from the perfection of being pleased with Allaah as Lord.

---

[125] Related by al-Bukhaaree (11/441); Muslim (2652); Maalik (2/898); Aboo Daawood (4701) and at-Tirmidhee (2135) from Aboo Hurayrah. This account is related by a number of Companions, refer to *as-Saheehah* (909 & 1702) of our Shaykh al-Albaanee.

[126] "And he did not question, 'Why did you disobey the Command?' People are bound to submit to *al-Qadar* and observe (Allaah's) Lordship when afflicted with calamities at the hands of others or otherwise." Mentioned by the author himself in his treatise *al-Ihtijaaj bi al-Qadar* (pg. 26), which he based on the commentary of this *hadeeth*. For more benefit refer to *Mirqaah al-Mafaateeh* (1/123-132) by Shaykh 'Alee al-Qaaree.

As for sins, it is not for the *'abd* to commit sins and if he does so, it is upon him to seek forgiveness and repent. Thus, He repents from all types of sins and is patient with calamities. Allaah (ﷻ) says:

فَٱصْبِرْ إِنَّ وَعْدَ ٱللَّهِ حَقٌّ وَٱسْتَغْفِرْ لِذَنۢبِكَ

"So be patient (O Muḥammad (ﷺ)). Verily the Promise of Allaah is true and ask forgiveness for your fault."[127]

Allaah (ﷻ) says:

وَإِن تَصْبِرُوا۟ وَتَتَّقُوا۟ لَا يَضُرُّكُمْ كَيْدُهُمْ شَيْـًٔا

"But if you remain patient and pious, not the least harm will their cunning do to you."[128]

Allaah (ﷻ) also says:

وَإِن تَصْبِرُوا۟ وَتَتَّقُوا۟ فَإِنَّ ذَٰلِكَ مِنْ عَزْمِ ٱلْأُمُورِ ۝

"But if you persevere patiently and are pious. Indeed, then that will be a matter of great resolution."[129]

Yoosuf (عليه السلام) said:

إِنَّهُۥ مَن يَتَّقِ وَيَصْبِرْ فَإِنَّ ٱللَّهَ لَا يُضِيعُ أَجْرَ ٱلْمُحْسِنِينَ

"Verily, he who fears (Allaah) and is patient, then surely Allaah makes not the reward of the good-doers to be lost."[130]

---

[127] Soorah al-Ghaafir (40):55.
[128] Soorah Aal-'Imraan (3):120.
[129] Soorah Aal-'Imraan (3):186.
[130] Soorah Yoosuf (12):90.

The Obligation of Commanding the Good

Similar is the case with the sins of the slaves;[131] it is a must upon the 'abd in this regard to command the good and forbid the evil in accordance with his capability.

He has to make *jihaad* in the way of Allaah against the disbelievers and the hypocrites, offer allegiance to the *awliyaa'* of Allaah and hold animosity towards the enemies of Allaah.

He has to love for Allaah and hate for Allaah, as Allaah (ﷻ) has said:

> يَٰٓأَيُّهَا ٱلَّذِينَ ءَامَنُواْ لَا تَتَّخِذُواْ عَدُوِّي وَعَدُوَّكُمْ أَوْلِيَآءَ تُلْقُونَ إِلَيْهِم بِٱلْمَوَدَّةِ وَقَدْ كَفَرُواْ بِمَا جَآءَكُم مِّنَ ٱلْحَقِّ يُخْرِجُونَ ٱلرَّسُولَ وَإِيَّاكُمْ أَن تُؤْمِنُواْ بِٱللَّهِ رَبِّكُمْ إِن كُنتُمْ خَرَجْتُمْ جِهَٰدًا فِي سَبِيلِي وَٱبْتِغَآءَ مَرْضَاتِي تُسِرُّونَ إِلَيْهِم بِٱلْمَوَدَّةِ وَأَنَا۠ أَعْلَمُ بِمَا أَخْفَيْتُمْ وَمَآ أَعْلَنتُمْ وَمَن يَفْعَلْهُ مِنكُمْ فَقَدْ ضَلَّ سَوَآءَ ٱلسَّبِيلِ ۝ إِن يَثْقَفُوكُمْ يَكُونُواْ لَكُمْ أَعْدَآءً وَيَبْسُطُوٓاْ إِلَيْكُمْ أَيْدِيَهُمْ وَأَلْسِنَتَهُم بِٱلسُّوٓءِ وَوَدُّواْ لَوْ تَكْفُرُونَ ۝ لَن تَنفَعَكُمْ أَرْحَامُكُمْ وَلَآ أَوْلَٰدُكُمْ يَوْمَ ٱلْقِيَٰمَةِ يَفْصِلُ بَيْنَكُمْ وَٱللَّهُ بِمَا تَعْمَلُونَ بَصِيرٌ ۝ قَدْ كَانَتْ لَكُمْ أُسْوَةٌ حَسَنَةٌ فِيٓ إِبْرَٰهِيمَ وَٱلَّذِينَ مَعَهُ إِذْ قَالُواْ لِقَوْمِهِمْ إِنَّا بُرَءَٰٓؤُاْ مِنكُمْ وَمِمَّا تَعْبُدُونَ مِن دُونِ ٱللَّهِ كَفَرْنَا بِكُمْ وَبَدَا بَيْنَنَا وَبَيْنَكُمُ ٱلْعَدَٰوَةُ وَٱلْبَغْضَآءُ أَبَدًا حَتَّىٰ تُؤْمِنُواْ بِٱللَّهِ وَحْدَهُ

---

[131] What has preceded concerns the *abd's* own sins. A person is not permitted to sin, but if he does, he should repent from it and he should also be patient during calamities. As for the sins of others around him, his stance is one of ordering the good and forbidding the evil and performing *jihaad* for Allaah's cause. [s]

"O you who believe! Do not take my enemies and your enemies as *awliyaa'*, offering them affection and love, whilst they have disbelieved in the truth that has come to you, and have driven out the Messenger (Muhammad (ﷺ)) and yourselves (from your homeland) because you believe in Allaah, your Lord!

If you have come forth to strive in My cause and to seek My Good Pleasure (then take not these disbelievers as your friends). You show friendship to them in secret, while I am fully aware of what you conceal and what you reveal. And whosoever of you does that, then he has indeed gone (far) astray, away from the Straight Path.

Should they gain the upper hand over you, they would behave to you as enemies, and stretch forth their hands and their tongues against you with evil and they desire that you should disbelieve.

Neither your relatives nor your children will benefit you on the Day of Resurrection (against Allaah). He will judge between you, and Allaah fully sees what you do.

Indeed there has been an excellent example for you in Ibraaheem and those with him, when they said to their people, 'Verily, we are disowning you and whatever you worship besides Allaah, we have rejected you, and there has arisen between us and you hostility and hatred for ever, until you believe in Allaah Alone."[132]

---

[132] Soorah al-Mumtahanah (60):1-4.

Allaah (ﷻ) says:

$$\text{لَّا تَجِدُ قَوْمًا يُؤْمِنُونَ بِاللَّهِ وَالْيَوْمِ الْآخِرِ يُوَآدُّونَ مَنْ حَآدَّ اللَّهَ وَرَسُولَهُ وَلَوْ كَانُوٓا۟ ءَابَآءَهُمْ أَوْ أَبْنَآءَهُمْ أَوْ إِخْوَانَهُمْ أَوْ عَشِيرَتَهُمْ أُو۟لَٰٓئِكَ كَتَبَ فِى قُلُوبِهِمُ الْإِيمَٰنَ وَأَيَّدَهُم بِرُوحٍ مِّنْهُ}$$

"You will not find any people who believe in Allaah and the Last Day, having friendship with those who oppose Allaah and His Messenger (Muḥammad (ﷺ)) even if they were their fathers, or their sons, or their brothers or their kindred. For such, He has written *eemaan* in their hearts and strengthened them with *roo<u>h</u>* (i.e., proofs, light and guidance) from Himself."[133]

Allaah says:

$$\text{أَفَنَجْعَلُ الْمُسْلِمِينَ كَالْمُجْرِمِينَ ۝}$$

"Shall We then treat the Muslims the same as the *mujrimoon* (criminals, *mushrikoon* and disbelievers)?"[134]

Allaah says:

$$\text{أَمْ نَجْعَلُ الَّذِينَ ءَامَنُوا۟ وَعَمِلُوا۟ الصَّٰلِحَٰتِ كَالْمُفْسِدِينَ فِى الْأَرْضِ أَمْ نَجْعَلُ الْمُتَّقِينَ كَالْفُجَّارِ}$$

"Shall We treat those who believe and do righteous deeds the same as those who do mischief on earth? Or shall We treat the pious the same as the unrighteous?"[135]

---

[133] Soorah al-Mujaadalah (58):22.

[134] Soorah al-Qalam (68):35.

[135] Soorah <u>S</u>aad (38):28.

Allaah (ﷻ) also says:

أَمْ حَسِبَ ٱلَّذِينَ ٱجْتَرَحُوا ٱلسَّيِّئَاتِ أَن نَّجْعَلَهُمْ كَٱلَّذِينَ
ءَامَنُوا وَعَمِلُوا ٱلصَّٰلِحَٰتِ سَوَآءً مَّحْيَاهُمْ وَمَمَاتُهُمْ سَآءَ
مَا يَحْكُمُونَ ﴿٢١﴾

"Or do those who earn evil deeds think that We shall
hold them equal to those who believe and do righteous deeds, — in (both) their present life and after
their death? Worst is the judgement that they
make."[136]

Allaah (ﷻ) also says:

وَمَا يَسْتَوِى ٱلْأَعْمَىٰ وَٱلْبَصِيرُ ﴿١٩﴾ وَلَا ٱلظُّلُمَٰتُ وَلَا ٱلنُّورُ
﴿٢٠﴾ وَلَا ٱلظِّلُّ وَلَا ٱلْحَرُورُ ﴿٢١﴾ وَمَا يَسْتَوِى ٱلْأَحْيَآءُ وَلَا ٱلْأَمْوَٰتُ

"Not alike are the blind and the seeing. Nor are
darkness and light. Nor are the shade and the sun's
(full) heat. Nor are the living and the dead."[137]

Allaah (ﷻ) also says:

ضَرَبَ ٱللَّهُ مَثَلًا رَّجُلًا فِيهِ
شُرَكَآءُ مُتَشَٰكِسُونَ وَرَجُلًا سَلَمًا لِّرَجُلٍ هَلْ يَسْتَوِيَانِ مَثَلًا

"Allaah puts forth a parable: a (slave) man belonging to many partners (like those who worship others along with Allaah) disputing with one another,
and a (slave) man belonging entirely to one master
(like those who worship Allaah Alone), are those two
equal in comparison?"[138]

---

[136] Soorah al-Jaathiyah (45):21.
[137] Soorah Faatir (35):19-22.
[138] Soorah az-Zumar (39):29.

Allaah (ﷻ) says:

ضَرَبَ ٱللَّهُ مَثَلًا عَبْدًا
مَّمْلُوكًا لَّا يَقْدِرُ عَلَىٰ شَىْءٍ وَمَن رَّزَقْنَٰهُ مِنَّا رِزْقًا حَسَنًا
فَهُوَ يُنفِقُ مِنْهُ سِرًّا وَجَهْرًا هَلْ يَسْتَوُۥنَ ٱلْحَمْدُ لِلَّهِ
بَلْ أَكْثَرُهُمْ لَا يَعْلَمُونَ ﴿٧٥﴾ وَضَرَبَ ٱللَّهُ مَثَلًا رَّجُلَيْنِ
أَحَدُهُمَا أَبْكَمُ لَا يَقْدِرُ عَلَىٰ شَىْءٍ وَهُوَ كَلٌّ عَلَىٰ
مَوْلَىٰهُ أَيْنَمَا يُوَجِّههُّ لَا يَأْتِ بِخَيْرٍ هَلْ يَسْتَوِى هُوَ وَمَن
يَأْمُرُ بِٱلْعَدْلِ وَهُوَ عَلَىٰ صِرَٰطٍ مُّسْتَقِيمٍ ﴿٧٦﴾

"Allaah puts forward the example (of two men - a disbeliever and a believer): a slave (disbeliever) under the possession of another, he has no power of any sort, and (the other), and one (believer) on whom We have bestowed a good provision from Ourselves, and he spends thereof secretly and openly. Can they be equal? (By no means) All Praise is for Allaah. Nay! (But) most of them know not.

And Allaah puts forward (another) example of two men, one of them, dumb (disbeliever), who has no power over anything, and he is a burden to his master, whichever way he directs him, he brings no good. Is such a man equal with one (i.e., the believer) who commands justice, and is himself on a Straight Path?"[139]

Allaah (ﷻ) also says:

لَا يَسْتَوِىٓ أَصْحَٰبُ ٱلنَّارِ وَأَصْحَٰبُ
ٱلْجَنَّةِ أَصْحَٰبُ ٱلْجَنَّةِ هُمُ ٱلْفَآئِزُونَ ﴿٢٠﴾

---

[139] Soorah an-Na<u>h</u>l (16):75-76.

"Not equal are the dwellers of the Fire and the dwellers of Paradise. It is the dwellers of Paradise that will be successful."[140]

Similarly, there are other *aayaat*, in which Allaah differentiates the people of truth from the people of falsehood; the people of obedience from the people of disobedience; the people of righteousness from the people of unrighteousness; the people of guidance from the people of deviation; the people of error from the people of reason and the people of truthfulness from the people of deceit.

Thus, one who witnesses the universal realities only and not the religious realities has (in effect) equated these different groups, which Allaah has differentiated in the most decisive of manners.

This equalisation eventually leads the person to equating Allaah with the idols, as Allaah has related from them:

$$ \text{تَٱللَّهِ إِن كُنَّا لَفِى ضَلَٰلٍ مُّبِينٍ ۝ إِذْ نُسَوِّيكُم بِرَبِّ ٱلْعَٰلَمِينَ ۝} $$

"By Allaah, we were truly in manifest error. When we held you (false deities) as equals (in worship) with the Lord of the Worlds."[141]

In fact, the situation with these people is such that they eventually equated Allaah with every existing thing. They declared the worship and obedience deserving (solely) for Allaah true for everything in existence, for they declared Allaah to be the very existence of all creation![142] This is the most monstrous *kufr* and *ilhaad* in the Lord of the Worlds.

Kufr absorbs these people to the point that they do not (even) witness that they are the *'ibaad* of Allaah, not in the sense of them

---

[140] Soorah al-Hashr (57):20.

[141] Soorah ash-Shu'araa (26):97-98.

[142] They are the professors of *Wahdah al-Wujood* (i.e., unity of existence, pantheism), May Allaah protect us from that.

being subdued, nor in the sense of them being worshippers, since they bear witness that their own selves are the Truth, as is explicitly stated by their false deities. Such as Ibn 'Arabee,[143] the author of *al-Fusoos*[144] and his likes of the *mulhidoon* and the slanderers and like Ibn Sab'een[145] and his likes. They bear witness that they are (simultaneously) the worshippers and the ones being worshipped.

This is not witnessing of the Reality, neither the universal nor the religious. Rather, it is deviation and blindness from witnessing the universal reality, by the virtue that they declared the existence of the Creator to be the existence of the Creation and they made every censured and praiseworthy description an attribute of (both) the Creator and the Creation, as the existence of the former is the (very) existence of the latter in their view!

As for the believers in Allaah and His Messenger, the elite and masses of them, who are the people of the Qur'aan, as the Prophet (ﷺ) has said: *"To Allaah belongs two types of people."* He was questioned: *"Who are they O Messenger of Allaah?"* He answered: *"The people of the Qur'aan, they are the people of Allaah and His elite."*[146]

---

[143] Muhyee ad-Deen (!) Ibn 'Arabee, passed away 638H. For knowledge of the statements of the scholars concerning him, refer to *Ibn 'Arabee 'Aqeedatuhu wa Hayaatuhu wa Aqwaal al-'Ulamaa' feehi* by Shaykh Taqee ad-Deen al-Hilaalee with my comments.

[144] The title of this book is *Fusoos al-Hikam*. It contains varieties of *Kufr* and *Shirk*. Ibn Taymiyyah, may Allaah have mercy upon him, has an unprecedented refutation of it titled *ar-Rad al-Aqwam 'alaa maa fee Fusoos al-Hikam*. It is printed within *Majmoo' al-Fataawaa* (2/362).

[145] He is 'Abdur-Rahmaan Ibn Sab'een, passed away 669H. He has statements of *Kufr* that are well known. See *al-Bidaayah wa an-Nihaayah* (13/261) and *Lisaan al-Meezaan* (1/188). Also refer to *Majmoo' al-Fataawa* (2/115, 123, 220, & 294).

[146] Related by at-Tayaalisee (2124); Ibn Maajah (215); Ahmad (3/127, 127-128 & 242) and Aboo Na'eem in *al-Hilyah* (3/63 & 9/40) from a number of chains from 'Abdur-Rahmaan Ibn Budayl from his father from Anas. Al-Busayree declared in *Misbaah az-Zujaajah*: "Its chain of narration is *saheeh*." I say, 'Rather, it is *hasan*, because of what has been said of 'Abdur-Rahmaan Ibn Budayl'.

These people know that Allaah is the Lord, Owner and Creator of everything and that the Creator (ﷻ) is separate from the creation. He is not incarnate within the creation, He is not united with it and nor is His existence, its very existence.

Moreover, Allaah declared the Christians to be **disbelievers** because of the fact that they professed (the doctrine of) the incarnation and unification of the Lord with *al-Maseeh*, **exclusively**. So how is the (state of the) one who declares that to be comprehensive, encompassing every creation?

Furthermore, they are aware in addition to this, that Allaah commanded obedience of Him and of His Messenger, that He prohibited disobedience of Him and His Messenger, that He does not like *fasaad*, He does not like *kufr* for His slaves and that it is upon creation to worship Him and therefore obey His command and to seek His assistance in all of this, as He has mentioned in the opening of the Book:

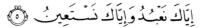

"It is You alone we worship and it is You alone we ask for help."[147]

Commanding the good and forbidding the evil according to ones capability, and *jihaad* in his cause against the people of *kufr* and hypocrisy are manifestations of his worship and obedience.

Thus, they (i.e., the believers) exhort efforts in establishing his religion, seek assistance from him, thereby uplifting and effacing as a result, the evils that had been decreed and at the same time repelling with that any feared consequences. This is similar to when a person vanquishes his present hunger by eating, at the same time he also repels future hunger; likewise, when a spell of coldness appears, he repels it with (extra) clothing.

---

[147] Soorah al-Faatihah (1):5.

Similar is the case with every thing desired that is used to repel something undesired. Just as they (i.e., the Companions) said to the Prophet (ﷺ): *"O Messenger of Allaah! Concerning the medicine that we use to cure ourselves, the ruqaa that we use as remedies (by reciting Qur'aan and du'aa) and the shelters that we use to protect ourselves (from the enemies), do these repel the Qadar of Allaah in any way? He answered: "These are from the Qadar of Allaah."*[148,149]

Also, in the *hadeeth*: *"Indeed, supplication and calamity meet and wrestle with each other between the heaven and earth."*[150]

Hence, this is the condition of the believers of Allaah and his Messenger, who worship Allaah.

All of these (aforementioned) matters are of worship.

As for these people who witness the universal reality - and that is His Lordship over everything - and they make that an obstacle to following his legal and religious command, they are of varying levels of deviation:

---

[148] i.e., Allaah has measured effects by their causes, and interlinked them. Hence, the presence of effects due to the presence of causes is also from the *Qadar* of Allaah. [t]

[149] Related by at-Tirmidhee (2148); Ibn Maajah (3437); al-Haakim (4/199); Ahmad (3/421) and al-Kharaa'itee in *Makaarim al-Akhlaaq* (pg. 94-95) from a number of chains from az-Zuhree from Aboo Khizaamah from his father. Aboo Khizaamah is unknown. It has a supporting *hadeeth* in *Mu'jam at-Tabaraanee al-Kabeer* (12784) by way of Saalih al-Murree from Qataadah from Zuraarah Ibn Abee Awfaa from Ibn 'Abbaas. Al-Haythamee says in *al-Majma'* (5/85): "It contains Saalih Ibn Basheer al-Murree and he is weak."
I say, 'In addition, there exists the *'an'anah* of Qataadah and he is a *mudallis*.' The *hadeeth* has other chains of narration, which are all not free of errors by narrators or mistakes. Refer to these in *Takhreej Ahaadeeth Mushkilah al-Faqr* (pg. 13-15) of our Shaykh al-Albaanee.

[150] Related by al-Haakim, 1/492; al-Bazzaar, 2165; al-Khateeb, 8/453 and Ibn al-Jawzee in *al-Waahiyaat*, 1411 from 'Aa'ishah. Its *sanad* contains Zakariyyaa Ibn Manthoor and he is weak. The *hadeeth* however is attested to by the saying of the Prophet (ﷺ): *"Nothing repels al-Qadaa except supplication."* This is related by at-Tirmidhee,2140 and at-Tahaawee in *al-Mushkil*, 4/169 from Salmaan with a *sanad* that also has weakness. It has other supporting narrations, refer to *as-Saheehah*, 154.

The extreme of them declares that to be absolute and general. They use *al-Qadar* as proof for every thing in which they oppose the *Sharee'ah*.

The statement of these people is more evil than that of the Jews and Christians. It is from the category of the statement of the *Mushrikoon* who said:

لَوْ شَاءَ ٱللَّهُ مَآ أَشْرَكْنَا وَلَآءَابَآؤُنَا وَلَاحَرَّمْنَا مِن شَىْءٍ

"If Allaah had willed, we would not have taken partners (in worship with Him) nor would our fathers, and we would not have forbidden anything (against His Will)."[151]

They also said:

لَوْشَاءَ ٱلرَّحْمَنُ مَاعَبَدْنَهُمْ

"If it had been the Will of the Most Beneficent (Allaah), we should not have worshipped them."[152]

Moreover, these people are the most contradictory people upon the earth. In fact, every person who uses *al-Qadar* as a proof, then he contradicts himself.

The reasoning is that it is not possible to endorse every single person in that which he does. Since, it is a must that if an oppressor oppresses him (i.e., the upholder of this argument) or oppresses the people and he goes on traversing across the land with mischief, spilling the blood of people, declaring illicit relations lawful, destroying crops and cattle and other similar types of harm, with which the people are not able to have any lifeline, it is a must that this *Qadar* be repelled and that the oppressor be punished so that his aggression and the aggression of others like him are prevented.

---

[151] Soorah al-An'aam (6):148.
[152] Soorah az-Zukhruf (43):20.

Thus, it is said to him (i.e., the upholder of this argument), *'If al-Qadar is a proof, then allow everyone to do what they want with you and anyone else, and if it is not a proof, your original statement that al-Qadar is a proof is falsified.'*[153]

Indeed, the maintainers of this statement, who use as proof the universal reality, do not (fully) reject it nor do they (fully) adhere to it. In fact, they merely follow their opinions and desires as some of the *Salaf* have said of them: "You are at times of (enacting) obedience a *Qadaree*, and at times of (committing) disobedience a *Jabree*; any school of thought that agrees with your desires, you adopt."

Another type of these people allege *taḥqeeq* and *ma'rifah* and they claim that the Command and Prohibition is binding for the one who witnesses for himself actions and affirms for himself attributes. As for the one who witnesses that these actions are created or that he is compelled to do such and that Allaah controls him in the same way that he manages all other moving things, in such a case this person is not accountable to the Command and Prohibition and to the Promise and Threat.

Furthermore, they might assert: *"Whoever witnesses the Will, the takleef has been removed from him and they also claim that the takleef had been removed from al-Khidhr because he had witnessed the Will."*

Hence, these people (of this particular group) differentiate between the masses and the elite who witnessed the universal reality; they witness that Allaah is the Creator of the actions of the slaves and that He wills and governs all beings.

They may differentiate between one who simply knows that and between one who sees that by witnessing. They do not remove the *takleef* from one who simply believes in it and knows it only, but

---

[153] This a rational and solid argument that invalidates their saying from its very foundation.

they remove it from one who witnesses that, whereby he does not see himself as having any action at all, from the outset.

These people declare *al-Jabr* and the affirmation of *al-Qadar* as an obstacle to the enjoining of *takleef* from this angle.

A number of groups that are attributed to *tahqeeq*, understanding and *tawheed* have fallen into this.

The reason behind this is that their comprehension was too narrow to understand the fact that the *'abd* can be commanded with something that opposes what has been decreed for him, just as the comprehension of the *Mu'tazilah* and their likes from the *al-Qadariyyah* was too narrow to understand that.

Thereafter, the *Mu'tazilah* affirmed the legal Command and Prohibition without affirming *al-Qadar* and *al-Qadaa*, which are the general will of Allaah and His creation of the actions.

These people (i.e., the former), affirmed *al-Qadar* and *al-Qadaa* and negated the command and the prohibition with regards to the one who witnesses *al-Qadar*, since they could not negate that in an absolute sense.

The statement of these people is worse than the statement of the Mu'tazilah, for this reason, not a single one of these people was of the *Salaf*.

These people declare the Command and Prohibition (enforceable) upon the *barred* ones, who have not witnessed the universal reality and this is why they deem the one who has arrived at witnessing this reality as being unaccountable to the Command and Prohibition. They say that he has become one of the elite and they may even construe for this purpose His (ﷻ) saying:

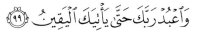

"And worship your Lord until there comes unto you the certainty (i. e., death)."[154]

This 'certainty' in their view, is the knowledge of this reality. **The saying of these people is unequivocal _Kufr_,** although some sects fell into this without knowing that it is _kufr_.

It is known, by necessity, from the _Deen_ of Islaam, that the Command and Prohibition are binding upon every single _'abd,_ so long as his sanity remains intact, up until he dies. The Command and Prohibition are never invalidated in his regard, not because of witnessing _al-Qadar_ or any other matter.

One who is unaware of this (basic fact) is to be taught and informed, if he persists in upholding the belief of the invalidation of the Command and Prohibition, he is to be killed.

Such similar doctrines and statements are numerous amongst the later generations, as for the predecessors of this _ummah_, these types of statements were not known amidst them.

These doctrines are (in essence) in opposition to Allaah and His Messenger, animosity towards them, an obstruction towards His path, contention with Him, denial of His Messengers, antagonistic to Him with regard to His rule, even though it may be possible that the one who professes such doctrines may be ignorant of this and believes that this path he is upon is the way of the Messenger and the way of the _awliyaa'_ of Allaah, the people of _tahqeeq_.

Under such circumstances, he bears resemblance to a person who believes that prayer is not obligatory over him because of his lack of need of it, as a result of the states and experiences of the heart he has undergone, or that intoxicating drinks are permissible for him because he is of the elite, who are not harmed by the consumption of intoxicating beverages, or that lewd deeds are lawful for him

---

[154] Soorah al-Hijr (15):99.

66

because he has become similar to an ocean, which cannot be marred by sins and other such accounts!

There is no doubt that the *Mushrikoon* who belied the Messenger (ﷺ), alternated between (committing) innovations that oppose the Law of Allaah and between adopting *al-Qadar* as proof for opposing the Command of Allaah.

Hence, these (aforementioned) groups bear some resemblance to the *Mushrikoon*, because they (also) either commit innovations or uphold *al-Qadar* as proof, or they may (even) combine both matters, as Allaah has informed us regarding the *Mushrikoon*:

وَإِذَا فَعَلُواْ

فَٰحِشَةً قَالُواْ وَجَدْنَا عَلَيْهَآ ءَابَآءَنَا وَٱللَّهُ أَمَرَنَا بِهَا قُلْ إِنَّ ٱللَّهَ لَا يَأْمُرُ بِٱلْفَحْشَآءِ أَتَقُولُونَ عَلَى ٱللَّهِ مَا لَا تَعْلَمُونَ ﴿٢٨﴾

"When they commit a lewd sin, they say, 'We found our fathers doing it, and Allaah has commanded it on us.' Say, 'Nay, Allaah never commands what is lewd. Do you say of Allaah what you know not?'"[155]

He has also said concerning them,

سَيَقُولُ ٱلَّذِينَ أَشْرَكُواْ

لَوْ شَآءَ ٱللَّهُ مَآ أَشْرَكْنَا وَلَآ ءَابَآؤُنَا وَلَا حَرَّمْنَا مِن شَيْءٍ

"Those who commit *shirk* with Allaah will say, 'If Allaah had willed, we would not have committed *shirk*, nor would our fathers, and we would not have forbidden anything (against His will).'"[156]

The innovations committed in the *Deen*, such as declaring lawful the unlawful and worshipping Allaah with what He has not legis-

---

[155] Soorah al-A'raaf (7):28.
[156] Soorah al-An'aam (6):148.

lated, have also been mentioned in connection with the *Mushrikoon*, as in His (ﷻ) saying:

$$وَقَالُوا هَٰذِهِ أَنْعَامٌ وَحَرْثٌ حِجْرٌ لَا يَطْعَمُهَا إِلَّا مَن
نَشَاءُ بِزَعْمِهِمْ وَأَنْعَامٌ حُرِّمَتْ ظُهُورُهَا وَأَنْعَامٌ لَا يَذْكُرُونَ
اسْمَ اللَّهِ عَلَيْهَا افْتِرَاءً عَلَيْهِ$$

"And according to their claim, they say that such and such cattle and crops are forbidden, and none should eat of them except those whom we allow. And (they say) there are cattle forbidden to use for burden (or any other work), and cattle on which (at slaughtering) the Name of Allaah is not pronounced; lying against Him (Allaah)."[157]

To the end of the *Soorah*. Likewise, in *Soorah al-A'raaf:*[158]

$$يَٰبَنِي ءَادَمَ لَا يَفْتِنَنَّكُمُ
الشَّيْطَانُ كَمَا أَخْرَجَ أَبَوَيْكُم مِّنَ الْجَنَّةِ يَنزِعُ عَنْهُمَا لِبَاسَهُمَا
لِيُرِيَهُمَا سَوْءَاتِهِمَا إِنَّهُ يَرَاكُمْ هُوَ وَقَبِيلُهُ مِنْ حَيْثُ لَا تَرَوْنَهُمْ
إِنَّا جَعَلْنَا الشَّيَاطِينَ أَوْلِيَاءَ لِلَّذِينَ لَا يُؤْمِنُونَ ﴿٢٧﴾ وَإِذَا فَعَلُوا
فَاحِشَةً قَالُوا وَجَدْنَا عَلَيْهَا ءَابَاءَنَا وَاللَّهُ أَمَرَنَا بِهَا قُلْ إِنَّ اللَّهَ
لَا يَأْمُرُ بِالْفَحْشَاءِ أَتَقُولُونَ عَلَى اللَّهِ مَا لَا تَعْلَمُونَ ﴿٢٨﴾ قُلْ
أَمَرَ رَبِّي بِالْقِسْطِ وَأَقِيمُوا وُجُوهَكُمْ عِندَ كُلِّ مَسْجِدٍ
وَادْعُوهُ مُخْلِصِينَ لَهُ الدِّينَ كَمَا بَدَأَكُمْ تَعُودُونَ ﴿٢٩﴾ فَرِيقًا
هَدَىٰ وَفَرِيقًا حَقَّ عَلَيْهِمُ الضَّلَالَةُ إِنَّهُمُ اتَّخَذُوا الشَّيَاطِينَ
أَوْلِيَاءَ مِن دُونِ اللَّهِ وَيَحْسَبُونَ أَنَّهُم مُّهْتَدُونَ ﴿٣٠﴾$$

---

[157] *Soorah al-An'aam* (6):138.

[158] *Aayaat* 27-33.

يَبَنِىٓ ءَادَمَ خُذُوا۟ زِينَتَكُمْ عِندَكُلِّ مَسْجِدٍ وَكُلُوا۟ وَٱشْرَبُوا۟ وَلَا تُسْرِفُوٓا۟ إِنَّهُۥ لَا يُحِبُّ ٱلْمُسْرِفِينَ ﴿٣١﴾ قُلْ مَنْ حَرَّمَ زِينَةَ ٱللَّهِ ٱلَّتِىٓ أَخْرَجَ لِعِبَادِهِۦ وَٱلطَّيِّبَٰتِ مِنَ ٱلرِّزْقِ قُلْ هِىَ لِلَّذِينَ ءَامَنُوا۟ فِى ٱلْحَيَوٰةِ ٱلدُّنْيَا خَالِصَةً يَوْمَ ٱلْقِيَٰمَةِ كَذَٰلِكَ نُفَصِّلُ ٱلْءَايَٰتِ لِقَوْمٍ يَعْلَمُونَ ﴿٣٢﴾ قُلْ إِنَّمَا حَرَّمَ رَبِّىَ ٱلْفَوَٰحِشَ مَا ظَهَرَ مِنْهَا وَمَا بَطَنَ وَٱلْإِثْمَ وَٱلْبَغْىَ بِغَيْرِ ٱلْحَقِّ وَأَن تُشْرِكُوا۟ بِٱللَّهِ مَا لَمْ يُنَزِّلْ بِهِۦ سُلْطَٰنًا وَأَن تَقُولُوا۟ عَلَى ٱللَّهِ مَا لَا تَعْلَمُونَ ﴿٣٣﴾

"O Children of Aadam! Let not *Shaytaan* deceive you, as he got your parents (Aadam and Hawwaa') out of Paradise, stripping them, of their clothing, to show them their private parts. Verily, he and his sort (i.e., his soldiers from the *jinn* or his tribe) see you from where you cannot see them. Verily, We made the *Shayaateen awliyaa'* for those who do not believe.

And when they commit a lewd deed, they say, 'We found our fathers doing it, and Allaah has commanded it on us.' Say, 'Nay, Allaah never commands what is lewd. Do you say of Allaah what you know not?'

Say (O Muhammad (ﷺ)), 'My Lord has commanded justice and (said) that you should face Him only (i.e., worship none but Allaah and face the *Qiblah*, i.e., the Ka'bah at Makkah during prayers) in each and every place of worship, in prayers (and not to face other false deities and idols), and invoke Him only making your religion sincere to Him by not joining in worship any partner to Him and with the intention that you are doing your deeds for Allaah's sake only. As He brought you (into being) in the beginning, so shall you be brought into being (on the Day of Resurrection) (in two groups, one as a blessed one (believers), and the other as a wretched one (disbelievers). A group He has guided, and a group deserved to be in error; (because) surely they took the *Shayaateen* (devils) as *awliyaa'* instead of Allaah, and consider that they are guided.

O Children of Aadam! Take your adornment (by wearing your clean clothes), when praying and circling the Ka'bah, and eat and drink but waste not by extravagance, certainly He (Allaah) does not like the *musrifoon* (those who waste by extravagance).

Say (O Muhammad (ﷺ)), 'Who has forbidden the adoration with clothes given by Allaah, which He has produced for His slaves, and *at-Tayyibaat* (all kinds of lawful things) of food?' Say, 'They are, in the life of this world, for those who believe, (and) exclusively for them (believers) on the Day of Resurrection (the disbelievers will not have a share of them).' Thus, We explain the *Aayaat* (Islamic laws) in detail for people who have knowledge.

Say (O Muhammad (ﷺ)), '(But) the things that my Lord has indeed forbidden are the *Fawaahish* (great evil sins, every kind of unlawful sexual intercourse, etc.) whether committed openly or secretly, sins (of all kinds), unrighteous oppression, joining partners (in worship) with Allaah for which He has given no authority, and saying things about Allaah of which you have no knowledge.'"[159]

These people may label the innovations they have invented as a reality or truth, just as they label the *Qadar* they witness to be a reality or truth.

---

[159] Soorah al-A'raaf (7):27-33.

The path pertaining to this reality, according to them, is the type of conduct in which the person does not confine himself to the Command and Prohibition of the Legislator (i.e., Allaah), but to what he himself sees, *tastes* and experiences in his heart - **in spite** of the inadvertence of Allaah that he actually has in his heart, etc.

These people do not adopt *al-Qadar* as proof in an unbound sense. Actually, their (prime) foundation is one of adherence to their own opinions and desires, and declaring what they see and what they desire to be a reality.

They instruct the people to follow this instead of the Command of Allaah and His Messenger (ﷺ), in similar standing to the people of *Kalaam* such as the *Jahmiyyah* and others, who declare the doctrines that they had innovated, which oppose the Book and *Sunnah*, to be rational realities that must be believed, in place of what the revealed texts point towards.

As for (their stance towards) the Book and the *Sunnah*, they either misconstrue the texts out of their proper context, or they neglect it completely, thereby not contemplating over it nor comprehending it, but instead declare, 'We entrust its meaning back to Allaah' whilst at the very same time they hold beliefs that are contrary to the indications of such texts.

If these people (i.e., people of *Kalaam*) actually fulfil these mentalities, which they maintain and which oppose the Book and *Sunnah*, absurd heresies and corrupt beliefs emerge.

Likewise, if they (i.e., the former groups) fulfil what they maintain to be the realities of the *awliyaa'* of Allaah, which oppose the Book and *Sunnah*, desires will emerge of which it is the enemies of Allaah who actually follow them and not the (real) *awliyaa'* of Allaah.

The root deviation of anyone who goes astray, is in placing forward ones own inference before the text that has been revealed

from Allaah and by placing forward the following of one's desires before that of following the Command of Allaah.

Since, taste, passion and such matters are relative to what the *'abd* loves and desires. Hence, every lover has a taste and passion that is relative to his love and desire.

The people of *eemaan* for instance, possess a taste and passion that is congruent to what the Prophet (ﷺ) has clarified in the <u>saheeh</u> <u>h</u>adeeth: *"Three (qualities), whoever possesses them, will find the sweetness of eemaan: that Allaah and His Messenger are more beloved to him besides anyone else, that he loves someone only for the sake of Allaah and that he hates to return to kufr after Allaah has delivered him from it just as he hates to be slung into the fire."*[160]

He (ﷺ) also said in a <u>saheeh</u> <u>h</u>adeeth: *"He indeed has tasted the relish of Eemaan: one who is pleased with Allaah as a Lord, with Islaam as a Deen, and with Mu<u>h</u>ammad as a Prophet."*[161]

As for the people of *kufr*, *bid'ah* and lusts, each one of them (also has a taste which) is relative to his own individuality.

Sufyaan Ibn 'Uyaynah was asked: "What is it with the people of desires in that they have extreme passion for their desires." His reply was something similar to: "Have you forgotten the saying of Allaah (ﷻ):

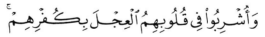

$$\text{وَأُشْرِبُوا۟ فِى قُلُوبِهِمُ ٱلْعِجْلَ بِكُفْرِهِمْ}$$

---

[160] Related by al-Bukhaaree (16, 21, 6041 & 6941); Muslim (43); Ibn Maajah (4033); an-Nasaa'ee (8/94-96); at-Tirmidhee (2626); A<u>h</u>mad (3/103, 172, 174, 230, 245, 275 & 288); a<u>t</u>-<u>T</u>ayaalisee (1959) and Ibn Mandah in *al-Eemaan* (281, 282 & 284) from Anas, may Allaah be pleased with him.

[161] Related by Muslim (24); at-Tirmidhee (2623); A<u>h</u>mad (1/208); al-Baghawee (1/52) and al-Bayhaqee in *al-Asmaa wa a<u>s</u>-<u>S</u>ifaat* (73) from al-'Abbaas Ibn 'Abdul-Mu<u>tt</u>alib, may Allaah be pleased with him.

"And their hearts absorbed (the worship of) the calf because of their disbelief."[162]

Thus, the worshippers of the idols love their deities, as Allaah (ﷻ) has said:

وَمِنَ ٱلنَّاسِ مَن يَتَّخِذُ مِن دُونِ ٱللَّهِ أَندَادًا يُحِبُّونَهُمْ كَحُبِّ ٱللَّهِ وَٱلَّذِينَ ءَامَنُوٓاْ أَشَدُّ حُبًّا لِّلَّهِ

"And of mankind are some who take (for worship) others besides Allaah as rivals (to Allaah). They love them as they love Allaah. But those who believe love Allaah more (than anything else)."[163]

He also said:

فَإِن لَّمْ يَسْتَجِيبُواْ لَكَ فَٱعْلَمْ أَنَّمَا يَتَّبِعُونَ أَهْوَآءَهُمْ وَمَنْ أَضَلُّ مِمَّنِ ٱتَّبَعَ هَوَىٰهُ بِغَيْرِ هُدًى مِّنَ ٱللَّهِ

"But if they answer you not (i.e., do not believe in your doctrine nor follow you) then know that they only follow their own lusts and who is more astray than one who follows his own lusts without any guidance from Allaah?"[164]

He also said

إِن يَتَّبِعُونَ إِلَّا ٱلظَّنَّ وَمَا تَهْوَى ٱلْأَنفُسُ وَلَقَدْ جَآءَهُم مِّن رَّبِّهِمُ ٱلْهُدَىٰ ﴿٢٣﴾

"They follow but conjecture and that which their souls desire. And indeed there has already come to them the Guidance from their Lord!"[165]

---

[162] Soorah al-Baqarah (2):93.
[163] Soorah al-Baqarah (2):165.
[164] Soorah al-Qasas (28):50.
[165] Soorah Najm (53):23.

This is the reason why these people deviate and become very fond of listening to poetry and sounds that stimulate general love, which is not specific to the people of *eemaan*. In fact, it is common to the lover of the Beneficent; the lover of the idols; the lover of the crosses; the lover of one's native lands, the lover of brethren, the lover of *murdaan* and the lover of women.

These are ones who follow their own tastes and passions without any consideration given to the Book, the *Sunnah* and the way the *Salaf* of this *ummah* were upon.

Consequently, the one who opposes that which Allaah sent His Messenger with of worship of Allaah alone and obedience to Him and His Messenger, can never be one who is following a *Deen* that Allaah has legislated, as Allaah (ﷻ) has said:

$$ ثُمَّ جَعَلْنَٰكَ عَلَىٰ شَرِيعَةٍ مِّنَ ٱلْأَمْرِ فَٱتَّبِعْهَا وَلَا تَتَّبِعْ أَهْوَآءَ ٱلَّذِينَ لَا يَعْلَمُونَ ۝ إِنَّهُمْ لَن يُغْنُوا۟ عَنكَ مِنَ ٱللَّهِ شَيْـًٔا وَإِنَّ ٱلظَّٰلِمِينَ بَعْضُهُمْ أَوْلِيَآءُ بَعْضٍ وَٱللَّهُ وَلِىُّ ٱلْمُتَّقِينَ $$

"Then We have put you (O Muḥammad (ﷺ)) on an evident way of Our Commandment. So follow that, and do not follow the desires of those who know not. Verily, they can avail you nothing against Allaah. Verily, the _dhaalimoon_ are _awliyaa'_ of one another, but Allaah is the _Walee_ of the _muttaqoon_." [166]

He is instead, following his own desire without any guidance from Allaah. Allaah (ﷻ) says:

$$ أَمْ لَهُمْ شُرَكَٰٓؤُا۟ شَرَعُوا۟ لَهُم مِّنَ ٱلدِّينِ مَا لَمْ يَأْذَن بِهِ ٱللَّهُ $$

"Or do they have partners with Allaah who have legislated for them a _Deen_ which Allaah has not allowed?" [167]

---

[166] Soorah al-Jaathiyah (45):18-19.
[167] Soorah ash-Shoora (42):21.

In this, they are sometimes upon innovation, which they label as being a reality and place before Allaah's legislation. At other times, they adopt the universal *Qadar* as proof against the *Sharee'ah* just as Allaah had stated about the *Mushrikoon,* as mentioned previously.

Another section of these people, is a group that is held in the highest regard by them. They (i.e., the people of this faction) adhere to what they have chosen by their own desires of the *Deen* concerning performing the obligatory well-known duties and refraining from the well-known prohibitions.

Yet, they deviate by abandoning the causes, which they have been commanded with and which are actually manifestations of worship. They do this under the presumption that as for the *'aarif,* if he witnesses *al-Qadar,* he is to abandon such causes. An example of this is like the one amongst them who considers *tawakkul,* supplication, etc. as befitting the levels of the general populace and not for the elite, by virtue of the point that the one who witnesses *al-Qadar,* knows that what has been decreed will come to pass, so there is no need for that (i.e., to have *tawakkul* and supplicate and so on)!

This is manifest deviation. Since, Allaah measures matters by their causes, just as He measured happiness and misery by their causes. This is just as the Prophet (ﷺ) said: *"Allaah has for paradise a (specific) people. He created it for them whilst they were still in their fathers' loins **and with the actions of the people of paradise, they act.** He created for the Fire a (specific) people. He created it for them whilst they were still in their fathers' loins and **with the actions of the people of the Fire, they act.** "*[168]

The Prophet (ﷺ) further told them (i.e., the Companions) when he informed them that Allaah had recorded every measure and they

---

[168] Related by Muslim (2662); Aboo Daawood (4713); an-Nasaa'ee (4/57); Ibn Maajah (82); Ahmad (6/41 & 208) and al-Aajurree in *ash-Sharee'ah* (196) from 'Aa'ishah.

replied, *'O Messenger of Allaah! Shall we then not abandon performing actions and rely upon the Book?"* He said: *"No, perform deeds, as each one of you is facilitated towards that which he was created for. Those who are among the people of happiness, they will be helped to do the deeds of the people of happiness. As for those who are among the people of misery, they will be helped to do the deeds of the people of misery."*[169]

Thus, all of the causes that Allaah has ordered His *'ibaad* with, they are of worship. Moreover, *tawakkul* is associated with worship, as in the saying of Allaah (ﷻ):

$$فَٱعْبُدْهُ وَتَوَكَّلْ عَلَيْهِ$$

"So worship Him (O Muhammad (ﷺ)) and have *tawakkul* in Him."[170]

And His (ﷻ) saying:

$$قُلْ هُوَ رَبِّى لَآ إِلَهَ إِلَّا هُوَ عَلَيْهِ تَوَكَّلْتُ وَإِلَيْهِ مَتَابِ ۝$$

"Say, 'He (Allaah) is my Lord! None has the right to be worshiped but He! On Him I have *tawakkul* and to Him will be my return with repentance."[171]

And the saying of Shu'ayb:

$$عَلَيْهِ تَوَكَّلْتُ وَإِلَيْهِ أُنِيبُ ۝$$

"In Him (Allaah) I have *tawakkul* and unto Him I repent."[172]

---

[169] Related by al-Bukhaaree (1362, 4945 & 4946); Muslim (2647); Aboo Daawood (4694); at-Tirmidhee (2136 & 3344); Ahmad (1/82, 129, 132 & 140); Ibn Maajah (78); an-Nasaa'ee in *al-Kubraa* as mentioned in *Tuhfah al-Ashraaf* (7/399); 'Abdur-Razzaaq in *al-Musannaf* (20074); Ibn Hibbaan (34 & 35) and al-Aajurree (171-172) from 'Alee, may Allaah be pleased with him.

[170] Soorah Hood (11):123.

[171] Soorah ar-Ra'd (13):30.

[172] Soorah Hood (11):88.

Another (section) of these people, is a group who may abandon the recommended deeds but not the obligatory duties and thus, they lessen accordingly (because of their abandonment of the recommended duties).

Another type, is a group that is deluded by the extraordinary occurrences that befall them,[173] such as *mukaashafah*, an answer of a supplication in an unusual manner and so on. Consequently, they become preoccupied with these matters instead of the worship and gratitude they have been commanded with.

Such matters commonly occur to the people of *Sulook* and *Tawajjuh*. Indeed however, the *'abd* can only save himself from such matters by holding fast to Allaah's Command, with which He sent His Messenger, at all times.

As az-Zuhree said: "Those who passed of our *Salaf* used to proclaim, 'Adherence to the *Sunnah*, is the salvation.'"[174]

The reasoning is that the *Sunnah* is as Maalik, may Allaah have mercy upon him, said: "Like the ark of Nooh; whoever embarks upon it will be saved and whoever stays behind, drowns."

Worship, obedience, uprightness, holding fast to the Straight Path and the like of such terms, which have one sole purpose, possess two pillars:

The first, that none should be worshipped except Allaah.

The second, that He should not be worshipped except with what has been commanded and legislated; He should not be worshipped with

---

[173] Like many who claim to perform miracles, the vast majority of them are great liars, deceivers and fraudulent!

[174] Refer to *Miftaah al-Jannah fee al-Ihtijaaj bi as-Sunnah*, pg. 129

other than that, such as with desires, conjectures and innovations. Allaah (ﷻ) said:

فَمَن كَانَ يَرْجُواْ لِقَآءَ رَبِّهِۦ فَلْيَعْمَلْ عَمَلًا صَٰلِحًا وَلَا يُشْرِكْ بِعِبَادَةِ رَبِّهِۦٓ أَحَدًۢا ۝

"So whoever hopes for the meeting with his Lord, let him do righteous deeds and associate none as partner in worship of his Lord."[175]

Allaah (ﷻ) also said:

بَلَىٰ مَنْ أَسْلَمَ وَجْهَهُۥ لِلَّهِ وَهُوَ مُحْسِنٌ فَلَهُۥٓ أَجْرُهُۥ عِندَ رَبِّهِۦ وَلَا خَوْفٌ عَلَيْهِمْ وَلَا هُمْ يَحْزَنُونَ ۝

"Yes, but whoever submits himself to Allaah and he is a good-doer, his reward is with his Lord, on such shall be no fear, nor shall they grieve."[176]

He (ﷻ) also said:

وَمَنْ أَحْسَنُ دِينًا مِّمَّنْ أَسْلَمَ وَجْهَهُۥ لِلَّهِ وَهُوَ مُحْسِنٌ وَٱتَّبَعَ مِلَّةَ إِبْرَٰهِيمَ حَنِيفًا وَٱتَّخَذَ ٱللَّهُ إِبْرَٰهِيمَ خَلِيلًا ۝

"And who can be better in *Deen* than one who submits to Allaah, and he is a doer of good (deeds) and follows the way of Ibraaheem, the worshipper of none but Allaah Alone? Indeed, Allaah did take Ibraaheem as a *khaleel*."[177]

The righteous deed is *Ihsaan* and that is to perform good acts. Good acts are those which are loved by Allaah and His Messenger and which have either been commanded as an obligation or recommendation.

---

[175] Soorah al-Kahf (18):110.
[176] Soorah al-Baqarah (2):112.
[177] Soorah an-Nisaa (4):125.

78

Therefore, whatever is found amidst the *Deen* by way of innovations that are not in the Book, nor in the authentic *Sunnah*, then these are not legislated, regardless of who professes them and of who performs them. Since, Allaah does not love them nor does His Messenger, so they are not of the good acts or righteous deeds.

This is the same as when one commits impermissible actions such as lewd sins and oppression, they are not good acts or righteous deeds.

As for His saying:

وَلَا يُشْرِكْ بِعِبَادَةِ رَبِّهِ أَحَدًا ۝

"…And (let him) associate none as partner in worship of his Lord."[178]

And His saying:

مَنْ أَسْلَمَ وَجْهَهُ لِلَّهِ

"…He who submits himself to Allaah…"[179]

This is in reference to purifying the *Deen* for Allaah alone.

'Umar bin al-Khattaab used to say, "O Allaah, make all my actions righteous and make them purely for your Face and do not let anyone have a share in them."

Al-Fudayl ibn 'Iyaad[180] stated in explanation to His (ﷻ) saying:

لِيَبْلُوَكُمْ أَيُّكُمْ أَحْسَنُ عَمَلًا

"That He (Allaah) may test you as to which of you is best in deed."[181]

---

[178] Soorah al-Kahf (18):110.

[179] Soorah al- Baqarah (2):112.

[180] An *Imaam*, a model and ascetic. He passed away in the year 186H. His biography can be found in *Siyar al-'Alaam an-Nubalaa'* (8/372).

[181] Soorah al-Mulk (67):2.

"The most sincere and most correct." The people questioned: "O Aboo 'Alee, how does it become the most sincere and the most correct?" He answered: "Indeed, the action, if it is done sincerely but not correctly, it is not accepted and if it is done correctly but not sincerely, it is not accepted, until it is done sincerely and correctly. The sincere deed is that it is for Allaah (alone) and the correct deed is that it conforms to the *Sunnah*."[182]

If one questions: "If everything that Allaah loves is encompassed by the term *'ibaadah*, why did Allaah connect other terms to it (in one clause) as in His saying in the opening of the Book:

$$\text{إِيَّاكَ نَعْبُدُ وَإِيَّاكَ نَسْتَعِينُ ﴿٥﴾}$$

"You (Alone) we worship *and* You (Alone) we ask for help."[183]

And in His saying to His Prophet:

$$\text{فَاعْبُدْهُ وَتَوَكَّلْ عَلَيْهِ}$$

"So worship Him (O Mu<u>h</u>ammad (ﷺ)) *and* have *tawakkul* in Him."[184]

And the saying of Noo<u>h</u> (to his people):

$$\text{أَنِ اعْبُدُوا اللَّهَ وَاتَّقُوهُ وَأَطِيعُونِ ﴿٣﴾}$$

"You should worship Allaah *and* protect yourselves from Him (by warding off evil) *and* obey me."[185]

In similar regard, there are statements of other Messengers.

The answer is: This (literary style) has many comparable examples, as in His saying:

---

[182] Within my book *'Ilm U<u>s</u>ool al-Bida'* is a substantial account - Allaah willing - of this principle.

[183] Soorah al-Faati<u>h</u>ah (1):5.

[184] Soorah Hood (11):123.

[185] Soorah Noo<u>h</u> (71):3.

$$إِنَّ ٱلصَّلَوٰةَ تَنْهَىٰ عَنِ ٱلْفَحْشَآءِ وَٱلْمُنكَرِ$$

"Verily, Prayer prevents (one) from (committing) al-Faḥshaa (lewd sins) and al-Munkar (reprehensible deeds)."[186]

Al-Faḥshaa (blatant sin) is a type of al-Munkar (the reprehensible deeds). Likewise, His saying:

$$إِنَّ ٱللَّهَ يَأْمُرُ بِٱلْعَدْلِ وَٱلْإِحْسَٰنِ وَإِيتَآئِ ذِى ٱلْقُرْبَىٰ وَيَنْهَىٰ عَنِ ٱلْفَحْشَآءِ وَٱلْمُنكَرِ وَٱلْبَغْىِ$$

"Verily! Allaah enjoins al-Adl (justice) and al-Iḥsaan (beneficence), and giving (help) to kith and kin and He forbids al-Faḥshaa (lewd sins) and al-Munkar (reprehensible deeds), and al-Baghy (all kinds of oppression)."[187]

Giving help to kith and kin is part of al-'Adl (justice) and Iḥsaan (beneficence) just as al-Faḥshaa and al-Baghy are of al-Munkar. Also, in His saying,

$$وَٱلَّذِينَ يُمَسِّكُونَ بِٱلْكِتَٰبِ وَأَقَامُوا۟ ٱلصَّلَوٰةَ$$

"And as to those who hold fast by the Book and establish Prayer (perfectly)."[188]

Establishing prayer is of the greatest ways of holding fast to the Book. In addition, Allaah's statement about His Prophets:

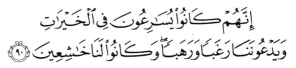

---

[186] Soorah al-'Ankaboot (29):45.

[187] Soorah an-Naḥl (16):90.

[188] Soorah al-A'raaf (7):170.

"Verily, they used to rush to do good deeds, *and* they used to call on Us with hope and fear and they used to humble themselves before Us."[189]

Their supplication out of hope and fear is part of doing good deeds. Examples of such kind are numerous in the Qur'aan.

As for (the signification of) this type (of literary style), in certain instances, one of the terms is a constituent of the other, and thus, the specific term is connected to the broader term to specifically single it out by mentioning it. This is done (in such occasions) when the single term is sought after from (both) the general meaning (found in the broad term) as well as from the specific meaning (found in the specific term).

In other instances, the connotation of the very term itself varies in accordance to whether it is mentioned separately or when mentioned in a connected manner (with other terms).

If the term is mentioned independently, it takes on a general meaning and when it is connected to other terms, it takes on a specific meaning. For example, the terms '*al-Faqeer*' (the poor) and the term '*al-Miskeen*' (the needy); when any one of them is mentioned separately, the other term also becomes included in it, as in His (ﷻ) saying:

"(Charity is) for the *fuqaraa*,[190] **who in Allaah's Cause are restricted (from travel)."**[191]

And His (ﷻ) saying:

إِطْعَامُ عَشَرَةِ مَسَـٰكِينَ

---

[189] Soorah al-Anbiyaa (21):90.

[190] The plural of *faqeer*. So here, the *fuqaraa* include the *masaakeen* as well. [t]

[191] Soorah al-Baqarah (2):273.

"…or feeding ten *masaakeen*[192] persons."[193]

However, when they are used in conjunction with each other, as in His saying:

$$\text{إِنَّمَا ٱلصَّدَقَٰتُ لِلْفُقَرَآءِ وَٱلْمَسَٰكِينِ}$$

*"Zakaat is only for the *fuqaraa* and the masaakeen…"*[194]

They become two distinct categories (i.e., each taking on a specific meaning). It has also been maintained that, whenever a specific term is connected after a general term, the specific term no longer remains embedded within the general term, but instead belongs to this (aforementioned) type (above).

The correct position however, is that this is not always necessarily true. Allaah (ﷻ) says:

$$\text{مَن كَانَ عَدُوًّا لِّلَّهِ وَمَلَٰٓئِكَتِهِۦ وَرُسُلِهِۦ وَجِبْرِيلَ وَمِيكَٰلَ}$$

"Whoever is an enemy to Allaah and His angels and His Messengers *and* Jibreel and Meekaal…"[195, 196]

He (ﷻ) also said:

$$\text{وَإِذْ أَخَذْنَا مِنَ ٱلنَّبِيِّـۧنَ مِيثَٰقَهُمْ وَمِنكَ وَمِن نُّوحٍ وَإِبْرَٰهِيمَ وَمُوسَىٰ وَعِيسَى ٱبْنِ مَرْيَمَ}$$

---

[192] The plural of *miskeen*. Likewise here, the *masaakeen* include the *fuqaraa* as well. [t]

[193] Soorah al-Maaidah (5):89.

[194] Soorah at-Tawbah (9):60.

[195] Soorah al-Baqarah (2):98.

[196] The point being made here is that *Jibreel* and *Meekaal* are specific terms that have been mentioned after a general term: *Angels*. At the same time however, they still remain well embedded within the meaning of this general term. Thus, they are referred to in this general term and again in their own specific terms for the purpose of specification and individualisation, which emanates from various reasons, some of which are about to be mentioned by Shaykhul-Islaam in the forthcoming paragraph. [t]

"And (remember) when We took from the prophets their covenant *and* from you (O Mu<u>h</u>ammad (ﷺ)) *and* from Noo<u>h</u> *and* Ibraaheem *and* Moosa, *and* 'Eesa Ibn Maryam."[197]

Mentioning the specific term alongside the general term can be for a variety of reasons. Sometimes, it might be because this specific term possesses a particular speciality that is not found in the remaining single terms that form the general term. This is the case of (the mentioning of) Noo<u>h</u>, Ibraaheem, Moosa and 'Eesa (in the previous *aayah*).

On another occasion, it may be because the general term is so absolute, that one might not comprehend (the detail of) its generality, as in His saying:

"…a guidance to the *muttaqoon*. Who believe in the *Ghayb* (the Unseen), establish Prayer, and spend out of what We have provided for them. *And* who believe in that which has been sent down (revealed) to you (Mu<u>h</u>ammad (ﷺ)) and in that which was sent down (revealed) before you."[198]

Thus, His saying, "They believe in *al-Ghayb* (the Unseen)", encompasses all the *ghayb* which one must believe in, however, it is very extensive. There is not within it an indication that part of the *ghayb* is "What has been revealed to you (Mu<u>h</u>ammad (ﷺ)) and what has been revealed before you."

---

[197] Soorah al-A<u>h</u>zaab (33):7.
[198] Soorah al-Baqarah (2):2-5.

84

Another example befitting this sort is the saying of Allaah (ﷻ):

اتْلُ مَآ أُوحِىَ إِلَيْكَ مِنَ ٱلْكِتَبِ وَأَقِمِ ٱلصَّلَوٰةَ

"Recite what is revealed to you of the Book *and* establish Prayer."[199]

And His (ﷻ) saying:

وَٱلَّذِينَ يُمَسِّكُونَ بِٱلْكِتَبِ وَأَقَامُوا ٱلصَّلَوٰةَ

"And those who hold fast by the Book *and* establish Prayer."[200]

The *tilaawah* (recitation) of the Book is actually following it and acting by it, as Ibn Mas'ood has commented on the saying of Allaah (ﷻ):

ٱلَّذِينَ ءَاتَيْنَهُمُ ٱلْكِتَبَ يَتْلُونَهُۥ حَقَّ تِلَاوَتِهِ

"Those to whom We have given the Book, recite It as It should be recited."[201]

He said: "They declare its lawful to be lawful, its unlawful to be unlawful, believe in its *mutashaabih* and they act by its *muhkam* (clear and conclusive *aayaat*)."[202]

Following the Book encompasses Prayer as well as other matters. However, Allaah mentioned it specifically because of its excellence. Another example is His statement to Moosa:

إِنَّنِىٓ أَنَا ٱللَّهُ لَآ إِلَهَ إِلَّآ أَنَا۠ فَٱعْبُدْنِى وَأَقِمِ ٱلصَّلَوٰةَ لِذِكْرِىٓ

"Verily! I am Allaah, there is no deity but I, so worship Me *and* establish Prayer for My remembrance."[203]

---

[199] Soorah al-'Ankaboot (29):45.

[200] Soorah al-A'raaf (7):170.

[201] Soorah al-Baqarah (2):121.

[202] Related by Ibn Jareer in *Jaami' al-'Uloom* (2/519) and 'Abdur-Razzaaq in his *Tafseer* (1/56).

[203] Soorah Taa Haa (20):14.

85

Establishing prayer for His remembrance is one of the most exalted manifestations of worshipping Allaah. Also, His (ﷻ) saying:

$$اَتَّقُواْ ٱللَّهَ وَقُولُواْ قَوْلًا سَدِيدًا ﴿٧٠﴾$$

"…have *taqwaa* of Allaah and (always) speak the truth."[204]

His saying:

$$اَتَّقُواْ ٱللَّهَ وَٱبْتَغُوٓاْ إِلَيْهِ ٱلْوَسِيلَةَ$$

"…have *taqwaa* of Allaah and seek the means of approach to Him."[205]

His saying:

$$اَتَّقُواْ ٱللَّهَ وَكُونُواْ مَعَ ٱلصَّـٰدِقِينَ$$

"…have *taqwaa* of Allaah and be with the truthful."[206]

All these matters constitute the perfection of having *taqwaa* of Allaah. Also, His saying,

$$فَٱعْبُدْهُ وَتَوَكَّلْ عَلَيْهِ$$

"So worship Him (Allaah) and have *tawakkul* in Him."[207]

Tawakkul is to seek aid, and this pertains to worship. It has been specifically mentioned here however, so that the worshipper may attune himself to it and seek it specifically as it is the aid to (enacting) all other types of worship. Indeed, Allaah (ﷻ) cannot be worshipped except through His assistance (afforded to the slave).

---

[204] Soorah al-Ahzaab (33):71.
[205] Soorah al-Maa idah (5):35.
[206] Soorah at-Tawbah (9):119.
[207] Soorah Hood (11):123.

If this matter becomes clear, the perfection of the creature, is dependent on the accomplishment of his *'uboodiyyah* to Allaah. The more the *'abd* fulfils *al-'uboodiyyah*, the greater his perfection will be and the higher his rank will be. As for whoever supposes that creation can draw away from *'uboodiyyah* in any manner whatsoever or that drawing away from it is a greater perfection, he is indeed of the most ignorant amongst all the creation. In fact, he is of the most astray amongst them. Allaah (ﷻ) has said:

وَقَالُواْ ٱتَّخَذَ ٱلرَّحْمَٰنُ وَلَدًا سُبْحَٰنَهُۥ ۚ بَلْ عِبَادٌ مُّكْرَمُونَ ﴿٢٦﴾ لَا يَسْبِقُونَهُۥ بِٱلْقَوْلِ وَهُم بِأَمْرِهِۦ يَعْمَلُونَ ﴿٢٧﴾ يَعْلَمُ مَا بَيْنَ أَيْدِيهِمْ وَمَا خَلْفَهُمْ وَلَا يَشْفَعُونَ إِلَّا لِمَنِ ٱرْتَضَىٰ وَهُم مِّنْ خَشْيَتِهِۦ مُشْفِقُونَ

"And they say, 'ar-Rahmaan has begotten children.' How perfect He is! They are but honoured *'Ibaad*. They do not speak until He has spoken and they act by His Command. He knows what is before them and what is behind them. They cannot intercede except for one whom He (Himself) is pleased with, and they stand in awe for fear of Him."[208]

He (ﷻ) also said:

وَقَالُواْ ٱتَّخَذَ ٱلرَّحْمَٰنُ وَلَدًا ﴿٨٨﴾ لَّقَدْ جِئْتُمْ شَيْئًا إِدًّا ﴿٨٩﴾ تَكَادُ ٱلسَّمَٰوَٰتُ يَتَفَطَّرْنَ مِنْهُ وَتَنشَقُّ ٱلْأَرْضُ وَتَخِرُّ ٱلْجِبَالُ هَدًّا ﴿٩٠﴾ أَن دَعَوْا لِلرَّحْمَٰنِ وَلَدًا ﴿٩١﴾ وَمَا يَنبَغِي لِلرَّحْمَٰنِ أَن يَتَّخِذَ وَلَدًا ﴿٩٢﴾ إِن كُلُّ مَن فِي ٱلسَّمَٰوَٰتِ وَٱلْأَرْضِ إِلَّا ءَاتِي ٱلرَّحْمَٰنِ عَبْدًا ﴿٩٣﴾ لَّقَدْ أَحْصَىٰهُمْ وَعَدَّهُمْ عَدًّا ﴿٩٤﴾ وَكُلُّهُمْ ءَاتِيهِ يَوْمَ ٱلْقِيَٰمَةِ فَرْدًا ﴿٩٥﴾

---

[208] Soorah al-Anbiyaa (21):26-28.

"And they say, 'ar-Rahmaan has begotten children.' Indeed, you have brought forth a terrible evil thing. The heavens are about to rip apart, the earth to split asunder and the mountains to fall in ruins; in that, they ascribed children to ar-Rahmaan. It is not be-fitting (the Majesty) of ar-Rahmaan that He should beget children. There is none in the heavens and the earth but comes unto ar-Rahmaan as an *'abd*. Verily He knows their number and has enumerated them most definitely and precisely. Every one of them will come to Him on the Day of Resurrection, alone."[209]

Allaah (ﷻ) said concerning the *Maseeh* (i.e., 'Eesa Ibn Maryam):

إِنْ هُوَ إِلَّا عَبْدٌ أَنْعَمْنَا عَلَيْهِ وَجَعَلْنَهُ مَثَلًا لِّبَنِىٓ إِسْرَءِيلَ

"He (i.e., 'Eesaa) was no more than an *'abd*. We favoured him and made him an example for the Children of Israa'eel."[210]

He (ﷻ) also said:

وَلَهُۥ مَن فِى ٱلسَّمَٰوَٰتِ وَٱلْأَرْضِ وَمَنْ عِندَهُۥ لَا يَسْتَكْبِرُونَ عَنْ عِبَادَتِهِۦ وَلَا يَسْتَحْسِرُونَ ۝ يُسَبِّحُونَ ٱلَّيْلَ وَٱلنَّهَارَ لَا يَفْتُرُونَ ۝

"To Him belongs whoever is in the heavens and the earth. And those who are with Him (i.e., the An-gels) do not disdain to worship Him and they never become weary. They exalt Him night and day, never slackening."[211]

---

[209] Soorah Maryam (19):88-95.
[210] Soorah az-Zukhruf (43):59.
[211] Soorah al-Anbiyaa (21):19-20.

He (ﷺ) said:

$$\text{لَّن يَسْتَنكِفَ ٱلْمَسِيحُ أَن يَكُونَ عَبْدًا لِّلَّهِ وَلَا ٱلْمَلَـٰٓئِكَةُ ٱلْمُقَرَّبُونَ ۚ وَمَن يَسْتَنكِفْ عَنْ عِبَادَتِهِۦ وَيَسْتَكْبِرْ فَسَيَحْشُرُهُمْ إِلَيْهِ جَمِيعًا ۝ فَأَمَّا ٱلَّذِينَ ءَامَنُوا۟ وَعَمِلُوا۟ ٱلصَّـٰلِحَـٰتِ فَيُوَفِّيهِمْ أُجُورَهُمْ وَيَزِيدُهُم مِّن فَضْلِهِۦ ۖ وَأَمَّا ٱلَّذِينَ ٱسْتَنكَفُوا۟ وَٱسْتَكْبَرُوا۟ فَيُعَذِّبُهُمْ عَذَابًا أَلِيمًا وَلَا يَجِدُونَ لَهُم مِّن دُونِ ٱللَّهِ وَلِيًّا وَلَا نَصِيرًا}$$

"*Al-Maseeh* will never be too proud to reject to be an '*abd* to Allaah, nor even the Angels who are near (to Allaah). And whosoever rejects His worship and is proud, He (Allaah) will gather them all together unto Himself. So as for those who believed and did righteous deeds, He will give them their (due) rewards, and more out of His Bounty. But as for those who refuse His worship and were proud, He will punish them with a painful torment and they will not find for themselves besides Allaah any protector or helper."[212]

He (ﷺ) also said:

$$\text{وَقَالَ رَبُّكُمُ ٱدْعُونِىٓ أَسْتَجِبْ لَكُمْ ۚ إِنَّ ٱلَّذِينَ يَسْتَكْبِرُونَ عَنْ عِبَادَتِى سَيَدْخُلُونَ جَهَنَّمَ دَاخِرِينَ}$$

"And your Lord said, 'Invoke Me, I will respond to your (invocation)'. Verily, those who scorn My worship, will enter Hell in humiliation!"[213]

---

[212] Soorah an-Nisaa (4):172-173.
[213] Soorah al-Ghaafir (40):60.

Allaah (ﷻ) said:

وَمِنْ ءَايَـٰتِهِ
ٱلَّيْلُ وَٱلنَّهَارُ وَٱلشَّمْسُ وَٱلْقَمَرُ لَا تَسْجُدُوا۟ لِلشَّمْسِ
وَلَا لِلْقَمَرِ وَٱسْجُدُوا۟ لِلَّهِ ٱلَّذِى خَلَقَهُنَّ إِن كُنتُمْ
إِيَّاهُ تَعْبُدُونَ ﴿٣٧﴾ فَإِنِ ٱسْتَكْبَرُوا۟ فَٱلَّذِينَ عِندَ
رَبِّكَ يُسَبِّحُونَ لَهُۥ بِٱلَّيْلِ وَٱلنَّهَارِ وَهُمْ لَا يَسْـَٔمُونَ ﴿٣٨﴾

"And from among His Signs are the night and the day, and the sun and the moon. Prostrate not to the sun nor to the moon, but prostrate to Allaah Who created them if you (really) worship Him. But if they are too proud (to do so), then there are those who are with your Lord (Angels) exalting Him night and day and they never tire."[214]

He (ﷻ) also said:

وَٱذْكُر رَّبَّكَ
فِى نَفْسِكَ تَضَرُّعًا وَخِيفَةً وَدُونَ ٱلْجَهْرِ مِنَ ٱلْقَوْلِ بِٱلْغُدُوِّ
وَٱلْـَٔاصَالِ وَلَا تَكُن مِّنَ ٱلْغَٰفِلِينَ ﴿٢٠٥﴾ إِنَّ ٱلَّذِينَ عِندَ رَبِّكَ
لَا يَسْتَكْبِرُونَ عَنْ عِبَادَتِهِۦ وَيُسَبِّحُونَهُۥ وَلَهُۥ يَسْجُدُونَ ﴿٢٠٦﴾

"And (O Muhammad (ﷺ)) remember your Lord in your (very) soul, humbly and with fear, without loudness in words in the mornings and evenings, and be not of those who are neglectful. Surely those who are near to your Lord are never too proud to worship Him, and they exalt Him and prostrate before Him."[215]

---

[214] Soorah Fussilat (41):37-38.
[215] Soorah al-A'raaf (7):205-206.

These *aayaat* and their like, in which the best of creation are depicted with worship and in which those who come away from that are condemned, are numerous in the Qur'aan.

In fact, Allaah (ﷻ) explained that He sent all the Messengers with this (worship). He (ﷻ) said:

$$وَمَا أَرْسَلْنَا مِن قَبْلِكَ مِن رَّسُولٍ إِلَّا نُوحِىٓ إِلَيْهِ أَنَّهُ لَآ إِلَٰهَ$$
$$إِلَّآ أَنَا۠ فَٱعْبُدُونِ ٢٥$$

"And We did not send any messenger before you (O Muḥammad) but We revealed unto him that none has the right to be worshipped but I (Allaah), so worship Me (Alone)."[216]

Allaah said:

$$وَلَقَدْ بَعَثْنَا فِى كُلِّ أُمَّةٍ رَّسُولًا أَنِ ٱعْبُدُوا۟ ٱللَّهَ$$
$$وَٱجْتَنِبُوا۟ ٱلطَّٰغُوتَ$$

"And verily We have sent amongst every nation a messenger (saying), 'Worship Allaah (Alone) and avoid all false deities.'"[217]

Allaah (ﷻ) said to the Banee Israa'eel:

$$يَٰعِبَادِىَ ٱلَّذِينَ ءَامَنُوٓا۟ إِنَّ أَرْضِى وَٰسِعَةٌ فَإِيَّٰىَ فَٱعْبُدُونِ$$

"O My *'ibaad*, who believe! My earth is indeed spacious. Therefore, worship Me (Alone)."[218]

$$وَإِيَّٰىَ فَٱتَّقُونِ$$

"And of Me, have *taqwaa*."[219]

---

[216] Soorah al-Anbiyaa (21):25.
[217] Soorah an-Naḥl (16):36.
[218] Soorah al-'Ankaboot (29):56.
[219] Soorah al-Baqarah (2):41.

He said:

يَٰٓأَيُّهَا ٱلنَّاسُ ٱعۡبُدُواْ رَبَّكُمُ ٱلَّذِى خَلَقَكُمۡ وَٱلَّذِينَ مِن قَبۡلِكُمۡ لَعَلَّكُمۡ تَتَّقُونَ ﴿٢١﴾

"O mankind! Worship your Lord, Who created you
and those who were before you so that you may have
taqwaa."[220]

He said:

وَمَا خَلَقۡتُ ٱلۡجِنَّ وَٱلۡإِنسَ إِلَّا لِيَعۡبُدُونِ ﴿٥٦﴾

"And I did not create the *jinn* and men except that
they should worship Me (Alone)."[221]

Allaah (ﷻ) also said:

قُلۡ إِنِّىٓ أُمِرۡتُ أَنۡ أَعۡبُدَ ٱللَّهَ مُخۡلِصًا لَّهُ ٱلدِّينَ ﴿١١﴾ وَأُمِرۡتُ لِأَنۡ أَكُونَ أَوَّلَ ٱلۡمُسۡلِمِينَ ﴿١٢﴾ قُلۡ إِنِّىٓ أَخَافُ إِنۡ عَصَيۡتُ رَبِّى عَذَابَ يَوۡمٍ عَظِيمٍ ﴿١٣﴾ قُلِ ٱللَّهَ أَعۡبُدُ مُخۡلِصًا لَّهُۥ دِينِى ﴿١٤﴾ فَٱعۡبُدُواْ مَا شِئۡتُم مِّن دُونِهِۦٓ

"Say (O Mu<u>h</u>ammad (ﷺ)), 'Verily, I am commanded
to worship Allaah (Alone) making the *Deen* pure
for Him only and I am commanded to be the first of
those who are Muslims (those who surrender to
Allaah).' Say, 'Verily, I fear, if I disobey my Lord,
the torment of a great Day'. Say, '(It is) Allaah alone
that I worship making my *Deen* pure for Him only,
so worship what you like besides Him.'"[222]

Every one of the Messengers started his call with the invitation to
the worship of Allaah (alone), as (shown) in the saying of Noo<u>h</u> and
those who came after him (as revealed) in *Soorah ash-Shu'araa*
and other *Soorahs*:

---

[220] Soorah al-Baqarah (2):21.
[221] Soorah adh-Dhaariyaat (51):56.
[222] Soorah az-Zumar (39):11-15.

$$\text{أَنِ اعْبُدُواْ اللَّهَ مَالَكُم مِّنْ إِلَهٍ غَيْرُهُ}$$

"Worship Allaah! You have no other deity but Him."[223]

Moreover, in the *Musnad*[224] (of Imaam Ahmad), Ibn 'Umar relates that the Prophet (ﷺ) said: *"I was sent with the sword just before the Hour so that Allaah is worshipped, with no partner. My sustenance was made under the shadow of my spear, and humiliation and low-liness were made for those who disobey my order."*

Allaah (ﷻ) has clarified that His chosen *'ibaad* are the ones who escape from the evil that *Shaytaan* makes alluring. *Shaytaan* said (as Allaah (ﷻ) related on him):

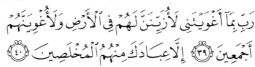

"O my Lord! Because You misled me I shall indeed adorn (the path of error) for them (i.e., mankind) on earth and I shall mislead them all; save Your chosen, guided *'Ibaad* amongst them."[225]

Allaah (ﷻ) said:

$$\text{هَذَا صِرَاطٌ عَلَيَّ مُسْتَقِيمٌ ﴿٤١﴾ إِنَّ عِبَادِى}$$
$$\text{لَيْسَ لَكَ عَلَيْهِمْ سُلْطَنٌ إِلَّا مَنِ اتَّبَعَكَ مِنَ الْغَاوِينَ ﴿٤٢﴾}$$

"This is the Way which will lead straight to Me. Certainly, you have no authority over My *'Ibaad*, except those who follow you of the errant."[226]

---

[223] Soorah al-Mu'minoon (23):32.

[224] (2/50 & 92) With a chain of narration that is *hasan*. I have discussed its ruling and chains of narrations at length in the beginning of the treatise on the commentary to the *hadeeth* authored by al-Haafidh Ibn Rajab, *al-Hikam al-Jadeerah bi al-Ithaa'ah*… May Allaah facilitate its publication.

[225] Soorah al-Hijr (15):39-40.

[226] Soorah al-Hijr (15):41-42.

Allaah also said (regarding *Shayṭaan*):

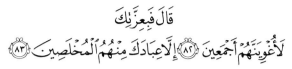

قَالَ فَبِعِزَّتِكَ لَأُغْوِيَنَّهُمْ أَجْمَعِينَ ۝ إِلَّا عِبَادَكَ مِنْهُمُ ٱلْمُخْلَصِينَ ۝

"Then *by Your Might*, I will surely mislead them all, except Your chosen *'ibaad* amongst them."[227]

Allaah said concerning Yoosuf:

كَذَٰلِكَ لِنَصْرِفَ عَنْهُ ٱلسُّوٓءَ وَٱلْفَحْشَآءَ إِنَّهُۥ مِنْ عِبَادِنَا ٱلْمُخْلَصِينَ ۝

"Thus it was, that We might turn away from him evil and the lewd sin (i.e., illicit relationship). Surely, he was one of Our chosen, guided *'ibaad*."[228]

Allaah (ﷻ) also said:

سُبْحَٰنَ ٱللَّهِ عَمَّا يَصِفُونَ ۝ إِلَّا عِبَادَ ٱللَّهِ ٱلْمُخْلَصِينَ ۝

"Exalted be Allaah from what they ascribe (to Him), except the chosen, guided *'ibaad* of Allaah (who do not attribute false things to Allaah)."[229]

He said:

إِنَّهُۥ لَيْسَ لَهُۥ سُلْطَٰنٌ عَلَى ٱلَّذِينَ ءَامَنُوا۟ وَعَلَىٰ رَبِّهِمْ يَتَوَكَّلُونَ ۝ إِنَّمَا سُلْطَٰنُهُۥ عَلَى ٱلَّذِينَ يَتَوَلَّوْنَهُۥ وَٱلَّذِينَ هُم بِهِۦ مُشْرِكُونَ

"Verily! He (i.e., *Shayṭaan*) has no power over those who believe and have *tawakkul* only in their Lord

---

[227] Soorah Ṣaad (38):82-83.
[228] Soorah Yoosuf (12):24.
[229] Soorah aṣ-Ṣaaffaat (37):159-160.

(Allaah). His (i.e., *Shaytaan*) power is only over those who take him as a *walee* and who join partners (with Allaah)."[230]

With *'uboodiyyah*, He described all of those whom He has chosen amongst His creation, as in His saying:

$$وَاذْكُرْ عَبْدَنَا إِبْرَٰهِيمَ وَإِسْحَٰقَ وَيَعْقُوبَ أُوْلِى الْأَيْدِى وَالْأَبْصَٰرِ ۝ إِنَّا أَخْلَصْنَٰهُم بِخَالِصَةٍ ذِكْرَى الدَّارِ ۝ وَإِنَّهُمْ عِندَنَا لَمِنَ الْمُصْطَفَيْنَ الْأَخْيَارِ ۝$$

"And remember Our *'ibaad*: Ibraaheem, Ishaaq and Ya'qoob, possessors of strength (in worshipping us) and understanding (of the *Deen*). Verily, We did choose them by granting them a special thing: the remembrance of *ad-Daar* (the home of the Hereafter), and they are in Our sight, verily of the chosen and the best."[231]

And in His saying:

$$وَاذْكُرْ عَبْدَنَا دَاوُۥدَ ذَا الْأَيْدِ ۖ إِنَّهُۥ أَوَّابٌ ۝$$

"And remember Our *'abd*, Daawood, the possessor of strength. Verily! He was ever oft-turning in repentance (towards Allaah)."[232]

He said of Sulaymaan:

$$نِّعْمَ الْعَبْدُ ۖ إِنَّهُۥ أَوَّابٌ$$

"How excellent an *'abd* (he is)! Verily, he was ever oft-returning in repentance (to Us)!"[233]

---

[230] Soorah an-Nahl (16): 99-100.
[231] Soorah Saad (38):45-47.
[232] Soorah Saad (38):17.
[233] Soorah Saad (38):30.

And regarding Ayyoob:

$$نِعْمَ ٱلْعَبْدُ$$

"How excellent an *'abd* **(he is)!"**[234]

He also said about him:

$$وَٱذْكُرْ عَبْدَنَآ أَيُّوبَ إِذْ نَادَىٰ رَبَّهُ$$

"And remember Our *'abd* **Ayyoob, when he invoked his Lord…"**[235]

Allaah said of Noo<u>h</u>:

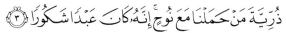

"O offspring of those whom We carried (in the ship) with Noo<u>h</u>! Verily, he was a grateful *'abd.*"[236]

He said concerning the *Seal of His Messengers:*

$$سُبْحَٰنَ ٱلَّذِىٓ أَسْرَىٰ بِعَبْدِهِۦ لَيْلًا مِّنَ ٱلْمَسْجِدِ ٱلْحَرَامِ إِلَى ٱلْمَسْجِدِ ٱلْأَقْصَا$$

"Exalted be He (Allaah) who took His *'abd* **(Mu<u>h</u>ammad (☼)) for a journey by night from the Sacred Mosque (at Makkah) to the farthest Mosque (at Bayt al-Maqdis)."**[237]

It (i.e., al-Masjid al-Aqsaa) was the first of the two *qiblahs* and Allaah favoured it by declaring worship within it to be of five hundred manifolds.[238] The intended place where the multiplication of reward is eligible is the actual mosque, which the Jews once burnt,

---

[234] Soorah <u>S</u>aad (38):44.

[235] Soorah <u>S</u>aad (38):41.

[236] Soorah al-Israa (17):3.

[237] Soorah al-Israa (17):1.

[238] As related by al-Bazzaar in his *Musnad* (422) by way of Sa'eed Ibn Saalim al-Qaddaa<u>h</u> from Sa'eed Ibn Basheer from Ismaa'eel Ibn 'Ubaydallaah from Umm ad-Dardaa' from Aboo ad-Dardaa'… It is also related by Ibn 'Abdil-Barr in *at-Tamheed* (6/30); a<u>t</u>-<u>T</u>ahaawee in　=

may the curse of Allaah be upon them. Some hold the opinion that al-Masjid al-Aqsaa (the farthest mosque) is the rock and its encompassing dome but that is not the case.

He also said:

$$وَأَنَّهُۥ لَمَّا قَامَ عَبۡدُ ٱللَّهِ يَدۡعُوهُ$$

"And when *'abdullaah* (i.e., the *'abd* of Allaah, Muhammad (ﷺ)) stood up, calling unto Him (i.e., Allaah)..."[239]

He said:

$$وَإِن كُنتُمۡ فِى رَيۡبٖ مِّمَّا نَزَّلۡنَا عَلَىٰ عَبۡدِنَا$$

"And if you are in doubt concerning that which We have sent down to Our *'abd*..."[240]

He said:

$$فَأَوۡحَىٰٓ إِلَىٰ عَبۡدِهِۦ مَآ أَوۡحَىٰ ۝$$

"So did Allaah reveal to His *'abd* what He revealed (through the Angel Jibraa'eel)."[241]

= *Mushkil al-Aathaar* (1/248); Ibn 'Adee in *al-Kaamil* (3/1234) by way of Sa'eed al-Qaddaah then by the same chain of narrators. As-Suyootee mentioned it in *ad-Durr al-Manthoor* (2/53) and added that it was also related by Ibn Khuzaymah, at-Tabaraanee and al-Bayhaqee in *ash-Shu'ab*. Al-Qaddaah and Sa'eed Ibn Jubayr are both weak! The correct position on this issue is what has been related by al-Haakim (4/509) and ad-Diyaa al-Maqdasee in *Fadaa'il Bayt al-Maqdis* (pg. 51) from Aboo Dharr that the Prophet (ﷺ) was questioned on praying in the Bayt al-Maqdis, does it hold a greater excellence or is the greater virtue in his (ﷺ) mosque? He replied, *'A prayer in this mosque of mine is better than four prayers in it...'* i.e., 250 prayers. The chain of this *hadeeth* is *hasan*. Al-Haythamee made mention of it in *al-Majma'* (4/7) and added that at-Tabaraanee related it in *al-Awsat*. He then said: "Its chain of narrators are people of the *Saheeh*"

[239] Soorah al-Jinn (72):19.
[240] Soorah al-Baqarah (2):23.
[241] Soorah an-Najm (53):10.

Allaah also said:

عَيْنًا يَشْرَبُ بِهَا عِبَادُ اللَّهِ يُفَجِّرُونَهَا تَفْجِيرًا ﴿٦﴾

"A fountain where the *'Ibaad* of Allaah will drink, making it gush forth in abundance."[242]

He also said:

وَعِبَادُ الرَّحْمَٰنِ الَّذِينَ يَمْشُونَ عَلَى الْأَرْضِ هَوْنًا وَإِذَا خَاطَبَهُمُ الْجَاهِلُونَ قَالُوا سَلَامًا ﴿٦٣﴾

"And the *'Ibaad* of ar-Rahmaan are those who walk upon the earth in humility, and when the foolish address them, they reply with words of gentleness"[243]

The like of these *aayaat* are numerous in the Qur'aan.

---

[242] Soorah al-Insaan (76):6.
[243] Soorah al-Furqaan (25):63.

On the Varying Levels of *Eemaan*

If the preceding discussion has become clear,[244] then it is well known that people vary very greatly in this concern and it is actually representative of their variance in the reality of *eemaan*.

They separate in this regard into a general category and a specific category. This is why their deification of the Lord is in a general and specific manner.

For this very reason, the presence of *shirk* in this *ummah* is more discrete than the creeping of an ant.[245]

Furthermore, in the *Saheeh*, it is reported that the Prophet (ﷺ) said: "*May the 'abd of the dirham perish, may the 'abd of the deenar perish, may the 'abd of the qateefah perish, may the 'abd of the khameesah perish. May he perish and regress and when he is pricked, may he not be able to extract the thorn. If he is given, he becomes pleased and if he is denied, he scorns.*"[246]

Thus, the Prophet (ﷺ) labelled such a person an *'abd* of the *dirham*, an *'abd* of the *deenaar*, an *'abd* of the *qateefah* and an *'abd* of the *khameesah*. He also made mention of him by way of supplication

---

[244] i.e., that people vary greatly in servitude to Allaah. [s]

[245] As has been authenticated from the Prophet (ﷺ) and related by Aboo Ya'laa (58), Ibn as-Sunnee (No. 281) and al-Marwazee in *Musnad Abee Bakr* (17) by way of Ibn Jurayj, who heard it from Layth Ibn Abee Sulaym from Aboo Muhammad from Hudhayfah from Aboo Bakr as-Siddeeq… Its chain is weak because of the weakness of Layth and the anonymity of Aboo Muhammad. This *hadeeth* is related by a number of companions via weak chains, which collectively strengthen each other, in: *al-Musnad* (4/403) from Aboo Moosa; *al-Hilyah* (7/112) via another chain from Aboo Bakr; by Ibn al-Jawzee in *al-'Ilal al-Mutanaahiyah* (1378), al-Haakim (2/291) and Aboo Nu'aym (8/368) from 'Aa'ishah; *al-Hilyah* (3/36) again from Ibn 'Abbaas. Refer to *Majma' az-Zawaa'id* (10/223); *Itthaaf as-Saadah al-Muttaqeen* (2/470, 7/304, 8/31); *al-Mataalib al-'Aaliyah* (3199) and *ad-Durr al-Manthoor* (2/17).

[246] *Saheeh al-Bukhaaree* (no. 6435) from Aboo Hurayrah. It is also related by Ibn Maajah (4136), al-Bayhaqee (9/159) and others.

(against him) and information (about him) and that is his saying: *"May he perish and regress and when he is pricked, may he not be able to extract the thorn. If he is given, he becomes pleased and if he is denied, he scorns."*

The word *an-Naqsh* means to remove a thorn from ones foot and *al-Minqaash* is the instrument used to remove the thorn.

This is the condition of one who when afflicted with evil, does not come away from it and he never succeeds because he has perished and regressed; he does not attain what he seeks nor does he deliver himself from adversity. This is the case of one who worships wealth.

This person has been depicted as such that when he is given he becomes pleased and when he is denied he scorns, as Allaah (ﷻ) has said:

وَمِنْهُم مَّن يَلْمِزُكَ فِي ٱلصَّدَقَٰتِ فَإِنْ أُعْطُوا۟ مِنْهَا رَضُوا۟ وَإِن لَّمْ يُعْطَوْا۟ مِنْهَآ إِذَا هُمْ يَسْخَطُونَ ﴿٥٨﴾

"And of them are some who accuse you (O Muḥammad (ﷺ)) in the matter of (the distribution of) the alms. If they are given part thereof, they are pleased, but if they are not given thereof, behold! They are enraged!"[247]

Their pleasure is for other than Allaah and their discontentment is for other than Allaah.

Such is the case for one who is attached to leadership, a *soorah* (image) or other such desires of his soul. If he attains it, he is pleased and if he unable to attain it, he becomes discontented. Such a person is the *'abd* of what he desires of these matters and he is a slave of it, since slavery and servitude in reality is the enslavement and

---

[247] Soorah at-Tawbah (9):58.

servitude of the heart, so whatever enslaves the heart and puts it under its servitude, the heart will be the *'abd* of that object. This is why it is said:

The 'abd is free as long as he is content
and the free one is an 'abd as long as he desires.

Another has said:

I obeyed my desires so they enslaved me
and if only I had been content, I would have been free

It is also said that desires are chains around one's neck and shackles around one's ankles; if the chains around the neck disappear, the shackles around the ankles disappear.

It is reported from 'Umar Ibn al-Kha<u>tt</u>aab that he said: "Desire is poverty and despair is enrichment and if one of you were to despair of something, he would become independent of it."

This is a matter that one finds in himself, for the thing that he becomes despondent of, he does not bother to seek it, nor desire it and his heart does not remain in need of it or in need of one who does it. However, if he desires a particular thing and hopes for it, his heart becomes attached to it and it becomes in need of attaining it and attaining anyone who he believes will constitute a cause towards acquiring that thing. This relates to wealth, power, *suwar* (images) and other things.

Al-Khaleel (i.e., Ibraaheem) said:

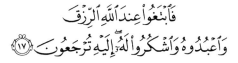

"So seek with Allaah your provision and worship Him (Alone), and be grateful to Him. To Him (Alone) you will be brought back."[248]

---

[248] Soorah al-Ankaboot (29):17.

The *'abd* has to have sustenance and he is need of it: If he seeks his sustenance from Allaah, he becomes an *'abd* of Allaah and in need of Him and if he seeks his sustenance from a creation, he becomes an *'abd* of that creation and in need of it.

This is why the issue of asking something of a creation is in principle, impermissible, and it is only permitted in a case of dire necessity.[249]

The prohibition of this is found in many *hadeeths* in the *Sihaah*, the *Sunan* and the *Masaaneed*, like his (ﷺ) saying: "*One of you would carry on asking until he comes on the Day of Resurrection without any flesh on his face.*"[250]

He also said: "*Whoever asks of the people whilst possessing what suffices him, what he asked for will appear on the Day of Judgement as scratches on his face.*"[251]

He said: "Asking is not permissible except for one who carries a burdensome debt, one who takes on an excruciating blood-money payment[252] or one who is in abasing poverty."[253]

---

[249] Refer to the author's discussion of this issue in *Majmoo' al-Fataawaa* (1/185-187).

[250] Related by al-Bukhaaree (3/268); Muslim (1040); an-Nasaa'ee (5/94) and Ahmad (2/15 & 88) from Ibn 'Umar.

[251] Related by Aboo Daawood (1626); an-Nasaa'ee (5/97); at-Tirmidhee (650); ad-Daarimee (1/386); Ibn Maajah (1840); Ahmad (1/388 & 441) and al-Haakim (1/408) from Ibn Mas'ood. Its chain of narration is *saheeh*.

[252] One who strives to secure peace between two sides disputing over blood or wealth by guaranteeing appropriate payments to the parties deserving it, in order to otherwise prevent an ill outcome. Refer to *Sunan Abee Daawood* with its commentary *Ma'aalim as-Sunan* by al-Khataabee (1640). [t]

[253] Related by Ahmad (3/100, 114 & 126); Aboo Daawood (1641); an-Nasaa'ee (7/259); Ibn Maajah (2189); at-Tayaalisee (285) and Aboo Na'eem)3/132) via a number of routes from Aboo Bakr al-Hanafee from Anas... Its chain is weak because of the anonymity of Aboo Bakr al-Hanafee. It is supported by the next *hadeeth* (indirectly referred to) as declared by the author himself.

This meaning (of the _hadeeth_) is found in the _Saheeh_.[254]

Also in the _Saheeh_ (is the _hadeeth_): _"It is better for one of you to take his rope and then togo and chop wood (for his livelihood) than to beg from people, whence they then (decide to) grant him or deny him."_[255]

He (ﷺ) also said: _"Whatever comes to you of this wealth without you asking for it or earnestly desiring it, then take it. As for anything besides that, then do not make yourself chase after it."_[256]

Thus, the Prophet (ﷺ) disliked one to take it by asking for it or earnestly desiring it within one's heart.

He (ﷺ) also said as in the _saheeh hadeeth_: _"Whoever abstains from asking others, Allaah will make him contented, and whoever tries to make himself self-sufficient, Allah will make him self-sufficient. And whoever remains patient, Allah will make him patient. No one has ever been given a bestowal better and more extensive than patience."_[257]

---

[254] He is probably referring to the _hadeeth_ related by Muslim (1044); Aboo Daawood (1640); an-Nasaa'ee (5/89 & 96-97); ad-Daarimee (1/333) and al-Bayhaqee (5/21 & 23) from Qabeesah that the Prophet (ﷺ) said: _"...begging is not permissible except for one of the three (classes) of people: one who has incurred debt, for him begging is permissible until he pays that off, after which he must stop; a man whose property has been destroyed by a calamity which has smitten him, for him begging is permissible until he receives enough sustenance, or reasonable subsistence; and a person who has been smitten by poverty, the genuineness of which is confirmed by three intelligent members of his people, for him begging is permissible..."_

[255] Related by al-Bukhaaree (1471 & 2373); Ahmad (1/168 & 164); al-Bayhaqee (4/195); Ibn Maajah (1836) and Wakee' in _az-Zuhd_ (141) from az-Zubayr Ibn al-'Awwaam.

[256] A _saheeh hadeeth_. Refer to the discussion on its ruling and chains of narration in my brief commentary to _ar-Rubaa'ee fee al-Hadeeth_ (pg. 17-18) by al-Haafidh 'Abdul-Ghanee Ibn Sa'eed al-Azdee. Also refer to _an-Nukat adh-Dhiraaf_ (8/39) and _Fath al-Baaree_ (13/153), both by al-Haafidh Ibn Hajar.

[257] Related by al-Bukhaaree (3/265); Muslim (1053); Maalik in _al-Muwatta_ (2/997); Aboo Daawood (1644); at-Tirmidhee (2025); an-Nasaa'ee (5/95); al-Bayhaqee (4/195) and al-Baghawee (6/110) from Aboo Sa'eed al-Khudree.

Furthermore, he (ﷺ) advised the elite of his Companions not to ask anything of anyone. In *al-Musnad*,[258] (is the narration): "Aboo Bakr's whip would fall from his hand and he would not ask anyone to hand it to him. He would comment, 'My *khaleel* instructed me never to ask anything of anyone.'"

In *Saheeh Muslim*[259] and other sources, 'Awf ibn Maalik relates that a group of people gave their pledge of allegiance to the Prophet (ﷺ) and he confided to them never to ask anything of anyone. Thereafter, whenever a whip used to drop from the hand of one of them, he would not say to anyone, 'Hand it to me.'

The command to ask from the Creator and the prohibition from asking from the created are well indicated by the texts in many places, like in His (ﷻ) saying:

فَإِذَا فَرَغْتَ فَٱنصَبْ ۝ وَإِلَىٰ رَبِّكَ فَٱرْغَب ۝

"So when you finish (from your occupation), stand up (for Allaah's worship i.e., stand up for prayer) and to your Lord (alone) turn (all your intentions, hopes and) your invocations."[260]

The Prophet (ﷺ) said to Ibn 'Abbaas: *"If you ask, then ask Allaah and if you seek help, then seek help from Allaah."[261]* Al-Khaleel

---

[258] No. 65, by way of Ibn Abee Mulaykah from Aboo Bakr. The great scholar Ahmad Shaakir said: "Its chain is weak because of a break in it; Ibn Abee Mulaykah whose name is 'Abdullaah Ibn 'Abdullaah, is a *taabi'ee* and *thiqah* but did not reach the time of Aboo Bakr. As-Suyootee mentioned in *Jam' al-Jawaami'* (17113 – his own arrangement) the statement of Ibn Hajar as in *al-Atraaf*: "This (chain) is unconnected." The part within the narration that is attributed to the Prophet is attested to by the *hadeeth* following it.

[259] No. 1043. It is also related by Aboo Daawood (1626); an-Nasaa'ee (1/229); Ibn Maajah (2868); at-Tabaraanee in *al-Kabeer* (18/33, 67 & 130) and in *Musnad ash-Shaamiyyeen* (335) and Ahmad (6/37) via two ways from 'Awf.

[260] Soorah al-Inshiraah (94):7-8.

[261] Related by Ahmad (1/293 & 307); at-Tirmidhee (2516); Ibn as-Sunnee in *'Amal al-Yawm* (425); Aboo Ya'laa (2556) and al-Bayhaqee in *al-Asmaa wa as-Sifaat* (pg. 75) from Ibn 'Abbaas with a chain that is *hasan*. The *hadeeth* has additional chains and other supporting *hadeeths*, which are not suitable to be presented here (to maintain brevity).

said:

$$\text{فَٱبْتَغُوا۟ عِندَ ٱللَّهِ ٱلرِّزْقَ}$$

"So seek with Allaah your provision..."[262]

He did not say: "So seek your provision with Allaah," because bringing forward the adverb denotes specialisation and restriction. It as if he said; "Do not seek provision except from Allaah."[263] Allaah (ﷻ) has also said:

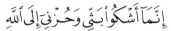

"And ask Allaah of His bounty."[264]

A person has to obtain the provision he is in need of and he has to repel what could harm him. With regard to both matters, it has been legislated for him that his supplication should be for Allaah. He does not ask for provision except from Allaah and does not complain except to Allaah, as Ya'qoob (عليه السلام) said:

$$\text{إِنَّمَآ أَشْكُوا۟ بَثِّى وَحُزْنِى إِلَى ٱللَّهِ}$$

"I complain of my grief and sorrow only to Allaah."[265]

Moreover, Allaah (ﷻ) mentioned in the Qur'aan a gracious separation,[266] a gracious pardon[267] and a gracious patience. It has been explained that a gracious separation is one without harm, a gracious pardon is one without blame and a gracious patience is one without complaint to creation. Consequently, when someone said to Ahmad

---

[262] Soorah al-Ankaboot (29):17, as Allaah relates from him.

[263] i.e., bringing forward the adverb (عِندَ), 'with' in front of the object *provision* imparts the meaning of restriction. If it had been deferred it would read 'seek your provision with Allaah' which does not signify the limitation as one could add, 'seek your provision with Allaah *and so-and-so and...*' [t].

[264] Soorah an-Nisaa' (4):32, as Allaah relates.

[265] Soorah Yoosuf (12):86, as Allaah relates.

[266] Allaah says: "And be patient (O Muhammad (ﷺ)) with what they say, and keep away from them in a good way." Soorah Muzzamil (73):10 [t].

[267] Allaah says: "...so overlook (O Muhammad (ﷺ)), their faults with a gracious forgiveness." Soorah al-Hijr (15):85. [t]

Ibn Hanbal during his illness that Taawoos used to dislike the groaning of a sick person and that he used to say that it was a form of complaining, Ahmad thereafter, never groaned until he passed away.

As for complaining to the Creator, this does not negate a gracious patience as Ya'qoob said:

فَصَبْرٌ جَمِيلٌ

"...so a gracious patience (is most fitting for me)..."[268]

He also said:

إِنَّمَآ أَشْكُواْ بَثِّى وَحُزْنِى إِلَى ٱللَّهِ

"...I only complain of my grief and sorrow to Allaah..."[269]

'Umar Ibn al-Khattaab, may Allaah be pleased with him, once recited in the *fajr* prayer, *Soorahs Yoonus, Yoosuf* and *an-Nahl*. When he passed by this *aayah* during his recitation he cried to the extent that his sobbing could be heard from the last set of rows.

(This is also indicated by) one of Moosa's supplications:[270] "O Allaah, for You is all praise and to You all complaints are directed. You are the One who is sought for help and You are the One who is called out for succour. Upon You we rely and there is no might nor power except with Allaah."

The supplication made by the Prophet (ﷺ) after the way he was treated by the people of at-Taa'if (contains a similar indication): *"O Allaah, to You I complain of the frailty of my strength, the defi-*

---

[268] Soorah Yoosuf (12):83, as related by Allaah.

[269] Soorah Yoosuf (12):86, as related by Allaah.

[270] It is most probably a narration emanating from Jewish sources, the mention of which is not objectionable on the condition that it does not embody anything contrary (to Islaamic teachings). This issue is elaborated upon in my treatise *at-Tahdheeraat min al-Fitan al-'Aasifaat* (pg. 18-20).

ciency of my stratagem and my humiliation at the people. O Most Merciful of those who show mercy, You are the Lord of the feeble and oppressed and You are my Lord. O Allaah, to whom will You entrust me? To a distant one who will receive me in an odious way or to an enemy, whom You will put me in the possession of? If You are not angry with me, then I am indifferent, save that Your 'aafiyah[271] is more expansive for me. I take refuge in the light of Your Face, which has radiated darkness and put the affair of this world and the Hereafter in order, from Your discontent descending upon me or that Your anger set down upon me. To You is al-'utbah[272] until You are pleased and there is no might nor power except by Allaah." In some narrations (the ending reads): *"there is no might nor power except by You."*[273]

The stronger the *'abd*'s desire is for the favour of Allaah and His Mercy, in accomplishing his needs and necessary requirements, the stronger his *'uboodiyyah* to Allaah will be and the greater becomes his freedom from every thing besides Allaah.

Just as the *'abd*'s desire for his Lord necessitates *'uboodiyyah* towards Him, likewise, his despair of creation will generate contentment in his heart, which (in turn) dispenses of creation. This is as has been said: "Manage without whomsoever you wish, you will become his peer, favour whomsoever you wish, you will become his leader and have need of whomsoever you wish, you will become his captive."

---

[271] A possible meaning here is *'your protection of me from the people'*. Refer to *an-Nihaayah fee Ghareeb al-Hadeeth*, lexical entry (عفا). [t]

[272] A possible meaning here is, 'I plead to you and constantly apologise for my wrong doings until you become pleased.' Refer to *Lisaan al-'Arab* of Ibn al-Mandhoor, lexical entry (عتب).[t]

[273] Related by Ibn Ishaaq in *as-Seerah* (2/70 – *Tahdheeb* edition) in *mursal* form and it is also related via him by at-Tabaree in his *at-Taareekh* (2/344). At-Tabaraanee connected it in *al-Mu'jam al-Kabeer* and its chain can be seen in *Taareekh Qazween* (2/82) as mentioned by al-Haythamee in *al-Majma'* (3/35) from 'Abdullaah Ibn Ja'far. He then said: "Its chain contains Ibn Ishaaq and he is a *mudallis thiqah* and the rest of the narrators are *thiqaat*." I say: "Moreover, Ibn Ishaaq has performed *'an'anah* here."

107

Similarly, the desire of the *'abd* for His Lord and his hope in Him generates *'uboodiyyah* of Him. The turning of his heart away from seeking from Allaah and hoping in Him causes his heart to turn away from having *'uboodiyyah* of Allaah, especially, in the case of one who hopes in creation and not in the Creator, in the sense that his heart is reliant on the leadership of that creation, his army, his followers and slaves. Or he could be reliant on his family and friends; his wealth and provisions; or his heads and elders such as his owner, king, *shaykh* and employer and so on of those who have passed away or who will die. Allaah (ﷻ) says:

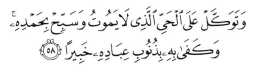

"And put your trust in the Living One, Who will never die, and glorify His praises; Sufficient He is, in being aware of the sins of His *'Ibaad*."[274]

Any person who attaches his heart to a creation for the purposes of aid, sustenance or guidance has submitted his heart to them and has given rise to a level of *'uboodiyyah* of that creation in accordance to the level of that (attachment), even if it appears that he is their leader who organises their affairs and manages them. The sensible person looks at the realities (of matters) and not at the superficialities.

If a man's heart becomes attached to a woman, even if it is a woman who is lawful for him, his heart will remain captive to her. She will rule him and manage him in any way she sees fit. On the surface, he is her master because he is her husband or owner but in reality he is her captive and is owned by her. This condition holds even more so if she is aware of his need for her, his passion for her and that he views her as irreplaceable. In such circumstances, she rules him in the manner a forceful and oppressive master rules his subjugated slave, who is unable to deliver himself from his master. In fact, this

---

[274] Soorah al-Furqaan (25):85.

condition (of a man attached to a woman in such a way) is much more severe (than the analogy put forward) because the captivity of the heart is more serious than the captivity of the body and the enslavement of the heart is more severe than the enslavement of the body.

Indeed, one whose body is enslaved and captured does not care (as much) so long as his heart is at ease and is appeased. In fact, he may even be able to employ some stratagem to liberate himself. However, if the heart, which is the king of the limbs, is taken captive, enslaved and holds the greatest type of love for other than Allaah, this is pure subservience and captivity and it is a servile *'uboodiyyah* of what the heart has been enslaved by.

Reward and punishment are the consequences of the *'uboodiyyah* and captivity of the **heart**. If a Muslim is taken captive by a *kaafir* or unlawfully subjugated by an evil person, it will not harm him if he performs the obligatory duties within his capability.

Likewise, whoever is enslaved lawfully, if he renders the rights of Allaah upon him and the rights of his master, he will receive two rewards,[275] even if he is forced to utter statements of *kufr* and does so, whilst his heart is content with *eemaan*, this will not harm him. As for the one whose heart is enslaved and has become an *'abd* for other than Allaah, this will harm him, even if he is the king of his people.

---

[275] As is authenticated from the Prophet (ﷺ). It is related by al-Bukhaaree (5/126); Muslim (154); an-Nasaa'ee (6/115); at-Tirmidhee (1116); ad-Daarimee (2/154-155); at-Tayaalisee (520); Sa'eed Ibn Mansoor (914) and Ahmad (4/402 & 405) from Aboo Moosa al-'Ash'aree, who relates that the Messenger of Allaah (ﷺ) said: *"Three types of people will be given their reward twice: A man who had a slave-girl, taught her good manners proficiently, improved her education proficiently and then manumitted her and married her; a slave who rendered the rights of his Lord and the rights of his master and a person who believed in his Book and then believed in Muhammad (ﷺ)."*

Thus, freedom is freedom of the heart and *'uboodiyyah* **is** *'uboodiyyah* **of the heart**, just as richness, is richness of the soul. The Prophet (ﷺ) said: *"Affluence is not the result of (possessing) the vanities of this world, but affluence is affluence of the heart."*[276]

By Allaah! This (i.e., the aforementioned account) is the case when the person is enslaved by a lawful <u>s</u>oorah.

As for the one who is enslaved by an unlawful <u>s</u>oorah: (be it) a woman or youth, this is indeed, a (type of) punishment that is unparalleled.

These people who are passionately fond of these <u>s</u>uwar are of the most severely punished types of people and the least of them rewarded; if the heart of the one who is passionately in love with a <u>s</u>oorah, remains attached to it and enslaved by it, the number of sorts of evils and corruption that band together within him are so great that none but the Lord of the *'Ibaad* can enumerate them.

Further, even if such a person were to be free of having committed the greater lewd sin (i.e., illicit sexual relation), the continuous attachment of the heart to this <u>s</u>oorah[277] without committing the lewd sin is more harmful to him than the case of one who embarks upon a sin and then repents and thereafter, the effect of the sin clears away from his heart.[278]

Such people are likened to drunkards and demented people, as has been said:

---

[276] Related by al-Bukhaaree (6446); Muslim (1051); at-Tirmidhee (2373); A<u>h</u>mad (2/389, 390 & 243); al-<u>H</u>umaydee (1063); Ibn Maajah (4137); al-Qudaa'ee (1211) and al-Baghawee (4040) from Aboo Hurayrah.

[277] Accompanied with heedlessness of the rememberance Allaah and without striving against one's soul.

[278] Thus, (the state of the former) weakens *eemaan*, diminishes the value of attachment to Allaah (ﷺ), which lead to disobedient acts and legal breaches.

*The two types of intoxication are the intoxication of
desire and of wine
And when will be the consciousness of the one who is
intoxicated?*

It has also been chanted:
*They said, 'You have become insane because of the one
you desire' so I replied to them
Passion is much more severe than what afflicts the insane
The holder of such passion cannot recover consciousness
throughout all time
Whereas the insane person falls down only at times.*

One of the greatest causes for this ordeal is the turning away of the heart from Allaah. If the heart tastes the sweetness of the worship of Allaah and of sincerity towards Him, nothing besides this will be sweeter, more delightful, pleasurable and agreeable.

Moreover, a person only abandons something beloved to him, when it is for something else even more beloved to him or because of fear of something harmful. Corrupt love can be relinquished by the heart as a result of a righteous love or fear of harm.

Allaah (عز وجل) says concerning Yoosuf:

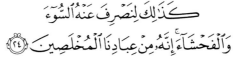

"Thus it was, that We might turn away from him evil and the lewd sin (i.e., illicit relationship). Surely, he was one of Our chosen, guided *'ibaad*."[279]

Thus, Allaah averts from his *'abd* any inclination he may have towards *suwar* and any attachment to them, which can bring harm

---

[279] Soorah Yoosuf (12):24.

upon him and He turns lewd sins away from him as a result of the *'abd's* sincerity towards Allaah.

This is why it[280] is before he tastes the sweetness of *'uboodiyyah* to Allah and sincerity to Him, whereby the soul overpowers him into following it's desire. Once he tastes the sweetness of sincerity and it strengthens in his heart, his desire will vanquish without any (other) remedy.

Allaah (ﷻ) says:

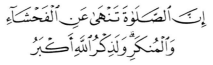

"Verily, Prayer prevents (one) from (committing) *al-Fahshaa* (lewd sins) *and al-Munkar* (reprehensible deeds) and indeed, the remembrance of Allaah is greater."[281]

The prayer prevents harmful matters, which are lewd sins and reprehensible deeds and it also brings about a beloved matter and that is the remembrance of Allaah. The attainment of this beloved matter is greater than the prevention of those harmful things because the remembrance of Allaah is *'ibaadah* of Allaah and the *'ibaadah* of Allaah, enacted by the heart, is a matter that is directly intended and sought after in itself. The prevention of harm on oneself however, is indirectly intended by way of consequence.

The heart has been created with love for truth and it wants and seeks it. When an intent for evil presents itself to the heart, it seeks to repel it because such an intent corrupts the heart in the same manner plantation is corrupted by thicket.

---

[280] i.e., having such an attachment to other than Allaah because of one's aversion to Allaah and His remembrance. [t]

[281] Soorah al-'Ankaboot (29):45.

That is why Allaah (ﷻ) has said:

$$قَدۡ أَفۡلَحَ مَن زَكَّىٰهَا ۝ وَقَدۡ خَابَ مَن دَسَّىٰهَا ۝$$

"Indeed, he succeeds who purifies it (i.e., his soul).
And indeed, he fails who corrupts it."[282]

Allaah (ﷻ) also said:

$$قَدۡ أَفۡلَحَ مَن تَزَكَّىٰ ۝ وَذَكَرَ ٱسۡمَ رَبِّهِۦ فَصَلَّىٰ ۝$$

"Indeed, he succeeds whosoever purifies himself,
and remembers (glorifies) the Name of his Lord and
prays."[283]

He said:

$$قُل لِّلۡمُؤۡمِنِينَ يَغُضُّوا۟ مِنۡ أَبۡصَـٰرِهِمۡ وَيَحۡفَظُوا۟ فُرُوجَهُمۡ ذَٰلِكَ أَزۡكَىٰ لَهُمۡ$$

"Tell the believing men to lower their gaze (from
looking at forbidden things), and protect their private parts (from illegal sexual acts, etc.). That is
purer for them."[284]

Allaah (ﷻ) also says:

$$وَلَوۡلَا فَضۡلُ ٱللَّهِ عَلَيۡكُمۡ وَرَحۡمَتُهُۥ مَا زَكَىٰ مِنكُم مِّنۡ أَحَدٍ أَبَدًا$$

"And had it not been for the Grace of Allaah and
His Mercy on you, not one of you would ever have
been sanctified (i.e., pure from sins)."[285]

Thus, Allaah (ﷻ) made the lowering of one's gaze and the protection of one's private organs as the strongest (method of) purification of the soul and He also explained that the shunning of lewd sins

---

[282] Soorah ash-Shams (91):9-10.

[283] Soorah al-'Alaa (87):14-15.

[284] Soorah an-Noor (24):30.

[285] Soorah an-Noor (24):21.

emanates from the purification of the soul. Purification of the soul implies the cessation of all evils, such as oppression, *shirk*, lying... etc.

Likewise,[286] (the case is the same with) the one who seeks leadership and superiority in the land. His heart is compassionate and enslaved towards the one who can assist him in this, even if he is, outwardly, placed ahead in front of them and the obeyed amongst them, he in reality, hopes in them and fears them. He extends to them wealth and offices and pardons them for what they perpetrate in order that they obey and assist him. **Hence, he is on the exterior their leader who is obeyed, but in reality (none other than) an *'abd* who obeys them.**

The precise determination is that each party exhibits *'uboodiyyah* of the other and both have abandoned the reality of the *'ibaadah* of Allaah. If their collaboration is undertaken for the purposes of (seeking) leadership in the land in an unlawful manner, they will be equivalent to those who cooperate to commit lewd sins or brigandry. Each one, as a result of the desires that have enslaved and subjugated him, is enslaved by the other. This is the same for the seeker of wealth, since that wealth enslaves and subjugates him.

These matters (that are sought) are of two types:

A type that the *'abd* is in need of, such as his need for food, drink, abode, marriage and their like. The *'abd* is to seek and request these from Allaah. Thus, the wealth he possesses - he employs it in accordance to his need - is synonymous to his donkey that he mounts and his rug that he sits on, or even more explicitly, his lavatory in which he relieves himself, in the sense that it does not enslave him whereby he then becomes anxious (over it):

---

[286] i.e., the attachment of a man to a woman (or vice versa) in such a way is one particular type of many types of attachment. [t]

$$\text{إِذَا مَسَّهُ ٱلشَّرُّ جَزُوعًا ﴿٢٠﴾ وَإِذَا مَسَّهُ ٱلْخَيْرُ مَنُوعًا ﴿٢١﴾}$$

"Irritable (discontented) when evil touches him and niggardly when good touches him."[287]

The other is the type of matters that the *'abd* is not in need of. It is not fitting that he affixes his heart on them. If he does attach his heart to them, they will enslave him. He may even become reliant upon other than Allaah and consequently, the reality of the *'ibaadah* of Allaah and *tawakkul* on Him may no longer subsist in him. Instead, within him forms an element of *'ibaadah* for other than Allaah and an element of *tawakkul* on other than Allaah and such a person merits the most, the saying of the Messenger (ﷺ): *"May the 'abd of the dirham perish, may the 'abd of the deenar perish, may the 'abd of the qateefah perish, may the 'abd of the khameesah perish."[288]* This person is an *'abd* of these things; if he asks Allaah for these things, Allaah either grants it to him and he becomes pleased or He denies him and he becomes enraged.

The (true) *'abd,* however, is the one who is pleased with what pleases Allaah and His Messenger; who has hatred for what Allaah and His Messenger hate; offers *walaa'* to the *awliyaa'* of Allaah and holds enmity towards the enemies of Allaah. This is the person who has fulfilled *eemaan* as in the *hadeeth: "Whoever loves for Allaah; hates for Allaah; gives for Allaah and denies for Allaah has fulfilled eemaan."[289]*

He (ﷺ) also said: *"The firmest bond of eemaan is love for Allaah and hate for Allaah."[290]*

---

[287] Soorah al-Ma'aarij (70):20-21.

[288] Its *takhreej* has already preceded, see footnote no. 246.

[289] Related by Aboo Daawood (4681), at-Tabaraanee in *al-Kabeer* (7613, 7737 & 7738) and al-Baghawee (13/54) with a *hasan* chain from Aboo Umaamah.

[290] A *hasan hadeeth* that has a number of chains from several Companions. The best of these chains is that related by Imaam at-Tabaraanee in *al-Mu'jam al-Kabeer* (10357) from Ibn Mas'ood with a *hasan* chain, Allaah willing. I have a separate treatise on the chains and *takhreej* of this *hadeeth*.

Also recorded in the _Saheeh,_[291] the Prophet (ﷺ) has said: _"Three (qualities), whoever possesses them, will find the sweetness of eemaan: that Allaah and His Messenger are more beloved to him besides anyone else, that he loves someone only for the sake of Allaah and that he hates to return to kufr after Allaah has delivered him from it just as he hates to be slung into the fire."_

Thus, this person agreed with His lord in that which He loves and hates. Allaah and His Messenger became the most beloved of all to him and he loved creation for Allaah, not for any other reason. This was as a result of his perfection of love for Allaah, since (also) having love for what one's beloved loves, constitutes perfection of having love for one's beloved.[292]

So if he loves the Prophets of Allaah and the _awliyaa_ of Allaah because of their accomplishment of what _al-Haqq_[293] loves, not for any other reason, he has then loved them for Allaah and none other. Allaah (ﷻ) has indeed said:

$$فَسَوْفَ يَأْتِي ٱللَّهُ بِقَوْمٍ يُحِبُّهُمْ$$

$$وَيُحِبُّونَهُۥٓ أَذِلَّةٍ عَلَى ٱلْمُؤْمِنِينَ أَعِزَّةٍ عَلَى ٱلْكَٰفِرِينَ$$

"Allaah will bring a people whom He will love and they will love Him; humble towards the believers, stern towards the disbelievers."[294]

This is why Allaah (ﷻ) has said:

$$قُلْ إِن كُنتُمْ تُحِبُّونَ ٱللَّهَ فَٱتَّبِعُونِي يُحْبِبْكُمُ ٱللَّهُ$$

---

[291] Its _takhreej_ has already preceded.

[292] Thus Allaah (ﷻ) loves the Prophets, the Angels and righteous people and if you also love them, this will constitute perfection of your love and agreement with Allaah. Likewise Allaah hates the disbelievers and the hypocrites, so if you also hate them, you have agreed with your Lord in that which He hates. [s]

[293] One of the names of Allaah (ﷻ), The True.

[294] Soorah al-Maa'idah (5):54.

**"Say (O Mu_h_ammad (ﷺ) to mankind): "If you (re-
ally) love Allaah then follow me (i.e. accept Islaamic
Monotheism, follow the Qur'aan and the _Sunnah_),
Allaah will love you."**[295]

The Messenger only commands that which Allaah loves, prohibits
that which Allaah hates, he only does that which Allaah loves and
informs of that which Allaah loves to ratify.

**Hence, whoever loves Allaah, has to follow the Messenger; by
believing him in that which he informs, obeying his orders and
emulating him in his actions. Whosoever does this has indeed
performed what Allaah loves and consequently, Allaah will love
him.**

Allaah has laid down two signs of the people who love Him: following the Messenger and performing _jihaad_ in his cause. This is
because the reality of _jihaad_ is to strive to attain what Allaah loves
of _eemaan_ and righteous action and of repelling what he hates such
as _kufr_, _fusooq_ and disobedience. Allaah (ﷻ) has said:

$$\text{قُلۡ إِن كَانَ ءَابَآؤُكُمۡ وَأَبۡنَآؤُكُمۡ وَإِخۡوَٰنُكُمۡ وَأَزۡوَٰجُكُمۡ وَعَشِيرَتُكُمۡ}$$
$$\text{وَأَمۡوَٰلٌ ٱقۡتَرَفۡتُمُوهَا وَتِجَٰرَةٌ تَخۡشَوۡنَ كَسَادَهَا وَمَسَٰكِنُ}$$
$$\text{تَرۡضَوۡنَهَآ أَحَبَّ إِلَيۡكُم مِّنَ ٱللَّهِ وَرَسُولِهِۦ وَجِهَادٍ}$$
$$\text{فِي سَبِيلِهِۦ فَتَرَبَّصُوا۟ حَتَّىٰ يَأۡتِيَ ٱللَّهُ بِأَمۡرِهِۦ}$$

**"Say: If your fathers, your sons, your brothers, your
wives, your kindred, the wealth that you have
gained, the commerce in which you fear a decline,
and the dwellings in which you delight are dearer
to you than Allaah and His Messenger, and striving
hard and fighting in His Cause, then wait until
Allaah brings about His Decision (torment)."**[296]

---

[295] Soorah Aal-'Imraan (3):31.
[296] Soorah at-Tawbah (9):24.

117

Allaah (ﷻ) warns one whose family and wealth are more beloved to him than Allaah and his Messenger and *jihaad* in his cause with such a threat.

In fact, it has been established from the Prophet (ﷺ) in the *Saheeh*[297] that he said: *"By Him in Whose Hand is my soul, not one of you will have (complete) eemaan until I am more beloved to Him than his children, father and all of mankind."*

Also recorded in the *Saheeh*,[298] 'Umar Ibn al-Khaṭṭaab said, *'O Messenger of Allaah, By Allaah, you are indeed more beloved to me than everything besides my own self'. The Prophet remarked, 'No O 'Umar (you will not possess complete eemaan), until I am more beloved to you than your own self'. He then replied, 'Then by Allaah, you are indeed more beloved to me than my own self'. The Prophet then said, 'Now, O 'Umar'.*

Thus, the reality of love can only be fulfilled by having *muwaalaah* of the beloved; this is by being agreement with him in loving that which the beloved loves and hating what the beloved hates and Allaah loves *eemaan* and *taqwaa* and hates *kufr, fusooq* and disobedience.

It is known that love stirs the will of the heart; the more the love strengthens in the heart, the (more the) heart calls for enacting the beloved things. If the love is complete it will necessitate a decisive intent for attaining the beloved matters and if the *'abd* possesses the ability to do so, he will achieve them.

If however, he is unable (to actually attain the beloved matter) and does what is within his capability, he will attain the reward of the one who does it (completely), as the Prophet (ﷺ) has said: *"Whoever invited to guidance, will have a reward (assured) for him equiva-*

---

[297] Related by al-Bukhaaree (1/58), Muslim (44) and an-Nasaa'ee (8/114) from Anas. It is also related by al-Bukhaaree (1/58) from Aboo Hurayrah.

[298] Related by al-Bukhaaree (11/523) from 'Umar.

lent to the rewards of those who adhered to that guidance, without their own rewards being diminished in any respect. Whoever called to deviation, will have to carry a sin equivalent to the sins of those who committed it, without their own sins being diminished in any respect." [299]

He (ﷺ) also said (whilst on an expedition): *"Indeed, there are men (right now) in al-Madeenah; there is not a distance that you traverse or a valley that you pass through, except that they are with you."* They (i.e., those accompanying him) remarked: *"Whilst they are in Madeenah?"* He replied: *"(Yes), whilst they are in Madeenah; they have been prevented (from joining you) by (justifiable) reasons."* [300]

Jihaad, is to extend one's utmost efforts - and these efforts are a reference to all the capabilities one possesses - in attaining that which al-Haqq loves and in repelling that which al-Haqq hates.

Consequently, if the *'abd* relinquishes the *jihaad* that is within his capability, this will be indicative of a weak love of Allaah and His Messenger that resides in his heart.

It is also common knowledge that in general one cannot attain that which is beloved, without enduring some form of hardship, regardless of whether the love in question is a righteous or unrighteous one. The lovers of wealth, leadership and *suwar* (for example), only obtain their pursuits after being afflicted with some harm in this world, along with the harms that befall them in this world and the hereafter.

Therefore, if the one who loves Allaah and His Messenger cannot endure what a discerning person from the lovers of other than Allaah

---

[299] Related by Muslim (2674); Aboo Daawood (4609); at-Tirmidhee (2674); ad-Daarimee (1/126-127); Ibn Maajah (206); Ahmad (2/397) and al-Baghawee (1/232) from Aboo Hurayrah.
[300] Related by al-Bukhaaree (6/34); Ahmad (3/103); Aboo Daawood (2508) and Ibn Maajah (2764) from Anas. It is also related by Muslim (1911), Ibn Maajah (2765) and Ahmad (3/341) from Jaabir.

sees as endurable for the sake of attaining his pursuits, it indicates a weakness of his love for Allaah, (especially) on account that the path they (i.e., lovers of other than Allaah) take, according to their view, is the path that the intellect points towards.

It is well known that the believer has a much more intense love for Allaah, as Allaah (ﷻ) says:

وَمِنَ ٱلنَّاسِ مَن يَتَّخِذُ مِن دُونِ ٱللَّهِ أَندَادًا يُحِبُّونَهُمْ كَحُبِّ ٱللَّهِ وَٱلَّذِينَ ءَامَنُوٓا۟ أَشَدُّ حُبًّا لِّلَّهِ

"And of mankind are some who take (for worship) others besides Allaah as rivals (to Allaah). They love them as they love Allaah. But those who believe, love Allaah more (than anything else)."[301]

Yes indeed, a lover may traverse – because of his feeble intellect and corrupt perception - a path in which he cannot attain his pursuit. Such a path is not commended if the love is a righteous and praise-worthy one, how is it then when the love in question is a corrupt one **and** the path does not lead (to it)? Such as the case of the impetuous folk who chase wealth, leadership and *suwar*, through having love for things that bring harm upon them and do not attain their goals. The point here however, is on the paths that are traversed upon by the possessor of sound intellect in pursuit of his demands.

If this becomes clear, then the greater the heart has of love of Allaah, the greater will be one's *'uboodiyyah*. The greater one's *'uboodiyyah* is, the greater one's love will be of Him and he will prefer Him above all else.

Moreover, the heart is intrinsically in need of Allaah from two angles: from the angle of *'ibaadah*, which is the ultimate reason (be-

---

[301] Soorah al-Baqarah (2):165.

hind the heart's creation) and from the angle of seeking assistance and *tawakkul*, which is the effective reason.[302]

The heart can only become sound, achieve success, take pleasure, be satisfied, experiencing enjoyment, become pleased, attain serenity and calmness through the *'ibaadah* of its Lord, having love of Him and turning to Him (in repentance). Even if it were to attain every type of pleasure from creation, it will not acquire serenity and tranquillity. This is because the heart possesses an intrinsic need for it's Lord, since He is its deity, love and pursuit and with Allaah, the heart achieves joy, pleasure, delight, amenity, serenity and tranquillity.

This can only be achieved through Allaah's assistance given to the *'abd*, since none other than Allaah has the ability to assure the *'abd* of such an achievement, thus, he is in constant need of the reality of:

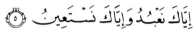

"You (Alone) we worship, and You (Alone) we ask for help (for each and everything)."[303]

If he was to be assisted in attaining all that he loves, desires and covets and does not attain any *'ibaadah* of Allaah, he actually attains nothing more than pain, regret and torment. Such a person will not be able to free himself from the pains of this world and its agonising life, except through sincere love of Allaah, whereby Allaah is his utmost pursuit and ultimate desire and that Allaah is his beloved from the initial intention and all others besides him are only loved for His sake, he does not love anything or anyone in a direct and independent way except Allaah.

---

[302] i.e., one can only establish the requisites and pillars of worship – which is the end reason - when Allaah facilitates such actions and the means towards enacting those actions. This facilitation is granted through seeking Allaah's assistance and having *tawakkul* upon him.
[303] Soorah al-Faatihah (1):5.

If the person does not achieve this, then he has not as of yet actualised the reality of لا إله إلا الله 'None has the right to be worshipped except Allaah'. Nor has he actualised tawheed, 'uboodiyyah and love of Allaah. Within him is a deficiency of tawheed and eemaan, rather, he has pains, regrets and torments, the magnitude of which, is a proportional amount (to his lack of fulfilment of those matters).

If he was to strive to attain this pursuit and not seek assistance from Allaah, have tawakkul in Him or feel in need of Him to achieve it, he will not achieve it, as what Allaah wills, comes to be and what He does not will, does not come to pass. Hence, the person is in need of Allaah, from the reasoning that Allaah is the end objective and the One that is beloved, the One desired and the object of worship and from the reasoning that He is the One who is be implored upon, sought assistance from and relied on. Allaah is his deity, whom there is no other (true) object of worship and Allaah is his Lord, whom there is no other (true) lord besides Him.

The 'uboodiyyah of Allaah cannot be accomplished by the person except by these two things. Hence, whenever the person loves other than Allaah in a direct and independent manner or he turns to other than Allaah for help, he will become an 'abd of whom he loves and an 'abd of whom he has hope in, according to the degree of love and hope he has for those besides Allaah.

If however, he does not love anyone directly or independently except Allaah. He loves others besides Him for Allaah's sake alone. He does not have hope in anyone or anything at all besides Allaah and when he undertakes the causes or achieves any of them, he witnesses that Allaah is the One who created them, decreed them and made them subservient to him and that Allaah is the Lord, Owner, Creator and Subjugator of everything in the heavens and earth and he feels a need for Him, (in such a situation therefore) he attains a level of complete 'uboodiyyah of Allaah in accordance to what has been apportioned for him.

People are of varying grades in this regard, none but Allaah can enumerate its paths.

From this perspective, the most perfect of creation, the best, most exalted, closest to Allaah, strongest and most guided is the one who has a more complete *'uboodiyyah* of Allaah.

This is the essence of the *Deen* of Islaam, with which Allaah sent the Messengers and revealed His Books and that is that the *'abd* submits to Allaah and none other. The one who submits to Allaah and other than Him is a *mushrik* and the one who refuses to submit to Allaah is an insolent person.

It is established in the *Saheeh*[304] that the Prophet (ﷺ): *"No one who has in his heart the weight of a mustard seed of pride shall enter Paradise."*

Likewise, no one who has the weight of a mustard seed of *eemaan* in his heart shall reside forever in the Fire.

The Prophet (ﷺ) declared pride to be opposite to *eemaan*, since pride negates the reality of *'uboodiyyah*, as has been established in the *Saheeh*[305] that the Prophet (ﷺ) said: *"Allaah says, 'Majesty is my lower garment and Pride is my upper garment; whoever contends Me on any of the two, I will punish him.'"*

---

[304] Related by Muslim (91); at-Tirmidhee (1998 1999); Aboo Daawood (4091); Ibn Maajah (59 & 4173) and at-Tabaraanee in *al-Kabeer* (10000) from Ibn Mas'ood.

[305] Related by Muslim (2620) with the Prophetic wording: *"Glory and Honour is His lower garment..."* and al-Humaydee said: "This is how we have seen it in the copies of Muslim's book and al-Barqaanee has related it from the chain related by Muslim from Aboo Sa'eed and Aboo Hurayrah..." and he mentioned it with the same wording mentioned by the author... al-Humaydee then said: "Aboo Mas'ood also related it in this way in his book." Likewise, it is like this in *Jaami' al-Usool* (10/613) and *at-Targheeb wa at-Tarheeb* (4/16). It is also related by Aboo Daawood (4090), Ibn Maajah (4174) and Ahmad (2/414, 248, 376, 427 & 442) with the same wording mentioned by the author.

Thus, pride and majesty are of the specialities of Lordship, and pride is superior to majesty; this is why He declared pride to be at the level of the higher garment, just as He declared majesty to be at the level of the lower garment.

Accordingly, the emblem of Prayer, *adhaan* and the days of *'eid* was made *at-Takbeer*[306] and its utterance was made recommended in high places, such as aṣ-Ṣafaa and al-Marwah;[307] when a person ascends a high point[308] or mounts an animal[309] and so on. With it, one extinguishes fire, even if it is of great magnitude,[310] and during the *adhaan*, *Shayṭaan* flees[311] (when it is mentioned).

Allaah (ﷻ) says:

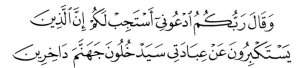

---

[306] i.e., saying, '*Allaahu Akbar*'. The words *Takbeer*, *Akbar* and *Kibar* (pride) are derived from the same root (ﻙ-ﺏ-ﺭ). [t]

[307] As related by Muslim (1218); Aboo Daawood (1907); Maalik (1/372) and Ibn Maajah (3074) from Jaabir.

[308] Related by al-Bukhaaree (6385); Muslim (1344); Ibn as-Sunnee (519); Maalik (1/421); Aboo Daawood (2770) and others from Ibn 'Umar.

[309] As related by Muslim (1342), at-Tirmidhee (3444) and Aboo Daawood (2599) from Ibn 'Umar.

[310] The author, may Allaah have mercy upon him, mentioned this *hadeeth* in *al-Kalim aṭ-Ṭayyib* (No. 221). He attributed it to the Prophet (ﷺ) in an unasserted manner. The *hadeeth* is related by al-'Uqaylee in *aḍ-Ḍu'afaa* (2/296), Ibn 'Adee in *al-Kaamil* (4/1469) and Ibn as-Sunnee in *'Amal al-Yawm wa al-Laylah* (289-292) via a number of routes from 'Amr Ibn Shu'ayb from his father from his grandfather. These chains up to 'Amr are all very weak. It has other chains in *Taareekh Jurjaan* (414); *al-Kunaa wa al-Asmaa* by ad-Doolaabee, (2/137); *ad-Du'aa* (1001); *al-Kaamil* (5/1767); *al-Maṭaalib al-'Aaliyah* (3424) and *al-Maqaasid al-Ḥasanah*. I may therefore, if Allaah wills, devote some time to scrutinise it further on a different occasion.

[311] As related by al-Bukhaaree (2/69-70); Muslim (389); Maalik (1/69 & 70); Aboo Daawood (516) and an-Nasaa'ee (2/21 & 22) from Aboo Hurayrah.

"And your Lord said, 'Invoke Me, I will respond to your (invocation)'. Verily, those who scorn My worship, will enter Hell in humiliation!"[312]

Anyone who is too proud to accede to the *'ibaadah* of Allaah, most definitely worships other than Allaah, since man is an emotional being, who stirs by means of volition.

In the _Saheeh_,[313] it is established that the Prophet (ﷺ) said: *"The most truthful of names are Ḥaarith*[314] *and Hammaam*[315]*."*

The Ḥaarith is a an achiever and worker and Hammaam fits the structure فَعَّال, which is derived from (الهم) 'al-Hamm'. Al-Hamm denotes the initial part of intention. A person always holds intention and every intention demands (the presence of) an end objective, which it eventually leads to. Thus, every *'abd* has a beloved goal that forms the conclusion of his love and intention. Whoever does not have Allaah as his object of worship and the conclusion of his love and intention and in fact, is too proud to accede to that, he will be an *'abd* of whatever his beloved desire is: whether it be wealth; status; _suwar_ or the false deities he takes besides Allaah such as the sun; moon; stars; idols; graves of the Prophets and righteous people or Angels and Prophets, whom they take as lords and all else that is worshipped besides Allaah.

---

[312] Soorah al-Ghaafir (40):60.

[313] Related by Muslim (2132), but with the wording: *"The most beloved names to Allaah are 'Abdullaah and 'Abdur-Raḥmaan"* from Ibn 'Umar. It is also related by at-Tirmidhee (2835) and Aboo Daawood (2/584). As for the wording: *"The most truthful of names are Ḥaarith and Hammaam,"* this has been related by Ibn Wahb in his *Jaami'* (pg. 7) from 'Abdullaah Ibn 'Aamir al-Yahsee in *mursal* form with a chain that is _saheeh_. It has a supporting _hadeeth_ that is unbroken (in it's chain), which is related by Aḥmad (4/345), Aboo Daawood (4950) and an-Nasaa'ee (6/218) from Aboo Wahb al-Jushamee with a chain that contains weakness. Thus, the narration strengthens by virtue of this one, Allaah willing. Also refer to *Mawaarid al-'Amaan...* pg. 65-66.

[314] Lexically, a ploughman and cultivator.

[315] Lexically, one who is energetic and active.

If he is an *'abd* to other than Allaah, he will be a *mushrik*. Every proud person is a *mushrik*; this is why Fir'awn was one of the most prominent of people who were too proud to accede to the *'ibaadah* of Allaah **and** he was a *mushrik*.

Allaah (ﷻ) says:

وَلَقَدْ أَرْسَلْنَا مُوسَىٰ بِـَٔايَـٰتِنَا وَسُلْطَـٰنٍ مُّبِينٍ ﴿٢٣﴾ إِلَىٰ فِرْعَوْنَ وَهَـٰمَـٰنَ وَقَـٰرُونَ فَقَالُوا۟ سَـٰحِرٌ كَذَّابٌ ﴿٢٤﴾ فَلَمَّا جَآءَهُم بِٱلْحَقِّ مِنْ عِندِنَا قَالُوا۟ ٱقْتُلُوٓا۟ أَبْنَآءَ ٱلَّذِينَ ءَامَنُوا۟ مَعَهُۥ وَٱسْتَحْيُوا۟ نِسَآءَهُمْ وَمَا كَيْدُ ٱلْكَـٰفِرِينَ إِلَّا فِى ضَلَـٰلٍ ﴿٢٥﴾ وَقَالَ فِرْعَوْنُ ذَرُونِىٓ أَقْتُلْ مُوسَىٰ وَلْيَدْعُ رَبَّهُۥٓ إِنِّىٓ أَخَافُ أَن يُبَدِّلَ دِينَكُمْ أَوْ أَن يُظْهِرَ فِى ٱلْأَرْضِ ٱلْفَسَادَ ﴿٢٦﴾ وَقَالَ مُوسَىٰٓ إِنِّى عُذْتُ بِرَبِّى وَرَبِّكُم مِّن كُلِّ مُتَكَبِّرٍ لَّا يُؤْمِنُ بِيَوْمِ ٱلْحِسَابِ ﴿٢٧﴾ وَقَالَ رَجُلٌ مُّؤْمِنٌ مِّنْ ءَالِ فِرْعَوْنَ يَكْتُمُ إِيمَـٰنَهُۥٓ أَتَقْتُلُونَ رَجُلًا أَن يَقُولَ رَبِّىَ ٱللَّهُ وَقَدْ جَآءَكُم بِٱلْبَيِّنَـٰتِ مِن رَّبِّكُمْ وَإِن يَكُ كَـٰذِبًا فَعَلَيْهِ كَذِبُهُۥ وَإِن يَكُ صَادِقًا يُصِبْكُم بَعْضُ ٱلَّذِى يَعِدُكُمْ إِنَّ ٱللَّهَ لَا يَهْدِى مَنْ هُوَ مُسْرِفٌ كَذَّابٌ ﴿٢٨﴾ يَـٰقَوْمِ لَكُمُ ٱلْمُلْكُ ٱلْيَوْمَ ظَـٰهِرِينَ فِى ٱلْأَرْضِ فَمَن يَنصُرُنَا مِنۢ بَأْسِ ٱللَّهِ إِن جَآءَنَا قَالَ فِرْعَوْنُ مَآ أُرِيكُمْ إِلَّا مَآ أَرَىٰ وَمَآ أَهْدِيكُمْ إِلَّا سَبِيلَ ٱلرَّشَادِ ﴿٢٩﴾ وَقَالَ ٱلَّذِىٓ ءَامَنَ يَـٰقَوْمِ إِنِّىٓ أَخَافُ عَلَيْكُم مِّثْلَ يَوْمِ ٱلْأَحْزَابِ ﴿٣٠﴾ مِثْلَ دَأْبِ قَوْمِ نُوحٍ

وَعَادٍ وَثَمُودَ وَالَّذِينَ مِنۢ بَعْدِهِمْ وَمَا اللَّهُ يُرِيدُ ظُلْمًا لِّلْعِبَادِ ۝ وَيَٰقَوْمِ إِنِّىٓ أَخَافُ عَلَيْكُمْ يَوْمَ التَّنَادِ ۝ يَوْمَ تُوَلُّونَ مُدْبِرِينَ مَا لَكُم مِّنَ اللَّهِ مِنْ عَاصِمٍ وَمَن يُضْلِلِ اللَّهُ فَمَا لَهُۥ مِنْ هَادٍ ۝ وَلَقَدْ جَآءَكُمْ يُوسُفُ مِن قَبْلُ بِالْبَيِّنَٰتِ فَمَا زِلْتُمْ فِى شَكٍّ مِّمَّا جَآءَكُم بِهِۦ حَتَّىٰٓ إِذَا هَلَكَ قُلْتُمْ لَن يَبْعَثَ اللَّهُ مِنۢ بَعْدِهِۦ رَسُولًا كَذَٰلِكَ يُضِلُّ اللَّهُ مَنْ هُوَ مُسْرِفٌ مُّرْتَابٌ ۝ الَّذِينَ يُجَٰدِلُونَ فِىٓ ءَايَٰتِ اللَّهِ بِغَيْرِ سُلْطَٰنٍ أَتَىٰهُمْ كَبُرَ مَقْتًا عِندَ اللَّهِ وَعِندَ الَّذِينَ ءَامَنُوا كَذَٰلِكَ يَطْبَعُ اللَّهُ عَلَىٰ كُلِّ قَلْبِ مُتَكَبِّرٍ جَبَّارٍ ۝

"And indeed We sent Moosa with Our *Aayaat* and a manifest authority to Fir'awn, Haamaan and Qaaroon, but they called (him), 'A sorcerer, a liar!' Then, when he brought them the Truth from Us, they said, 'Kill the sons of those who believe with him and let their women live' but the plots of the disbelievers are nothing but loss! Fir'awn said, 'Leave me to kill Moosa and let him call his Lord (to stop me from killing him)! I fear that he may change your religion, or that he may cause mischief to appear in the land!' Moosa said, 'Verily, I take refuge in my Lord and your Lord from every arrogant one who does not believe in the Day of Reckoning!'

And a believing man of Fir'awn's family, who hid his faith said, 'Would you kill a man because he says: "My Lord is Allaah, and he has come to you with clear signs (proofs) from your Lord?" And if he is a liar, upon him will be (the sin of) his lie; but if he is telling the truth, then some of that (calamity) wherewith he threatens you will befall you. Verily, Allaah guides not one who is a *Musrif* (a polytheist, or a murderer who sheds blood unlawfully, or those who commit great sins, oppressor, transgressor), a liar! O my people! Yours is the kingdom this day, you are uppermost in the land. But who will save us from the Torment of Allaah, should it befall us?'

Fir'awn said, 'I show you only that which I see (as being correct), and I guide you only to the path of right policy!' And the one who believed said, 'O my people! Verily, I fear for you a fate like that day (of disaster) of the Confederates (of old). Like the fate of the people of Nooh (Noah), and 'Aad, and Thamood and those who came after them. And Allaah wills no injustice for (His) slaves. And, O my people! Verily! I fear for you the Day when there will be mutual calling (between the people of Hell and of Paradise). A Day when you will turn your backs and flee having no protector from Allaah, And whomsoever Allaah sends astray, for him there is no guide'.

And indeed Yoosuf did come to you, in times gone by, with clear signs, but you ceased not to doubt in that which he did bring to you, till when he died you said, 'No Messenger will Allaah send after him'. Thus Allaah leaves astray him who is a *Musrif* (a polytheist, oppressor, a criminal, sinner who commit great sins) and a *Murtaab* (one who doubts Allaah's Warning and His Oneness). Those who dispute about the *Aayaat* (proofs, evidences, verses, lessons, signs, revelations, etc.) of Allaah, without any authority that has come to them, it is greatly hateful and disgusting to Allaah and to those who believe. Thus does Allaah seal up the heart of every arrogant, tyrant. (So they cannot guide themselves to the Right Path)."[316]

Allaah (ﷻ) also said:

وَقَٰرُونَ وَفِرْعَوْنَ وَهَٰمَٰنَ وَلَقَدْ جَآءَهُم مُّوسَىٰ بِٱلْبَيِّنَٰتِ فَٱسْتَكْبَرُوا۟ فِى ٱلْأَرْضِ وَمَا كَانُوا۟ سَٰبِقِينَ

"And (We destroyed also) Qaaroon, Fir'awn and Haamaan. And indeed Moosa came to them with clear *Aayaat* (proofs, evidences, verses, lessons, signs, revelations, etc.), but they were arrogant in the land, yet they could not outstrip Us (i.e., escape Our punishment)."[317]

He (ﷻ) said:

إِنَّ فِرْعَوْنَ عَلَا فِى ٱلْأَرْضِ وَجَعَلَ أَهْلَهَا شِيَعًا يَسْتَضْعِفُ طَآئِفَةً مِّنْهُمْ يُذَبِّحُ أَبْنَآءَهُمْ وَيَسْتَحْىِۦ نِسَآءَهُمْ

"Verily, Fir'awn (Pharaoh) exalted himself in the land and made its people into sects, weakening (oppressing) a group (i.e., Children of Israel) among them, killing their sons, and letting their females live."[318]

He (ﷻ) said:

وَجَحَدُوا۟ بِهَا وَٱسْتَيْقَنَتْهَآ أَنفُسُهُمْ ظُلْمًا وَعُلُوًّا فَٱنظُرْ كَيْفَ كَانَ عَٰقِبَةُ ٱلْمُفْسِدِينَ ﴿١٤﴾

"And they belied them (those *Aayaat*) wrongfully and arrogantly, though their own selves were con-

---

[316] Soorah Ghaafir (40):23-35.
[317] Soorah al-'Ankaboot (29):39.
[318] Soorah al-Qaṣas (28):4.

vinced thereof [i.e., that those (*Aayaat*) are from Allaah and Moosa is the Messenger of Allaah in truth, but they disliked to obey Moosa and hated to believe in his Message of Monotheism]. So see what was the end of the *Mufsidoon* (disbelievers, those who disobey Allaah, evildoers, liars)."[319]

The like of these (*aayaat*) are numerous in the Qur'aan.

Fir'awn has been depicted with *shirk* in Allaah's saying:

$$وَقَالَ ٱلۡمَلَأُ مِن قَوۡمِ فِرۡعَوۡنَ أَتَذَرُ مُوسَىٰ وَقَوۡمَهُۥ لِيُفۡسِدُواْ فِى ٱلۡأَرۡضِ وَيَذَرَكَ وَءَالِهَتَكَ$$

"The chiefs of Fir'awn's people said, 'Will you allow Moosa and his people to spread mischief in the land and to abandon you and your gods?'"[320]

In fact, examination and research indicate that the more a person is too proud to accede to the worship of Allaah, the greater will be the *shirk* he commits with Allaah. The reason is that the more he disdains to worship Allaah, the greater will be his poverty and need for a beloved pursuit, which culminates as his end desire: the primary desire of the heart. Thus, he becomes a *mushrik* on account of what has enslaved him of such end intents.

Furthermore, the heart can only dispense of all creation when Allaah is its patron and protector and when it worships none other; only seeking assistance from Allaah; relying on none besides Him; taking joy in only that which Allaah loves and is pleased with; disliking only that which the Lord hates and dislikes; not offering *walaa'* except to those whom Allaah has offered *walaa'*; having enmity only towards those whom Allaah has enmity towards; loving for Allaah solely; hating for Allaah solely; giving for Allaah only and denying for Allaah only.

---

[319] Soorah an-Naml (27):14.
[320] Soorah al-A'raaf (7):127.

The stronger the sincerity of one's *Deen* is for Allaah, the more complete will be his *'uboodiyyah* and his independence of the creation.

With the perfection of one's *'uboodiyyah* of Allaah, will be the completion of one's absolution of pride and *shirk*. *Shirk* is prevalent among the Christians and pride is prevalent among the Jews. Allaah (ﷻ) says concerning the Christians:[321]

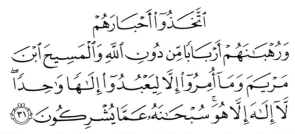

"They took their rabbis and their monks to be their lords besides Allaah (by obeying them in things which they made lawful or unlawful according to their own desires without being ordered by Allaah), and (they also took as their Lord) *al-Maseeh*, son of Maryam, while they were commanded to worship none but One Deity (i.e., Allaah); None has the right to be worshipped but He. Praise and glory be to Him, (far above is He) from having the partners they associate (with Him)."[322]

Regarding the Jews, Allaah says:

أَفَكُلَّمَا جَآءَكُمْ رَسُولٌ بِمَا لَا تَهْوَىٰٓ أَنفُسُكُمُ ٱسْتَكْبَرْتُمْ فَفَرِيقًا كَذَّبْتُمْ وَفَرِيقًا تَقْتُلُونَ ۝

---

[321] Although, this *aayah* is not specific to the Christians – a matter that the author is very much aware of - the intention from the author is to use the significant part from the *aayah* that demonstrates his specific point here. [t]

[322] Soorah at-Tawbah (9):31.

"Is it that whenever there comes to you a messenger with what you yourselves desire not, you treat him with disdain? Some you disbelieve in and some you kill."[323]

Allaah (ﷻ) also says:

سَأَصْرِفُ عَنْ ءَايَنتِيَ ٱلَّذِينَ يَتَكَبَّرُونَ فِى ٱلْأَرْضِ بِغَيْرِ ٱلْحَقِّ وَإِن يَرَوْاْ كُلَّ ءَايَةٍ لَّا يُؤْمِنُواْ بِهَا وَإِن يَرَوْاْ سَبِيلَ ٱلرُّشْدِ لَا يَتَّخِذُوهُ سَبِيلًا وَإِن يَرَوْاْ سَبِيلَ ٱلْغَيِّ يَتَّخِذُوهُ سَبِيلًا

"I shall turn away from My *Aayaat* (i.e., verses of the Qur'aan) those who behave arrogantly on the earth, without a right, and (even) if they see all the *Aayaat* (proofs, evidences, verses, lessons, signs, revelations, etc.), they will not believe in them. And if they see the way of righteousness (monotheism, piety, and good deeds), they will not adopt it as the Way, but if they see the way of error (polytheism, crimes and evil deeds), they will adopt that way."[324]

Since pride necessitates *shirk* and *shirk* is the antithesis of Islaam – and it is the sin that Allaah does not forgive - Allaah (ﷻ) has said:

إِنَّ ٱللَّهَ لَا يَغْفِرُ أَن يُشْرَكَ بِهِۦ وَيَغْفِرُ مَا دُونَ ذَٰلِكَ لِمَن يَشَآءُ وَمَن يُشْرِكْ بِٱللَّهِ فَقَدِ ٱفْتَرَىٰٓ إِثْمًا عَظِيمًا

"Verily, Allaah forgives not that *shirk* should be committed with Him, but He forgives (everything) besides that to whom He pleases, and whoever commits *shirk* with Allaah in worship, he has indeed invented a tremendous sin."[325]

---

[323] Soorah al-Baqarah (2):87.
[324] Soorah al-A'raaf (7):146.
[325] Soorah an-Nisaa' (4):48.

Allaah also says:

إِنَّ ٱللَّهَ لَا يَغْفِرُ أَن يُشْرَكَ بِهِۦ وَيَغْفِرُ مَا دُونَ ذَٰلِكَ لِمَن يَشَآءُ وَمَن يُشْرِكْ بِٱللَّهِ فَقَدْ ضَلَّ ضَلَٰلَۢا بَعِيدًا

"Verily, Allaah forgives not that *shirk* should be committed with Him, but He forgives (everything) besides that to whom He pleases, and whoever commits *shirk* with Allaah in worship, he has indeed strayed far away."[326]

All of the Prophets were sent with the *Deen* of Islaam. It is the only *Deen* that Allaah accepts, from the first to the last of people. Noo<u>h</u> said:[327]

فَإِن تَوَلَّيْتُمْ فَمَا سَأَلْتُكُم مِّنْ أَجْرٍ إِنْ أَجْرِىَ إِلَّا عَلَى ٱللَّهِ وَأُمِرْتُ أَنْ أَكُونَ مِنَ ٱلْمُسْلِمِينَ ٧٢

"But if you turn away [from accepting my doctrine of Islaamic Monotheism], then no reward have I asked of you, my reward is only from Allaah, and I have been commanded to be one of the Muslims (those who submit to Allaah's Will)."

Allaah said concerning Ibraaheem:

وَمَن يَرْغَبُ عَن مِّلَّةِ إِبْرَٰهِـمَ إِلَّا مَن سَفِهَ نَفْسَهُۥ وَلَقَدِ ٱصْطَفَيْنَٰهُ فِى ٱلدُّنْيَا وَإِنَّهُۥ فِى ٱلْءَاخِرَةِ لَمِنَ ٱلصَّٰلِحِينَ ١٣٠ إِذْ قَالَ لَهُۥ رَبُّهُۥ أَسْلِمْ قَالَ أَسْلَمْتُ لِرَبِّ ٱلْعَٰلَمِينَ ١٣١ وَوَصَّىٰ بِهَآ إِبْرَٰهِـمُ بَنِيهِ وَيَعْقُوبُ يَٰبَنِىَّ إِنَّ ٱللَّهَ ٱصْطَفَىٰ لَكُمُ ٱلدِّينَ فَلَا تَمُوتُنَّ إِلَّا وَأَنتُم مُّسْلِمُونَ ١٣٢

---

[326] Soorah an-Nisaa' (4):116.
[327] As related by Allaah, Soorah Yoonus (10):72.

"And who turns away from the religion of Ibraaheem (i.e., Islaamic Monotheism) except him who deludes himself? Truly, We chose him in this world and verily, in the Hereafter he will be among the righteous. When his Lord said to him, 'Submit (i.e., be a Muslim)!' He replied, 'I have submitted myself (as a Muslim) to the Lord of the 'Aalameen (mankind, *jinns* and all that exists)'. And this (sub-mission to Allaah, Islaam) was enjoined by Ibraaheem upon his sons and by Ya'qoob (saying), 'O my sons! Allaah has chosen for you the (true) religion, then die not except as Muslims.'"[327]

Yoosuf said:[328]

تَوَفَّنِي مُسْلِمًا وَأَلْحِقْنِي بِالصَّلِحِينَ ﴿١٠١﴾

"...and cause me to die as a Muslim (the one sub-mitting to Your Will), and unite me with the right-eous."

Moosa said:[329]

يَنقَوْمِ إِن كُنتُمْ ءَامَنتُم

بِاللَّهِ فَعَلَيْهِ تَوَكَّلُواْ إِن كُنتُم مُّسْلِمِينَ ﴿٨٤﴾ فَقَالُواْ عَلَى اللَّهِ تَوَكَّلْنَا

"...'O my people! If you have believed in Allaah, then put your trust in Him if you are Muslims'. They said, 'In Allaah we put our trust'..."

Allaah (ﷻ) also says:

إِنَّا أَنزَلْنَا التَّوْرَنةَ فِيهَا

هُدًى وَنُورٌ يَحْكُمُ بِهَا النَّبِيُّونَ الَّذِينَ أَسْلَمُواْ لِلَّذِينَ هَادُواْ

---

[327] Soorah al-Baqarah (2):130-2.
[328] As related by Allaah, Soorah Yoosuf (12):101.
[329] As related by Allaah, Soorah Yoonus (10):84-85.

"Verily, We did send down the Tawraat (to Moosa), therein was guidance and light, by which the Prophets, who submitted themselves to Allaah's Will, judged the Jews."[330]

Bilqees said:[331]

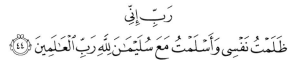

"My Lord! Verily, I have wronged myself, and I submit (in Islaam) together with Sulaymaan to Allaah, the Lord of the 'Aalameen (mankind, *jinn* and all that exists)."

Allaah said:

وَإِذْ أَوْحَيْتُ إِلَى ٱلْحَوَارِيِّنَ أَنْ ءَامِنُوا۟ بِي وَبِرَسُولِي قَالُوٓا۟ءَامَنَّا وَٱشْهَدْ بِأَنَّنَا مُسْلِمُونَ ﴿١١١﴾

"And when I (i.e., Allaah) put in the hearts of the *Hawaariyyeen* (i.e., the disciples of 'Eesa) to believe in Me and My Messenger, they said, 'We believe and bear witness that we are Muslims.'"[332]

Allaah also says:

إِنَّ ٱلدِّينَ عِندَ ٱللَّهِ ٱلْإِسْلَٰمُ

"Truly, the religion with Allaah is Islaam."[333]

Allaah says:

وَمَن يَبْتَغِ غَيْرَ ٱلْإِسْلَٰمِ دِينًا فَلَن يُقْبَلَ مِنْهُ وَهُوَ فِي ٱلْءَاخِرَةِ مِنَ ٱلْخَٰسِرِينَ ﴿٨٥﴾

---

[330] Soorah al-Maa'idah (5):44.

[331] As related by Allaah, Soorah an-Naml (27):44.

[332] Soorah al-Maa'idah (5):111.

[333] Soorah Aal-'Imraan (3):19.

"And whoever seeks a religion other than Islaam, it will never be accepted of him, and in the Hereafter he will be one of the losers."[334]

Allaah (ﷻ) also says:

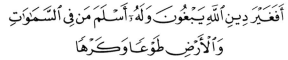

"Do they seek other than the religion of Allaah (the true Islaamic Monotheism worshipping none but Allaah Alone), while to Him all creatures in the heavens and the earth have submitted, willingly or unwillingly."[335]

Thus, Allaah (ﷻ) mentioned the *Islaam* of all beings, willingly or unwillingly, since all of creation worship Allaah with the general manifestation of worship, regardless of whether one (of them) acknowledges or denies that. They submit to Him and are managed by Him. Thus, they submit to Him, willingly or unwillingly; not a single one of His creation has the ability to escape that which Allaah wills, decrees and ordains. There is no might nor power except with Allaah and He is the Lord of the Worlds and their Owner. He disposes as He sees fits and He is the Creator, Originator and Fashioner of them all.

Everything besides Him is under the Lordship of Allaah, created, originated, destitute, indigent, subjugated and subdued. Whereas He (ﷻ) is the One, *al-Qahhaar,*[336] the Creator, Originator and Fashioner.

---

[334] Soorah Aal-'Imraan (3):85.

[335] Soorah Aal-'Imraan (3):83.

[336] One of Allaah's Names (ﷻ), it denotes the One Who has subdued all of creation and Whom all of creation are subservient to. All movements occur by His will. [t]

Furthermore, even though He created His creation through causes, He is also the Creator of cause and the One who decrees it.[337] Cause is in need of Him just as (other parts of) creation is in need of Him. There does not exist amidst creation, a cause that independently brings about good or repels harm. Indeed, everything that is a cause is in need of another cause that assists it and in need of that which repels the deterrent factor, which seeks to oppose and resist it.

He is solely, the Rich and independent of all besides Him; He does not have a partner that aids Him or a rival that is hostile towards Him and opposes Him. Allaah (ﷻ) says:

قُلْ أَفَرَءَيْتُم مَّا تَدْعُونَ مِن دُونِ ٱللَّهِ إِنْ أَرَادَنِيَ ٱللَّهُ بِضُرٍّ هَلْ هُنَّ كَٰشِفَٰتُ ضُرِّهِۦٓ أَوْ أَرَادَنِي بِرَحْمَةٍ هَلْ هُنَّ مُمْسِكَٰتُ رَحْمَتِهِۦۚ قُلْ حَسْبِيَ ٱللَّهُۖ عَلَيْهِ يَتَوَكَّلُ ٱلْمُتَوَكِّلُونَ ﴿٣٨﴾

"Say, 'Tell me then, the things that you invoke besides Allaah, if Allaah intended some harm for me, could they remove His harm, or if He (Allaah) intended some mercy for me, could they withhold His Mercy?' Say, 'Sufficient for me is Allaah; in Him those who trust (i.e., believers) must put their trust.'"[338]

---

[337] There are causes that Allaah has linked to effects. There is no single cause that independently attains one's pursuit. Rather, Allaah has linked everything through causes and obstacles. If such causes materialise and such obstacles disappear, the pursuit is achieved. There is nothing that has an independent and sole effect besides the Will of Allaah. Whatever He wills, comes to be and whatever he does not will, cannot be. [s]

[338] Soorah az-Zumar (39):38.

Allaah (ﷻ) also says:

$$وَإِن يَمْسَسْكَ ٱللَّهُ بِضُرٍّ فَلَا كَاشِفَ لَهُۥٓ$$

$$إِلَّا هُوَ ۖ وَإِن يَمْسَسْكَ بِخَيْرٍ فَهُوَ عَلَىٰ كُلِّ شَىْءٍ قَدِيرٌ ۝١٧$$

"**And if Allaah touches you with harm, none can remove it but He, and if He touches you with good, then He is Able to do all things.**"[339]

Allaah (ﷻ) relates regarding Ibraaheem:

$$قَالَ يَٰقَوْمِ إِنِّى بَرِىٓءٌ مِّمَّا تُشْرِكُونَ ۝٧٨$$

$$إِنِّى وَجَّهْتُ وَجْهِىَ لِلَّذِى فَطَرَ ٱلسَّمَٰوَٰتِ وَٱلْأَرْضَ$$

$$حَنِيفًا ۖ وَمَآ أَنَا۠ مِنَ ٱلْمُشْرِكِينَ ۝٧٩ وَحَآجَّهُۥ قَوْمُهُۥ ۚ قَالَ$$

$$أَتُحَٰٓجُّوٓنِّى فِى ٱللَّهِ وَقَدْ هَدَىٰنِ ۚ وَلَآ أَخَافُ مَا تُشْرِكُونَ بِهِۦٓ$$

$$إِلَّآ أَن يَشَآءَ رَبِّى شَيْـًٔا ۗ وَسِعَ رَبِّى كُلَّ شَىْءٍ عِلْمًا ۗ أَفَلَا$$

$$تَتَذَكَّرُونَ ۝٨٠ وَكَيْفَ أَخَافُ مَآ أَشْرَكْتُمْ وَلَا$$

$$تَخَافُونَ أَنَّكُمْ أَشْرَكْتُم بِٱللَّهِ مَا لَمْ يُنَزِّلْ بِهِۦ عَلَيْكُمْ$$

$$سُلْطَٰنًا ۚ فَأَىُّ ٱلْفَرِيقَيْنِ أَحَقُّ بِٱلْأَمْنِ ۖ إِن كُنتُمْ تَعْلَمُونَ ۝٨١$$

$$ٱلَّذِينَ ءَامَنُوا۟ وَلَمْ يَلْبِسُوٓا۟ إِيمَٰنَهُم بِظُلْمٍ أُو۟لَٰٓئِكَ لَهُمُ ٱلْأَمْنُ$$

$$وَهُم مُّهْتَدُونَ ۝٨٢$$

"**…'O my people! I am indeed free from all that you join as partners in worship with Allaah. Verily, I have turned my face towards Him Who has created the heavens and the earth soundly (i.e., with Islaamic Monotheism, worshipping none but Allaah Alone) and I am not of the *mushrikoon*.'**

---

[339] Soorah al-An'aam (6):17.

138

His people disputed with him. He said, 'Do you dispute with me concerning Allaah while He has guided me, and I fear not those whom you associate with Allaah in worship. (Nothing can happen to me) except when my Lord (Allaah) wills something. My Lord comprehends in His Knowledge all things. Will you not then remember? And how should I fear those whom you associate in worship with Allaah (though they can neither benefit nor harm), while you fear not that you have joined in worship with Allaah things for which He has not sent down to you any authority. (So) which of the two parties has more right to be in security? If you but know.'

It is those who believe (in the Oneness of Allaah and worship none but Him Alone) and mix not their belief with _dhulm_ (wrong, i.e., by worshipping others besides Allaah), for them (only) there is security and they are the guided."[340]

Recorded in the _Saheehayn_,[341] 'Abdullaah Ibn Mas'ood, may Allaah be pleased with him, relates that when this _aayah_[342] was revealed, it proved hard to bear by the Companions of the Prophet (ﷺ). They said: _"O Messenger of Allaah! Which one of us has not mixed his eemaan with dhulm[343]?"_ He replied: _"Indeed, it is (in reference to) none other than shirk. Have you not heard the statement of the righteous 'abd:_[344]

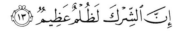

"Verily! _Shirk_ is a great _dhulm_ indeed."[345]

---

[340] Soorah al-An'aam (6):78-82.

[341] Related by al-Bukhaaree (1/81); Muslim (124); Ahmad (3589); at-Tirmidhee (3069) and Ibn Jareer (13476) from Ibn Mas'ood.

[342] i.e., the last _aayah_ from the passage just cited by the author, 6:82. [t]

[343] i.e., oppression of all sorts in its general meaning, which is what was initially understood by the Companions. [t]

[344] i.e., Luqmaan.

[345] Soorah Luqmaan (31):13.

Ibraaheem, the *Khaleel*, is the *Imaam* of the pure, sincere and up-right holders (of Islaam) as he was sent when the *Deen* of the *mushrikoon* was widespread throughout the whole world. Allaah (ﷻ) says:

$$\text{وَإِذِ ٱبْتَلَىٰٓ إِبْرَٰهِـۧمَ رَبُّهُۥ بِكَلِمَٰتٍ فَأَتَمَّهُنَّ قَالَ إِنِّي جَاعِلُكَ لِلنَّاسِ إِمَامًا قَالَ وَمِن ذُرِّيَّتِي قَالَ لَا يَنَالُ عَهْدِى ٱلظَّٰلِمِينَ ﴿١٢٤﴾}$$

"And (remember) when Ibraaheem was tried by his Lord with (certain) Commands, which he then ful-filled. He (i.e., Allaah) said, 'Verily, I am going to make you an Imaam (i.e., leader, Prophet) of man-kind.' Ibraaheem said, 'And (will You make lead-ers) from my offspring.' He (i.e., Allaah) replied, 'My Covenant (i.e., leadership, Prophethood, etc.) does not include the *dhaalimoon* (i.e., *mushrikoon* and wrong-doers)'."[346]

Allaah explained that His covenant of leadership does not encom-pass the oppressor and hence, Allaah (ﷻ) did not rule that an *op-pressor* be an *imaam*, and the most severe form of *oppression* is *shirk*.

Allaah (ﷻ) says:

$$\text{إِنَّ إِبْرَٰهِيمَ كَانَ أُمَّةً قَانِتًا لِّلَّهِ حَنِيفًا وَلَمْ يَكُ مِنَ ٱلْمُشْرِكِينَ}$$

"Verily, Ibraaheem was an *ummah* (i.e., a leader having all the good righteous qualities or a nation in himself), obedient to Allaah, upright (i.e., wor-shipping none but Allaah), and he was never of the *mushrikoon*."[347]

---

[346] Soorah al-Baqarah (2):124.
[347] Soorah an-Nahl (16):120.

140

The *ummah* is the instructor of good, who is imitated[348] just as the *qudwah* is the one whose example is followed.

Allaah (ﷻ) placed prophethood and the (revelation of) scriptures within Ibraaheem's offspring and the Prophets dispatched after him were sent with none other than his way. Allaah (ﷻ) says:

ثُمَّ أَوْحَيْنَا إِلَيْكَ أَنِ ٱتَّبِعْ مِلَّةَ إِبْرَٰهِيمَ حَنِيفًا وَمَا كَانَ مِنَ ٱلْمُشْرِكِينَ ﴿١٢٣﴾

"Then, We have inspired you (O Muhammad (ﷺ) saying), 'Follow the way of Ibraaheem, soundly (i.e., Islaamic Monotheism, to worship none but Allaah) and he was not of the *mushrikoon*."[349]

Allaah (ﷻ) also said:

إِنَّ أَوْلَى ٱلنَّاسِ بِإِبْرَٰهِيمَ لَلَّذِينَ ٱتَّبَعُوهُ وَهَٰذَا ٱلنَّبِىُّ وَٱلَّذِينَ ءَامَنُوا۟ وَٱللَّهُ وَلِىُّ ٱلْمُؤْمِنِينَ ﴿٦٨﴾

"Verily, among mankind who have the most deserving claim to Ibraaheem are those who followed him, and this Prophet (Muhammad (ﷺ)) and those who have believed (Muslims). And Allaah is the *Walee* of the believers."[350]

Allaah (ﷻ) says:

مَا كَانَ إِبْرَٰهِيمُ يَهُودِيًّا وَلَا نَصْرَانِيًّا وَلَٰكِن كَانَ حَنِيفًا مُّسْلِمًا وَمَا كَانَ مِنَ ٱلْمُشْرِكِينَ ﴿٦٧﴾

---

[348] Refer to *at-Tadhkirah wa al-I'tibaar wa al-Intisaar li al-Abraar*, pg. 23 of Ibn Shaykh al-Hazzaameen with my *ta'leeq*.

[349] Soorah an-Nahl (16):123.

[350] Soorah Aal-'Imraan (3):68.

"Ibraaheem was neither a Jew nor a Christian, but he was a true upright (i.e., Islaamic Monotheism, to worship none but Allaah Alone) Muslim and he was not of the *mushrikoon*."[351]

Allaah (ﷻ) also says:

وَقَالُواْ كُونُواْ هُودًا أَوْ نَصَـٰرَىٰ تَهْتَدُواْ قُلْ بَلْ مِلَّةَ إِبْرَٰهِـۦمَ حَنِيفًا وَمَا كَانَ مِنَ ٱلْمُشْرِكِينَ ﴿١٣٥﴾ قُولُوٓاْ ءَامَنَّا بِٱللَّهِ وَمَآ أُنزِلَ إِلَيْنَا وَمَآ أُنزِلَ إِلَىٰٓ إِبْرَٰهِـۦمَ وَإِسْمَـٰعِيلَ وَإِسْحَـٰقَ وَيَعْقُوبَ وَٱلْأَسْبَاطِ وَمَآ أُوتِيَ مُوسَىٰ وَعِيسَىٰ وَمَآ أُوتِيَ ٱلنَّبِيُّونَ مِن رَّبِّهِمْ لَا نُفَرِّقُ بَيْنَ أَحَدٍ مِّنْهُمْ وَنَحْنُ لَهُۥ مُسْلِمُونَ ﴿١٣٦﴾

"And they say, 'Be Jews or Christians, then you will be guided.' Say (to them, O Mu<u>h</u>ammad (ﷺ)), 'Nay, (We follow) only the religion of Ibraaheem, uprightly (i.e., Islaamic Monotheism, to worship none but Allaah Alone) and he was not of the *mushrikoon*.'

Say (O Muslims), 'We believe in Allaah and that which has been sent down to us and that which has been sent down to Ibraaheem, Ismaa'eel, Ishaaq, Ya'qoob, and to the *Asbaat* (i.e., the twelve sons of Ya'qoob), and that which has been given to Moosa and 'Eeesa, and that which has been given to the Prophets from their Lord. We make no distinction between any of them, and to Him we have submitted (in Islaam)'."[352]

---

[351] Soorah Aal-'Imraan (3):67.
[352] Soorah al-Baqarah (2):135-136.

It is established in the _Saheeh_[353] that the Prophet (ﷺ) said: "_Verily,_ _Ibraaheem is the best of creation._" He is the best of Prophets after the Prophet (ﷺ) (i.e., Muhammad) and he is the _khaleel_ of Allaah (ﷺ).

It is also established in the _Saheeh_[354] in a number of narrations that he (ﷺ) said: "_Indeed, Allaah has taken me as a khaleel just as He took Ibraaheem as a khaleel._"

He (ﷺ) also said: "_If I were to take a khaleel from the people of this earth, I would take Aboo Bakr as a khaleel but your companion is the khaleel of Allaah._"[355] The Prophet was referring to himself.

He (ﷺ) said: "_All wicket-doors leading into the mosque are to be blocked except Aboo Bakr's wicket-door._"[356]

He (ﷺ) also said: "_Verily, those who preceded you used to take the graves as mosques. Verily, do not take graves as mosques, for I forbid you to do that._"[357]

All of these (_hadeeths_) are in the _Saheeh_.

Likewise, it is also reported in the _Saheeh_[358] that he said this prior to his death by a few days and this is from the perfection of his message as it embodies the perfect actualisation of his _mukhaallah_

---

[353] Related by Muslim (2369); Aboo Daawood (4672); at-Tirmidhee (3352) and an-Nasaa'ee in _al-Kubraa_ as mentioned in _Tuhfah al-Ashraaf_ (1/403).

[354] Related by Muslim (532) from Jundub. This _hadeeth_ is narrated by a number of Companions, refer to _Jaami' al-Usool_ (8/584-590).

[355] Related by al-Bukhaaree (10/10), Muslim (2382) and at-Tirmidhee (3661) from Aboo Sa'eed al-Khudree.

[356] This is an excerpt from the previous _hadeeth_.

[357] Related by Muslim (532); Aboo 'Awaanah (1/401); at-Tabaraanee in _al-Kabeer_ (1686) and Ibn Sa'd (2/240) from Jundub Ibn 'Abdillaah.

[358] i.e., in the very same _hadeeth_: "...before he passed away by five (days)...". [t]

of Allaah, which is based on Allaah's (ﷻ) love for the *'abd* and the *'abd*'s love for Allaah, contrary to the (position of the) *Jahmiyyah.*[359]

It (i.e., the *hadeeth*) comprises the realisation of the *tawheed* of Allaah and that none but He be worshipped, in refutation of those who resemble the *mushrikoon.*

It also contains a refutation of the *Raafidah*, who withhold as-Siddeeq's[360] due, may Allaah be pleased with him. Of all those who attribute themselves to the *qiblah*[361] they commit the greatest *shirk* through worship of 'Alee and other individuals from mankind.[362]

Al-Khullah denotes the perfection of love, which necessitates from the *'abd* perfect *'uboodiyyah* of Allaah and from the Lord, perfect Lordship for his *'ibaad*, those whom He loves and they love Him.

The term *'uboodiyyah* embodies the utmost degree of submission and the utmost degree of love. They (i.e., the Arabs) say, 'a heart that is *mutayyam*' if it is worshipped by it's beloved. The *mutayyam* (المتيم) is the *muta'abbad* (المتعبد).

Tayyama Allaah (تيم الله) means (عبد الله) *'abada Allaah*, and this occurred on a perfect manner for Ibraaheem and Muhammad (ﷺ).

It was for this reason that the Prophet (ﷺ) did not take a single person from the people of this earth as a *khaleel*, since *khullah* is not open to apportionment; it is as has been said in meaning:

---

[359] Refer to *Dar Ta'aarud al-'Aql wa an-Naql* (6/59-63) by the author, may Allaah have mercy upon him.

[360] i.e., Aboo Bakr as-Siddeeq.

[361] i.e., to be of the Muslims.

[362] The author, may Allaah have mercy upon him, has elaborated extensively on invalidating their views and disproving their beliefs in his amazing book *Minhaaj as-Sunnah an-Nabawiyyah*. It has been printed – at long last - with a thorough verification, in 9 volumes.

You have indeed interpenetrated[363] within me the
passageway of the soul
> And as a result, the *khaleel* was named *khaleel*

This is contrary to the basic level of love (*mahabbah*), since he (ﷺ)
said of al-Hasan and Usaamah as in the *saheeh hadeeth*: "*O Allaah,
I love them, so love them and love those who love them.*"[364]

Furthermore, 'Amr Ibn Al-'Aas asked him: "*Who amongst the people is most beloved to you?*" He replied: "*Aa'ishah.*" He then asked:
"*From among the men?*" He answered: "*Her father.*"[365]

---

[363] The verb (تخلل) means to come between, intervene, etc. It and the word (خليل) *khaleel* are
both derivatives of the root (خلل). [t]

[364] Related by al-Bukhaaree (3735 & 3747); Ahmad in *al-Musnad* (5/210) and *Fadaa'il as-
Sahaabah* (1352); an-Nasaa'ee in *Fadaa'il as-Sahaabah* (no. 80); Ibn Sa'd (4/62); al-Baghawee
in *Sharh as-Sunnah* (14/143) and Aboo al-Qaasim al-Baghawee in *Musnad Zayd* (no. 8)
from Usaamah Ibn Zayd.
The narration however, does not contain the wording: "*and love those who love them.*" This
wording is from a narration concerning al-Hasan and al-Husayn, which is related by at-
Tirmidhee in his *Sunan* (3769); an-Nasaa'ee in *al-Khasaa'is* (136); Ibn Hibbaan (2234); Ibn
Abee Shaybah in *al-Musannaf* (12/97); al-Bukhaaree in *at-Taareekh al-Kabeer* (2/286) and
al-Mizzee in *Tahdheeb al-Kamaal* (6/55) by way of Moosa Ibn Ya'qoob az-Zam'ee from
'Abdullaah Ibn Aboo Bakr Ibn Zayd from Muslim Ibn Abee Sahl from Hasan Ibn Usaamah
from his father.
Ibn al-Madeenee said concerning this *hadeeth*: "The *hadeeth* of al-Hasan Ibn Usaamah is a
madeenee hadeeth, which is related by a *shaykh* who is weak and of *munkar* narration, he is
known as Moosa Ibn Ya'qoob, a son of 'Abdullaah Ibn Zam'ah, who relates it from an unknown person from another person who is also unknown." This statement is recorded by Ibn
'Asaakir in his *at-Taareekh*, (4/155 – a *tahdheeb* version).
It has also been declared as weak by adh-Dhahabee in *as-Siyar*, 3/252 and he then said: "This
is one of those (narrations) of which at-Tirmidhee is criticised for grading as *hasan*." Our
brother al-Huwaynee attributed it to al-Haakim in *al-Hulee…*, I have not however seen it in
al-Haakim's *Mustadrak*!
The wording, '*O Allaah, I love them, so love them.*' has a supporting *hadeeth*. It is related by
Ahmad in *al-Musnad*, 2/446 and *al-Fadaa'il*, 1371, Ibn Abee Shaybah in *al-Musannaf*, 12/
95 and al-Bazzaar, 3/226 via two ways from Aboo Hurayrah and its chain is *hasan*.

[365] Related by al-Bukhaaree, 3662; Muslim, 2384; at-Tirmidhee, 3879; an-Nasaa'ee in *Fadaa'il
as-Sahaabah*, no. 5 and Ahmad, 4/203 via many ways from 'Amr Ibn al-'Aas.

He also said to 'Alee,[366] may Allaah be pleased with him: *"Tomorrow, I will give this flag to a man who loves Allaah and His Messenger and whom is loved by Allaah and His Messenger."*[367]

Examples of this are numerous.

Furthermore, Allaah (ﷻ) has informed us:

$$فَإِنَّ ٱللَّهَ يُحِبُّ ٱلْمُتَّقِينَ ﴿٧٦﴾$$

"Allaah loves the *muttaqoon*."[368]

$$إِنَّ ٱللَّهَ يُحِبُّ ٱلْمُحْسِنِينَ ﴿١٩٥﴾$$

"Allaah loves the *muhsinoon* (the good-doers)."[369]

$$إِنَّ ٱللَّهَ يُحِبُّ ٱلْمُقْسِطِينَ$$

"Allaah loves those who are equitable."[370]

$$إِنَّ ٱللَّهَ يُحِبُّ ٱلتَّوَّٰبِينَ وَيُحِبُّ ٱلْمُتَطَهِّرِينَ ﴿٢٢٢﴾$$

"Allaah loves those who turn unto Him in repentance and loves those who purify themselves."[371]

$$إِنَّ ٱللَّهَ يُحِبُّ ٱلَّذِينَ يُقَٰتِلُونَ فِى سَبِيلِهِۦ صَفًّا كَأَنَّهُم بُنْيَٰنٌ مَّرْصُوصٌ ﴿٤﴾$$

"Allaah loves those who fight in His Cause in rows (ranks) as if they were a solid structure."[372]

---

[366] This is how the original reads, the author probably meant *'concerning 'Alee'* but wrote it *'to 'Alee'*.

[367] Related by al-Bukhaaree, (3009, 3701 & 4201); Muslim, 2406; Ahmad in his *Musnad*, 5/333 and *Fadaa'il*, 1037; an-Nasaa'ee in *al-Kubraa'*, (36 – *Fadaa'il as-Sahaabah*); al-Baghawee, 3906 and at-Tabaraanee in *al-Kabeer*, 5876 5950 & 5991 from Sahl Ibn Sa'd. This *hadeeth* has been narrated by a number of Companions.

[368] Soorah Aal-'Imraan (3):76.

[369] Soorah al-Baqarah (2):195.

[370] Soorah al-Hujuraat (49):9.

[371] Soorah al-Baqarah (2): 222.

[372] Soorah as-Saff (61):4.

He also said:

فَسَوْفَ يَأْتِي ٱللَّهُ بِقَوْمٍ يُحِبُّهُمْ وَيُحِبُّونَهُ

"...then Allaah will bring a people whom He will love and they will love Him."[373]

Hence, Allaah informs us of His love for the believers and of the love of the believers for Him, to the extent that He said:

وَٱلَّذِينَ ءَامَنُوٓاْ أَشَدُّ حُبًّا لِّلَّهِ

"But those who believe, love Allaah more (than anything else)."[374]

As for *al-Khullah*, it is exclusive.

The assertion of some that 'Muhammad (ﷺ) is the beloved of Allaah and Ibraaheem is the *Khaleel* of Allaah' along with the presumption that love (*mahabbah*) is of a higher rank than *khullah*, is a weak statement since Muhammad **is also** the *khaleel* of Allaah as has been established in ample and authentic *hadeeths*.[375]

In addition, the narration that relates that al-'Abbaas will be raised up (on the Day of Judgement) between (the level of) a beloved and a *khaleel*,[376] and the likes of such narrations, they are all fabricated *hadeeths* that are not fit to be used for any basis.

---

[373] Soorah al-Maa'idah (5):54.

[374] Soorah al-Baqarah (2):165.

[375] Some of which have just preceded.

[376] The author is probably referring to the narration attributed to the Prophet (ﷺ): "*...and al-'Abbaas is between us, a believer; between two khaleels.*" It is related by Ibn Maajah (141), al-'Aqeelee (3/78) and Ibn al-Jawzee in *al-Mawdoo'aat* (2/32) from Ibn 'Amr. al-Busayree states in *Misbaah az-Zujaajah* (no. 51): "This is a weak chain, because of their agreement on the weakness of 'Abdul-Wahhaab (Ibn ad-Dahhaak). In fact, Aboo Daawood said of him, 'He fabricates *hadeeths*' and al-Haakim said, 'He has related fabricated *hadeeths* and his shaykh, Ismaa'eel, commits *tadlees*." I say: "Therefore, the like of this is a fabricated *hadeeth* as asserted by Ibn al-Jawzee and as for as-Suyootee's criticism of Ibn al-Jawzee for this, as recorded in *al-Laali* (1/430), on the basis that it has been related by Ibn Maajah! This argument is refuted by the mere presentation of the argument!

We have already mentioned that love of Allaah is to love Him and to love that which He loves as recorded in the two *Saheehs*,[377] that the Prophet (ﷺ) said: *"Three (qualities), whoever possesses them, will find the sweetness of eemaan: that Allaah and His Messenger are more beloved to him besides anyone else, that he loves someone only for the sake of Allaah and that he hates to return to kufr after Allaah has delivered him from it just as he hates to be slung into the fire."*

The Prophet (ﷺ) informed that whoever possesses these three traits, will find the sweetness of *eemaan*. This is because experiencing the sweetness of something is preceded by love of that thing. One who loves or desires something, if he attains his pursuit, he then experiences the sweetness, pleasure and joy of that thing.

Pleasure is a matter that occurs directly after attaining that which is agreeable, which is the beloved or desired matter. As for the one who declares that pleasure is (itself) attaining the agreeable as alleged by some philosophers and doctors;[378] this is a gross mistake on their part since the attainment (of the agreeable) lies in between love and pleasure. A person for instance, desires food and when he eats it, he then experiences pleasure straight after that.

Pleasure follows on after viewing something (for example); when one looks at it, he takes pleasure in that. This pleasure, which follows on after looking at something is not the actual viewing itself and nor is it the object that is viewed, rather, it (i.e., pleasure) occurs immediately after viewing.[379]

---

[377] The *takhreej* for this *hadeeth* has already preceded.

[378] Refer to *Dar' Ta'aarud al-'Aql wa an-Naql*, 6/69-75 by the author for further elaboration.

[379] It is a very fine point that the author is mentioning here. For further clarification, if we take the scenario of a person taking pleasure at looking at Allaah's marvellous creation: the rivers, mountains and forestry for example. The pleasure that one feels is not the objects themselves and nor is it the act of looking. This pleasure is a matter that occurs as a result of looking at these objects. [t]

148

Allaah (جل جلاله) says:

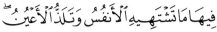

فِيهَا مَا تَشْتَهِيهِ ٱلْأَنفُسُ وَتَلَذُّ ٱلْأَعْيُنُ

"...(there will be) therein, all that the souls could desire and all that the eyes could delight in..."[380]

The case is the same for all types of pleasures and pains that befall the soul, such as happiness, sorrow and so on. They occur as a result of feelings towards something beloved or feelings towards something undesired and these feelings are not themselves happiness and sorrow.

Hence, the sweetness of *eemaan*, which embodies such pleasure for *eemaan* and joy of what the believer experiences as a result of finding the sweetness of *eemaan*, follows on **after** the perfection of the *'abd's* love of Allaah. This is (achieved) by three matters: the completion of this love, its apportionment and by repelling its opposite.

The meaning of its completion is that Allaah and His Messenger are more beloved to the person besides anyone else. Love of Allaah and His Messenger is not sufficed by having mere love for them, rather it is as has been previously explained, by loving Allaah and His Messenger **more** than anyone else.

Its apportionment means that a person loves another person **only** for Allaah's sake.

Repelling its opposite means that one has a greater hatred for the opposite of *eemaan* than he does for being thrown into the fire.

Hence, if love for the Messenger and the Muslims emanates from love of Allaah, and the Messenger of Allaah loved the believers, whom were loved by Allaah, because he has the most complete love of Allaah and he is the most deserving of those who love what Allaah loves and hate what Allaah hates, and if (as just established)

---

[380] Soorah az-Zukhruf (43):71.

al-Khullah is not apportioned to other than Allaah, but instead, he (i.e., the Prophet) said: *"If I were to take a khaleel from the people of this earth, I would take Aboo Bakr as a Khaleel,"*[381] the fact that *al-Khullah* is of a greater level than just love (*mahabbah*) can be recognised.

The point is that *al-Khullah* and love (*mahabbah*) of Allaah is the actualisation of *'uboodiyyah* to Allaah.

Those who err in this regard do so because they presume *al-'uboodiyyah* to connote only humbleness and submission, with no love alongside that. They further presume that love denotes a divulgence into desires or a divulgence void of fear, which is not sustained by Lordship.

For this reason it is said of Dhoo an-Noon,[382] that when some people spoke within his presence about the issue of love he remarked, 'Refrain from this matter; whenever the souls hear of it they allege to possess it.'[383]

Those of the people of knowledge disliked taking company with a folk that spoke greatly on love without (addressing) fear.

Some of the *Salaf* have said: "Whoever worships Allaah with love alone is a *zindeeq*; whoever worships Him with hope alone is a *Murji*; whoever worships Him with fear alone is a *Hurooree* and whoever worships Him with love, fear and hope is a *muwahhid*."[384]

---

[381] Its *takhreej* has already preceded.

[382] He is Thawbaan Ibn Ibraaheem, who was renown for asceticism. He passed away in the year 245H. His biography is in *Taareekh Baghdaad*, 8/393.

[383] Refer to his biography in *Hilyah al-'Awliyaa'*, 9/331 and onwards. A great number of his statements and reports about him have been mentioned therein.

[384] See *at-Takhweef min an-Naar* by al-Haafidh Ibn Rajab, pg. 15.

150

On account of this, some of the latter generations adulterated this claim of love to the point where it brought one of them out to some form of imprudence and allegation, which negates *al-'uboodiyyah* and places the *'abd* in (a position) of some form of Lordship, which befits Allaah alone. One of them would make claims that exceed the limits of the Prophets and Messengers or he would seek from Allaah that which can only be fitting for Allaah alone; it would not befit even the Prophets or the Messengers.

Many of the *shaykhs*[385] fell in error in this regard and its cause is the frailty of their actualisation of the *'uboodiyyah*, which was explained by the Messengers and was exactly defined by the Command and Prohibition that came with it. Indeed, (it is also because of) the weakness of their intellect, through which, the *'abd* recognises his own reality.

If the intellect becomes impaired and knowledge of the *Deen* becomes constricted and within the soul there exists a love that is rash and ignorant, the soul in all its stupidity, will extend towards that. This is similar to the case of a person who reaches out in love for another person with stupidity and ignorance and declares: "I am a lover, so I will not be held to account for certain actions I undertake that consist of wrongdoing and ignorance!"

This is pure ignorance and it resembles the statement of the Jews and Christians:

$$\text{نَحۡنُ أَبۡنَـٰٓؤُاْ ٱللَّهِ وَأَحِبَّـٰٓؤُهُۥ}$$

"We are the children of Allaah and His beloved ones."[386]

---

[385] The *shaykhs* that the author is referring to here are the *shaykhs* of the *Soofiyyah*. [s]

[386] Soorah al-Maa'idah (5):18.

151

Allaah (ﷻ) says (in response to their claim):

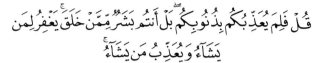

"Say, 'Why then does He punish you for your sins?'
Nay, you are but human beings, of those He has cre-
ated, He forgives whom He wills and He punishes
whom He wills."[387]

The punishment of Allaah inflicted upon them demonstrates that they are not beloved to Him and that they are not attributed to Him through son-ship. In fact, it shows that they are all under the Lord-ship of Allaah and created.

Whoever Allaah loves, Allaah will employ him in a manner that this beloved person will like, he will not perpetrate actions of *kufr*, *fusooq* and disobedience that are hated and scorned by *al-Haqq*.

One who commits major sins, persistently and does not repent from them, Allaah hates that of him, just as He loves of him the actions of goodness he does. As, His love for the *'abd* is dependent upon his (level) of *eemaan* and *taqwaa*.

As for one who presumes that sins do him no harm because Allaah loves him and at the same time he is continuously perpetrating such sins, he is equal to the one who alleges that the constant consumption of poison without taking medication to combat it does him no harm, because of his healthy disposition!

If the foolish person were to contemplate over the accounts of Allaah's Prophets, which He has related in his Book: the incidents that they went through pertaining to repentance and seeking for-giveness and the various types of trials that befell them, which were

---

[387] Soorah al-Maa'idah (5):18.

in effect a test and purification of them according to their conditions, he would become aware of some of the harms of sins upon its perpetrators, even if he held the loftiest of positions.

The reason for this is that, one who loves a creation, if he is unaware of his welfare or does not desire it, but instead acts to the dictates of his love – even if it is ignorant and oppressive – it will constitute cause for hatred and aversion on part of the beloved for the lover. Indeed, it may be a reason for chastising the lover.

Many of the travellers,[388] committed a number of matters of ignorance in the *Deen* in claiming love of Allaah. This was by transgressing the limits set by Allaah or by squandering the rights of Allaah. It was also through making false claims that have no reality whatsoever, like the saying of some of them, 'I disassociate myself from any *mureed* of mine who leaves a single person in the fire'. Another said, 'I disassociate myself from any *mureed* of mine who allows a believer to enter the fire'.

The first, declared that his *mureed* (has the authority to) take everyone out of the fire! Whereas, the second, declared that his *mureed* (had the authority to) prevent any of the people of major sins from entering the fire!

Some of them even state, 'On the Day of Standing, I will erect my pavilion over *Jahannam* so that none can enter it'!

There are other such statements, which are related from some of the well-known *shaykhs*. Such statements are either fabrications upon them or blunders from them.[389]

---

[388] *Saalik*, a traveller, a term which in its general sense can signify everyone as we are all on our way to Allaah. In a more specific sense as here, it refers to the *Soofiyyah*. [t]

[389] May Allaah have mercy upon Shaykhul-Islaam Ibn Taymiyyah, see how just and fair he is. If his adversaries and dissidents, may Allaah guide them, were to behave in the same manner that he behaved towards them, they would know of his standing and give him his due....

Such statements may emanate during states of intoxication, being overcome and *fanaa'*.[390] The ability of a person to distinguish in such states is non-existent or lessens to such an extent that a person does not know what he is saying.

Intoxication is a state of pleasure without the ability to distinguish. Subsequently, when some of these people awoke in the morning they would seek forgiveness from such statements.

This was the very intention behind those of the *shaykhs* who delved greatly into listening to poems of love, desire, reproach, admonition and passion. Since, this category (consisting of such poetry and its like) stirs the love within the heart, whatever type of love it is. As such, Allaah revealed a test, through which, He can test the holder of love. He said:

قُلۡ إِن كُنتُمۡ تُحِبُّونَ ٱللَّهَ فَٱتَّبِعُونِي يُحۡبِبۡكُمُ ٱللَّهُ

"Say (O Muḥammad (ﷺ) to mankind), 'If you (really) love Allaah then follow me (i.e. accept Islaamic Monotheism, follow the Qur'aan and the *Sunnah*), Allaah will love you'."[391]

A person therefore, cannot love Allaah except by following his Messenger. Obedience of the Messenger and following him can only be achieved through actualising *al-'uboodiyyah*.

Many of those who claim love (of Allaah) deviate and go beyond the *Sharee'ah* and *Sunnah* of the Prophet (ﷺ). Further, they claim to experience such conditions,[392] which this present time does not allow it's mention, to the extent that one of them holds the belief of no longer being subject to Commands and declaring unlawful mat-

---

[390] These matters are all of the deceptions of Iblees and the traps and snares of the accursed *Shayṭaan*.

[391] Soorah Aal-'Imraan (3):31.

[392] Like many of the proponents of *Tasawwuf* and those who claim to undergo miraculous feats, in all times.

ters to be lawful and other such matters, which oppose the *Sharee'ah* of the Messenger, his *Sunnah* and obedience to him.

Instead, Allaah has declared the foundation of love of Him and His Messenger to be *jihaad* in his cause. *Jihaad* signifies a complete love for what Allaah has commanded and a complete hatred for what Allaah has prohibited. Accordingly, Allaah says in describing those whom He loves and those who love him:

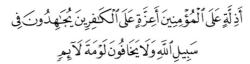

"…humble towards the believers, stern towards the disbelievers, fighting in the Way of Allaah, and never afraid of the blame of those who reproach."[393]

Consequently, the love of this *ummah* for Allaah is more complete than then of those before it and the *'uboodiyyah* of those from this *ummah* is more perfect than the *'uboodiyyah* of those before them.

The most complete of this *ummah* in this regard are the Companions of Muḥammad (ﷺ) and whoever resembles them greater, that will be a greater perfection for him.[394] Where does this (reality) stand against a people who allege love (of Allaah)?

One of the statements of some of the *shaykhs* is: "Love is a fire that burns in the heart everything except the will of the Beloved (i.e., Allaah)." They intended by this statement that Allaah intended the presence of the universe in its entirety and then presumed that perfection of love signifies that the *'abd* love every single thing, even the *kufr*, *fusooq* and disobedience (in existence)! It is not possible for a person to love every thing in existence. Rather, he loves what

---

[393] Soorah al-Maaʾidah (5):54.

[394] This is why we attribute ourselves to them, emulate them and adopt their guidance, may Allaah be pleased with them and unite us with them upon goodness.

agrees with him and what benefits him and he hates what he finds inconsistent to him and what harms him.

However, they (i.e., these *shaykhs*) benefited from this deviation in following their desires. This deviation further increased their ingrossment into their desires and lusts. Thus, they love what they desire, such as *suwar*, leadership, excess wealth and innovations that cause deviation, under the pretence that this is from having love of Allaah!

A part of love of Allaah, is to hate what Allaah and His Messenger hate and to perform *jihaad* with one's self and wealth.

The root of their deviation is that the one who said: "Love is a fire that burns in the heart everything except the will of the beloved (i.e., Allaah)." He intended by the phrase 'will of Allaah': The universal will encompassing every thing in existence.

If however, this statement was made by a believer in Allaah, His books and His Messengers, he would intend by it Allaah's Religious and Legislative will, which denotes His love and pleasure. It would be as if he said, 'It burns in the heart everything except that which is beloved to Allaah'.

This is a correct meaning, as loving only that which Allaah loves is from the completion of love. If you therefore, love what Allaah does not love, the love (you have for Allaah) will be deficient.

As for Allaah's *Qadaa* and *Qadar* (of evil), He hates, dislikes, scorns and prohibits it. If I do not therefore agree with Allaah in hating, disliking and scorning at it, I will not be one who loves Him but instead, one who loves what He hates.

Following this *Sharee'ah* and performing *jihaad* with it is one of the greatest distinguishing factors between the people of Allaah and his *awliyaa'*, whom are loved by Him and who love Him and between those who claim love of Allaah, observing (only) the generality of His Lordship or following some innovations that oppose Allaah's *Sharee'ah*. A claim of this type of love of Allaah is from the same sort of claim made by the Jews and Christians for love of Allaah. In fact, the claim of these people may be worse than the claim of the Jews and Christians because of the hypocrisy that is within them, which will cause them to be in the lowest depths of the Fire. Equally, the claim of the Jews and Christians can be worse than their claim if they do not reach the same level of *kufr* as that of the Jews and Christians.

Within the *Tawraat* and *Injeel*, there are many an enticement towards love of Allaah, which the Jews and Christians agree upon, to the extent that this is to them their greatest precepts of the Law.

In the *Injeel* it is recorded 'The greatest legacy left by *al-Maseeh̲* is to love Allaah with all your heart, intellect and soul.'

The Christians claim to enact this love and that the asceticism and worship they undergo emanates from this love. They are far-removed from having love of Allaah, as they did not follow what He loved, instead:

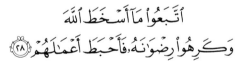

"...they followed that which angered Allaah, and hated that which pleased Him. So He made their deeds fruitless."[395]

Allaah hates the disbelievers, He detests them and curses them. He (سبحانه) loves those who love Him. It is not possible that an *'abd* have love for Allaah and for Allaah (جل جلاله) not to love him. Indeed, the level of love the *'abd* has for Allaah determines the level of love Allaah has for the *'abd*, even though, the reward of Allaah for the

---

[395] Soorah Muh̲ammad (47):28.

'*abd* is greater, as in the *saheeh* divine[396] *hadeeth* on Allaah (ﷻ), in which He said: "*Whoever draws near to Me the span of a hand I draw near to him the span of an arm. Whoever draws near to Me the span of an arm I draw near to him the span of two outstretched arms, and whoever takes a step towards Me I hastily step towards him.*"[397]

Allaah (سبحانه) informs that He loves people of *taqwaa*, doers of benevolence and the patient. He loves those who repent often and those who purify themselves.[398] Indeed, He loves those who perform what he orders of the obligatory and recommended duties, as in the *saheeh* divine *hadeeth*: "*My servant does not cease to draw near to me through supererogatory deeds until I love Him. When I do love him, I will be his hearing with which he hears, his seeing with which he sees...*"[399]

Many of those at fault who committed innovations in asceticism and worship, fell into that which the Christians fell into of claiming love of Allaah whilst opposing His *Sharee'ah* and abandoning striving in his cause and so on.

They hold on to the *Deen*, with which they seek a nearness to Allaah, with what the Christians held on to such as obscure statements as well as tales, of which the truthfulness of its sayers are not known, and if they were known, such sayers would not be infallible.

They allow the one they follow to legislate a *Deen* for them, just like the Christians, who allowed their priests and monks to legislate a *Deen* for them. Furthermore, they diminish *al-'uboodiyyah* and

---

[396] i.e., a *hadeeth* which the Messenger relates from Allaah (ﷻ).

[397] Related by al-Bukhaaree, 13/325 and Muslim, 2675 from Aboo Hurayrah. It is also related by al-Bukhaaree, 13/ 427 from Anas and related by Muslim, 2687 from Aboo Dharr.

[398] Some of these *aayaat* have already preceded.

[399] A *saheeh hadeeth*. It has many chains that individually are not void of weakness. Our Shaykh al-Albaanee has discussed this *hadeeth* fully in an admirable manner as in *as-Silsilah as-Saheehah*, 4/183-193.

allege that the elite transcend it, as the Christians did with *al-Maseeh* and the clergy. They affirm for their elite an association with Allaah similar to what the Christians affirm for *al-Maseeh*, his mother, the priests and monks and other categories of people - to discuss this would take too long in this present discussion.

The *Deen* of truth however, is none other than the actualisation of *'uboodiyyah* to Allaah in all respects, and this is the actualisation of love of Allaah in all degrees. The level of completion of *'uboodiyyah* determines the level of love the *'abd* has for Allaah and the level of love Allaah has for the *'abd*. Likewise, the level of deficiency in the former, determines the level of deficiency in the latter.

Whenever there is in the heart love for other than Allaah, there will be within it *'uboodiyyah* for other than Allaah and whenever there is with in it *'uboodiyyah* for other than Allaah, there will be in it love for other than Allaah in appropriate measure.

Any love that is not for Allaah is false and any action that is not sought for the Face of Allaah is false. The world is cursed; everything within it is cursed except that which is for Allaah.[400] It cannot be for Allaah unless it is something that Allaah and His Messenger loves and that is what has been legislated.

Thus, any action with which other than Allaah is sought, will not be for Allaah and any action that does not agree with the law of Allaah, will not be for Allaah. Rather, it will not be for Allaah unless it

---

[400] There is a *saheeh hadeeth* from the Prophet (ﷺ) which carries this meaning. It is related by at-Tirmidhee, 2323; Ibn Maajah , 4112; Ibn al-Jawzee in *al-'Ilal al-Mutanaahiyah*, 1330; al-Baghawee, 4028 and al-'Aqeelee in *ad-Du'afaa'*, 2/326 by way of 'Ataa Ibn Qurrah from 'Abdullaah Ibn Damrah from Aboo Hurayrah. Its *sanad* is *hasan*, a number of people have related from Ibn Damrah and he was declared *thiqah* by al-'Ijlee and Ibn Hibbaan. Dr Bashshaar 'Awwaad transmits in his *ta'leeq* of *Tahdheeb al-Kamaal*, 15/130 from Ibn Hajar his statement in *at-Taqreeb*: "Thiqah"! This has no basis, Ibn Hajar said instead: "He was declared *thiqah* by al-'Ijlee." The difference between the two is obvious! Refer to my book *ar-Radd al-'Ilmee* as it contains further explanation.

159

combines both descriptions: that it be for Allaah and that it agree with the love of Allaah and His Messenger. That (i.e., the second description) is (a reference to) the obligatory and recommended actions, as Allaah (ﷻ) has said:

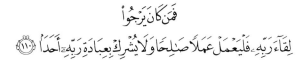

"So whoever hopes for the meeting with his Lord, let him do righteous deeds and associate none as partner in worship of his Lord."[401]

Hence, righteous deeds are a necessity and they are the obligatory and recommended actions. The action must also be sincerely for Allaah's Face (ﷻ), as Allaah (ﷻ) has said:

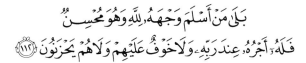

"Yes, but whoever submits his face (himself) to Allaah and he is a *Muhsin* (i.e., doer of good) then his reward is with his Lord, on such shall be no fear, nor shall they grieve."[402]

The Prophet (ﷺ) has said: *'Whosoever does a deed which is not sanctioned by us will have it rejected.'*[403]

The Prophet (ﷺ) also said: *"Actions are (determined) by their intentions and every person shall have that which he intended. Thus, he whose hijrah was for Allaah and His Messenger, his hijrah was for Allaah and His Messenger. He whose hijrah was for achieving*

---

[401] Soorah al-Kahf (18):110.

[402] Soorah al-Baqarah (2):112.

[403] Related by al-Bukhaaree, 2697; Muslim, 1718; Aboo Daawood, 4606; Ibn Maajah, 14; Ahmad, (6/146, 180, 240, 256 & 270) and al-Qudaa'ee in *Musnad ash-Shihaab*, (359 & 360) and others. Refer to *Juz Ittibaa' as-Sunan*, pg. 33-34 by ad-Diyaa' al-Maqdasee along with my *ta'leeq*.

some worldly thing or to take a woman in marriage, his hijrah was for that which he made hijrah for. ”[404]

This principle is the foundation of the *Deen*. The measure of its realisation determines one's measure of the realisation of the *Deen*. With it, the Messengers were sent; the Books were revealed; to it the Messenger invited; for it, he performed *jihaad*; with it, he ordered and towards it, he enticed. It is the pivot of the *Deen*, which the entire *Deen* revolves around.

Shirk is prevalent over the souls, it is as mentioned in the *hadeeth*: *"It is in this ummah, more discrete than the creeping of an ant."*[405]

In another *hadeeth*, Aboo Bakr says: *"O Messenger of Allaah, how do we deliver ourselves from it, when it is more discrete than the creeping of an ant?"* The Prophet (ﷺ) replied to Aboo Bakr: *"I will teach you an expression, if you say it, you will deliver yourself from its minute and great (form). Say,*

اللهم إني أعوذ بك أن أشرك بك وأنا أعلم، وأستغفرك لما لا أعلم

'O Allaah, I take refuge in You lest I should commit shirk with You knowingly and I seek Your forgiveness for what I do unknowingly'. ”[406]

'Umar used to say in his supplication: "O Allaah, make all my actions righteous and make them purely for your Face and do not let anyone have a share in them."

---

[404] Related by al-Bukhaaree, (1, 45 & 2529); Muslim, 1907; Aboo Daawood, 220; at-Tirmidhee, 1647; Ibn Maajah, 2427; an-Nasaa'ee, 1/58 and others from 'Umar, may Allaah be pleased with him. Refer to the book *al-Hittah fee Dhikr as-Sihaah as-Sittah*, pg. 141, 289 & 309) of Siddeeq Hasan Khaan, with my *ta'leeq*. It contains a mention of many beneficial points related to this *hadeeth*.

[405] Its *takhreej* has already preceded.

[406] Its *takhreej* has already preceded within the previous *hadeeth*.

It is very often that the souls become mingled with discrete lusts that corrupt the souls from actualising love of Allaah, *'uboodiyyah* to Him and having sincerity of *Deen* to him alone. This is as stated by Shaddaad Ibn Aws: *"Yaa Na'aayaa al-'Arab,*[407] the greatest fear I have over you is concerning *ar-Riyaa'* and discrete desires."[408]

Aboo Daawood as-Sijistaanee[409] was questioned: "What are discrete desires?" He replied: "Love for leadership."

Ka'b Ibn Maalik relates that the Prophet (ﷺ) said: *"Two hungry wolves set loose in a sheep pen are not more damaging to them than a persons craving after wealth and status is to his Deen."*[410] at-Tirmidhee declared: "A *hadeeth* that is *hasan saheeh*."[411]

He (ﷺ) explained that the corruptive effect of striving after wealth and status has on the *Deen*, is not less than the damage two hungry wolves do within the confines of a sheep pen.

---

[407] A phrase signifying that the Arabs are destroyed or on the verge of destruction. Refer to Ibn al-Atheer's *an-Nihaayah fee Ghareeb al-Hadeeth*, lexical entry (نعى). [t]

[408] The attribution of this statement to the Prophet (ﷺ) has been ascertained. It is related by al-Bayhaqee in *az-Zuhd*, pg.319; Bahshal in *Taareekh Waasit*, pg. 220; Ibn 'Adee in *al-Kaamil*, 4/1529 and Aboo Na'eem in both *al-Hilyah*, 7/122 and *Akhbaar Asbahaan*, 2/66 by way of 'Abdullaah Ibn Budayl from az-Zuhree from 'Abbaad Ibn Tameem from his paternal uncle from the Prophet (ﷺ). There is some slight discussion on (the dependability of) Ibn Budayl, but there is another narration that supports him. It is related by ash-Shajaree in *al-Amaalee*, 2/220 by way of 'Ubaydullaah Ibn 'Umar from az-Zuhree, then from the same chain as the previous one. 'Ubaydullah is *thiqah*. The *sanad* is therefore, *saheeh*, Allaah willing.

[409] He is the Imaam al-Haafidh Sulaymaan Ibn al-Ash'ath, the author of *as-Sunan* (i.e., *Sunan Abee Daawood*). He passed away in the year 278H, may Allaah have mercy upon him. His biography is in *as-Siyar*, 13/203.

[410] Related by Ahmad, (3/356 & 460); at-Tirmidhee, 2482; an-Nasaa'ee in *al-Kubraa* as mentioned in *Tuhfah al-Ashraaf*, 8/316; Ibn Hibbaan in his *as-Saheeh*, 2472; Ibn al-Mubaarak in *az-Zuhd* (181 – additions of Nu'aym); ad-Daarimee, 2733 and at-Tabaraanee in *al-Kabeer*, 19/88/189. [**Publisher's Note**: For a detailed explanation of this *hadeeth* refer to *The Evil of Craving for Wealth and Status* by Haafidh Ibn Rajab al-Hanbalee (al-Hidaayah Publishing and Distribution, 1995, U.K.)].

[411] It is as he said.

This is very evident, as the *Deen* that is sound and proper, does not contain such a striving. This is because when the heart tastes the sweetness of its *'uboodiyyah* of Allaah and love of Him, nothing besides this is more beloved to the heart whereby it would give it a greater precedence. As a result, Allaah turns away evil and lewd sins from the people, who have sincerity towards Allaah, as Allaah (ﷻ) has said:

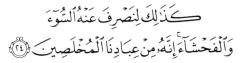

"Thus it was, that We might turn away from him evil and the lewd sin (i.e., illicit relationship). Surely, he was one of Our chosen, guided *'ibaad*."[412]

The one who is sincere to Allaah has tasted such a sweetness of his *'uboodiyyah* of Allaah that prevents him from any *'uboodiyyah* towards anyone else. He tastes such a sweetness of love of Allaah that prevents him from loving other than Him (directly and independently). The heart that is sound and proper, finds nothing more sweeter, pleasurable, agreeable, gratifying and blissful than the sweetness of *eemaan*, which embodies *'uboodiyyah* of Allaah, love of Him and sincerity of *Deen* to him alone.

This necessitates the hearts attraction towards Allaah. The heart then becomes repentant and turns back to Allaah, it becomes fearful of Him, desiring (Allaah and what He has in store for it) and in apprehension (of Him and His chastisement), as Allaah (ﷻ) said:

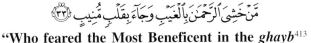

"Who feared the Most Beneficent in the *ghayb*[413]

---

[412] Soorah Yoosuf (12):24.

[413] i.e., that which is beyond man's senses. The meaning would therefore refer to one who worshipped Allaah in this worldly life before seeing and meeting Him. Another interpretation is when the word *ghayb* is not attached to 'the Most beneficent' but instead to 'feared'. It would therefore mean whoever feared Allaah when in the state of *ghayb*, i.e., not in the presence or view of the people, for example when one worships Allaah in seclusion in his own home during the night. [t]

and brought a heart turned in repentance (to Him)."[414]

The one who has love, fears the cessation of what he pursues [or the occurrence of what he desires].[415] He cannot be therefore an *'abd* of Allaah or one who loves Him unless he is between (the states of) fear and hope, as Allaah (ﷻ) has said:

أُوْلَـٰٓئِكَ ٱلَّذِينَ يَدْعُونَ يَبْتَغُونَ إِلَىٰ رَبِّهِمُ ٱلْوَسِيلَةَ أَيُّهُمْ أَقْرَبُ وَيَرْجُونَ رَحْمَتَهُۥ وَيَخَافُونَ عَذَابَهُۥٓ إِنَّ عَذَابَ رَبِّكَ كَانَ مَحْذُورًا ٥٧

"Those whom they call upon (i.e., such as 'Eesaa, 'Uzayr, the Angels, etc.) desire (for themselves) a means of access to their Lord, as to which of them should be the nearest and they (i.e., 'Eesaa, 'Uzayr, the Angels, etc.) hope for His Mercy and fear His Torment. Verily, the Torment of your Lord is something to be afraid of!"[416]

If the *'abd* is sincere to Allaah, His Lord will select him. Allaah will give life to his heart and draw him close to Himself. He will turn away from him the evil and lewd sins that oppose this (state) and the *'abd* will be fearful of the occurrence of anything contrary to this (state). This is in contrast to the heart that is not sincere to Allaah. Such a heart contains a pursuit, desire and love that is unrestricted. This heart takes to anything that presents itself and it clings to whatever it desires, like a twig; any gentle breeze that experiences, causes it to bend and incline. On occasions, unlawful *suwar* or lawful ones attract it and thus, he remains a captive and an *'abd* of something,

---

[414] Soorah Qaaf (50):33.

[415] In the text of Shaykh 'Abdul'Azeez's commentary, pg. 139, it reads 'or the occurrence of what he *fears*'. It is evident that this is the correct meaning. It seems probable that what is established above from Shaykh 'Alee's version is a printing error as only a change of one single letter (a ع to a م) transforms it from *desires* to *fears*. [t]

[416] Soorah al-Israa' (17):57.

who if instead, this object were to him as an *'abd*, it would be regarded as something shameful, deficient and blameworthy.

On other occasions, status and leadership attract him. Certain words please him and other words anger him. One who praises him enslaves him, even if he praises him with something that is false. He has enmity towards one who censures him, even if such a reproach was a legitimate one.

At other times, he is enslaved by the *Dirham* and the *Deenar* and other similar things that enslave the hearts, which the hearts desire and cause one to take his desires as his deity and to follow them void of any guidance from Allaah.

Whoever is not sincere to Allaah, an *'abd* of Him and whoever's heart has not become enslaved by his Lord, alone without any partner, whereby Allaah is more beloved to him than anything or anyone else and that he is subservient and obedient to Him, will be otherwise enslaved by (created) entities. The *Shayaateen* will take hold of his heart and he will be of the errant, the brothers of the *Shayaateen*. He will retain such a degree of evil and lewd sins that only Allaah can enumerate. This is a necessary fact, of which there is no other possibility.

If the heart is not straight, approaching Allaah and turning away from anything besides Him, it will be one that commits *shirk*:

فَأَقِمْ وَجْهَكَ لِلدِّينِ حَنِيفًا فِطْرَتَ ٱللَّهِ ٱلَّتِي فَطَرَ ٱلنَّاسَ عَلَيْهَا لَا تَبْدِيلَ لِخَلْقِ ٱللَّهِ ذَٰلِكَ ٱلدِّينُ ٱلْقَيِّمُ وَلَٰكِنَّ أَكْثَرَ ٱلنَّاسِ لَا يَعْلَمُونَ ۝ مُنِيبِينَ إِلَيْهِ وَٱتَّقُوهُ وَأَقِيمُوا ٱلصَّلَوٰةَ وَلَا تَكُونُوا مِنَ ٱلْمُشْرِكِينَ ۝ مِنَ ٱلَّذِينَ فَرَّقُوا دِينَهُمْ وَكَانُوا شِيَعًا كُلُّ حِزْبٍ بِمَا لَدَيْهِمْ فَرِحُونَ ۝

"So set you (O Muhammad (ﷺ)) your face towards the *Deen*, soundly (i.e., worship none but Allaah Alone): Allaah's *Fitrah* (i.e., Allaah's Islaamic Monotheism), with which He has created mankind. No change let there be in the creation of Allaah (i.e., the Religion of Allaah Islaamic Monotheism), that is the straight religion, but most of mankind do not know.

(Always) Turning in repentance to Him (only), and be afraid and dutiful to Him; and establish Prayer and be not of the *Mushrikoon*; of those who split up their religion (i.e., who left the true Islaamic Mono-theism) and became sects (i.e., they invented new things in the religion and followed their vain de-sires], each sect rejoicing in that which is with it."[417]

Allaah made Ibraaheem and his family the leaders of these upright and sincere people, those who love Allaah, worship Him, and make their *Deen* sincere for Him, just as He made Fir'awn and his clan leaders of the *Mushrikoon*, who follow their desires. Allaah (تعالى) says concerning Ibraaheem:

وَوَهَبْنَا لَهُۥٓ إِسْحَٰقَ وَيَعْقُوبَ نَافِلَةً وَكُلًّا جَعَلْنَا صَٰلِحِينَ ۝ وَجَعَلْنَٰهُمْ أَئِمَّةً يَهْدُونَ بِأَمْرِنَا وَأَوْحَيْنَآ إِلَيْهِمْ فِعْلَ الْخَيْرَٰتِ وَإِقَامَ الصَّلَوٰةِ وَإِيتَآءَ الزَّكَوٰةِ ۖ وَكَانُوا۟ لَنَا عَٰبِدِينَ ۝

"And We bestowed upon him Ishaaq, and (a grand-son) Ya'qoob as a favour (after having become of old age and his wife became barren). Each one We made righteous. And We made them leaders, guid-ing (mankind) by Our Command, and We inspired in them the enactment of good deeds, establishment of Prayer and the giving of *Zakaat* and of Us (Alone) they were worshippers."[418]

---

[417] Soorah ar-Room (30):30-32.
[418] Soorah al-Anbiyaa' (21):72-73.

He says about Fir'awn and his people:

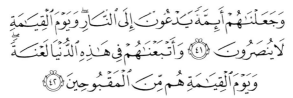

"And We made them leaders inviting to the Fire, and on the Day of Resurrection, they will not be helped. And We made a curse to follow them in this world, and on the Day of Resurrection, they will be among the *Maqbuhoon* (those who are prevented to receive Allaah's Mercy or any good, despised or destroyed, etc.)."[419]

On account of this, the followers of Fir'awn, initially do not distinguish between what Allaah loves and is pleased with and between what He has decreed and ordained. Instead, they only take observation of the general comprehensive will and then ultimately, they do not distinguish between the Creator and the creation. Rather, they declare the presence of the former to be the very presence of the latter.

Their most prominent people of *tahqeeq* declare: "The *Sharee'ah* contains obedience and disobedience. [The *haqeeqah* contains disobedience without any obedience][420] and the *tahqeeq* contains no obedience or disobedience."![421]

---

[419] Soorah al-Qasas (28):41-42.

[420] In the text of Shaykh ar-Raajihee's commentary, pg. 143, this excerpt reads in the opposite, 'The *haqeeqah* contains **obedience** without any **disobedience**'. This meaning seems to be correct in contrast to what is above because of the explanation given to it by Shaykh 'Abdul'Azeez ar-Raajihee as can be read in the next footnote. [t]

[421] This is the categorisation of people as done by the *Soofiyyah*. They categorise people into three ranks. The rank of *Sharee'ah*, which contains obedience and disobedience. Who is the *Sharee'ah* for? They say that it is for the common folk. They categorise the people into the common folk, the elite, and the cream of the elite. The common folk are the people of the *Sharee'ah*, who commit acts of obedience and disobedience. All the Prophets and ⸗

167

This (in reality) is the *tahqeeq* of the path of Fir'awn and his people, who renounced the Creator and denied that Allaah spoke to Moosa as well as the Command and Prohibition he was sent with.

= Messengers are amongst the common folk in their view... as for the elite, there is no such thing as disobedient acts; everything they do is obedience. If they commit fornication or adultery, steal or consume intoxicant beverages, this is all regarded to be obedience... because they do not affirm attributes and actions for themselves and they attribute it all to Allaah. Thus everything that emanates from one of these people (from this second rank: the people of *haqeeqah*) is regarded to be obedience, whether it be something truthful or false, even *Kufr* – may Allaah protect us from this. The third rank is that of the cream of the elite, where there is no disobedience or obedience, because they have arrived at the doctrine of the unity of existence (*wahdah al-wujood*). The existence is one, which is the Lord and the *'abd*...**This is the most extreme form of Kufr**. [s]

The Difference Between the Creator and the Creation

As for Ibraaheem and the followers of Ibraaheem, the pure and upright from the Prophets and those who believer in them, they know that a differentiation between the Creator and creation and a differentiation between obedience and disobedience is something essential. They also know that the more an *'abd* actualises this difference, the greater will be his love for Allaah, his *'uboodiyyah* to Him, his obedience of Him and his aversion to worshipping, loving and obeying others besides Him.

These astray *mushrikoon* equate Allaah with His creation, whereas the *khaleel* (i.e., Ibraaheem) says:[422]

قَالَ أَفَرَءَيْتُم مَّا كُنتُمْ تَعْبُدُونَ ۞ أَنتُمْ
وَءَابَآؤُكُمُ ٱلْأَقْدَمُونَ ۞ فَإِنَّهُمْ عَدُوٌّ لِّيٓ إِلَّا رَبَّ ٱلْعَٰلَمِينَ

"Do you observe that which you have been worshipping, you and your ancient fathers? Verily! They are enemies to me, save the Lord of the worlds."

Further, they adhere to words of the *shaykhs* that are *mutashaabih* just as the Christians did.

An example of this is the term *al-Fanaa'* (الفناء); *al-Fanaa'* is of three types:

1. A type pertaining to the perfect and complete, from the Prophets and the *awliyaa'*.
2. A type pertaining to the average people from the *awliyaa* and the righteous people.
3. A type pertaining to the hypocrites, the *mulhidoon,* those who liken (Allaah to His creation).

---

[422] As Allaah relates from him, Soorah ash-Shu'araa' (26):75-77.

169

The first type is *fanaa'* from intending other than Allaah, in that one loves none but Allaah; worships none but Allaah; has *tawakkul* only on Allaah and seeks from none other than Allaah. This is the interpretation that has to be provided for the statement of Shaykh Aboo Yazeed,[423] in which he says: "I want to only want what He wants." i.e., the desire that is beloved and pleasing, which is the desire for the religious will.

The perfection of the *'abd* is that he does not desire, love and become pleased with anything but what Allaah wants, is pleased with and loves, and that is in reference to what Allaah has commanded, either in an obligatory or recommended way. He should also only love those that Allaah loves, such as the Angels, the Prophets and the righteous people. This is the meaning of their statement regarding His saying:

"...except him who brings to Allaah a clean heart."[424]

They explain: "He is the one who is clean and free from other than the worship of Allaah or from that which is besides the will of Allaah or that which is besides the love of Allaah." The meaning is one.

This understanding, **whether it is labelled *al-Fanaa'* or not,**[425] is the beginning and end of Islaam, the inner and outer (form of) Islaam.

As for the second type, it is *fanaa'* from witnessing other than Allaah.

---

[423] He is al-Bistaamee, he passed away in the year 261H. Ad-Dhahabee provided a biography of him in many of his books, such as *Meezan al-I'tidaal*, 2/346.

[424] Soorah ash-Shu'araa (26):89.

[425] The significant matter therefore is the actual thing that is named and the reality, not the name or superficial exterior. However, terms that connote some form of opposition (to Islaamic teachings) or have obscurity about them, are to avoided.

This occurs to many of the travellers. As a result of the immoderation of the attraction of their hearts to the remembrance of Allaah, his worship and love and because of the failing of their hearts to witness other than what they worship or see anything besides what they pursue, none but Allaah appear to their hearts. In fact, they are not aware of anything besides Him, as it is said concerning the statement of Allaah (ﷻ):

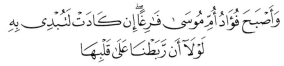

"And the heart of the mother of Moosa became void. She came very near to disclose his case (i.e., that the child is her son) had We not strengthened her heart..."[426]

They say that her heart became void of every thing except the thought of Moosa.

This occurs very often to one whom becomes overtaken by a matter, either pertaining to love, fear or hope. One's heart remains averse to everything besides what it has now loved, feared or is seeking, to the extent that such an ingrossment in this causes him not to be aware of anything else.

If the person of such *fanaa'* strengthens in this regard, he separates from his own existence because of the existence he has found, he separates from his own observation to what he is now observing, he separates from his own remembrance to what he now has remembrance of and he separates from his own awareness to what he is now aware of. This is to the level whereby all things that were not (always in existence) vanish - and this refers to all of creation: the *'abd* himself and all else - and only He who has never ceased to be, remains - and that is the Lord. The meaning here, is the *fanaa'* (ob-

---

[426] Soorah al-Qasas (28):10.

livion) of creation as far as the observation and remembrance of the *'abd* is concerned[427] and his own *fanaa'* whereby he is unable to comprehend and witness the creation.

If this strengthens, the lover weakens until his ability to distinguish goes into disarray. He may actually believe himself to be his very beloved! Such a thing is mentioned about a person who fell into the open sea. His lover then plunged himself after him. At that, the beloved said: "I fell in, but what caused you to fall in after me?" He (i.e., the lover) replied: "I separated from my (own existence) because of you and thus thought that you were me!"

Many people have erred in this regard and they presumed this to be a union and that the lover merges with the beloved, whereby there ceases to be a difference between their existence. **This is a gross mistake as nothing merges with the Creator, not at all**. In fact, no two things can merge and unite unless they transform and the essence of each spoils, resulting in a third existence because of the union of the two entities. The first is not the second and nor is the second the first. This is similar to when water merges with milk or when water merges with an intoxicating liquid and so on.

However, what can merge are their desire for what is beloved and their desire for what is disliked. Both agree on the type of like and dislike. One loves what the other loves; he hates what the other hates; is pleased with what the other is pleased with; scorns at what the other scorns at; hates what the other hates; offers *walaa'* to whom the other offers *walaa'* to and holds enmity towards those whom the other holds enmity towards.

Anyhow, this type of *fanaa'* is completely defective.

---

[427] The *fanaa'* of the *Soofiyyah* in this second type is one where all of creation is still in existence but the person has arrived at such a state where he is unable to bear witness or observe that! The third type of *fanaa'*, which will be explained shortly, is when all of existence actually does go into oblivion! May Allaah protect us from such deceptions of *Shaytaan*[t]

The senior *awliyaa'*, such as Aboo Bakr, 'Umar and the vanguard (of Islaam), the first of the *Muhaajiroon* and the *Ansaar*, did not enter into such a *fanaa'*, let alone the Prophets who are superior to them. **Such a thing occurred only after (the era of) the Companions**.

This is the same for everything that is of this manner that involves the absence of the intellect, the inability to distinguish the conditions of *eemaan* that appear on the heart. The Companions, may Allaah be pleased with them, were too complete, strong and established in their states of *eemaan* for their intellects to be absent or to experience trances, shock, intoxication, *fanaa'*, confusion (because of extreme love) or dementia.[428]

The fundamental basics of these matters appeared in the (era of) the *Taabi'oon*, from some worshippers at Basra. There was amongst them, those that would fall unconscious when listening to the Qur'aan and others would even die, such as Aboo Juhayr ad-Dareer[429] and Zuraarah Ibn Awfaa,[430] the magistrate of Basra.

The *shaykhs* of *Soofiyyah* likewise underwent experiences of *fanaa'* and intoxication, which would weaken their ability to distinguish until one of them would say under such conditions words that he knows he is mistaken in as soon as he regains consciousness. Such

---

[428] This is the path of the complete people amongst the worshippers of Allaah. The Prophets and the Messengers are at the foremost, then the Companions, then the *Taabi'oon* and the *Imaams* and the scholars. None of them underwent such witnessing, which the *Soofiyyah* maintain. Instead, their state of mind was sound and they possessed only love of Allaah and His desire. They differentiated between the Creator and creation. They witness that the Creator is a creator and arranger and they witness that creation are created and subject to His order… [s]

[429] I have not been able to come across his biography so his name as appears above may have been subject to some distortion.

[430] His biography is in *Hilyah al-Awliyaa'*, 2/258 and this account is mentioned within it. Refer to my work *al-Muntaqaa an-Nafees*…, pg. 329-335.

matters are related on Aboo Yazeed, Aboo al-Hasan an-Nooree,[431] Aboo Bakr ash-Shiblee and their likes. This was in contrast to the likes of Aboo Sulaymaan ad-Daaraanee, Ma'roof al-Karkhiyy and al-Fudayl Ibn al-'Iyyaad, in fact, even al-Junayd and his likes. The intellect and ability to distinguish were present with such people during their conditions and they would not undergo experiences of *fanaa'*, intoxication and others similar to them.[432]

Indeed, the hearts of those who are complete do not contain anything but the love of Allaah, His will and worship of Him. Alongside that, they possess abundant knowledge and perception, which allows them to observe matters as they truly are. They observe the creation being in existence by the command of Allaah and managed by His will, indeed, even answering and submitting to Him.

Within the creation is an insight and reminder[433] for them. What they witness of that supports and extends the sincerity of *Deen*, *tawheed* of Him alone and the worship of Him alone without any partner, which is in their hearts.

---

[431] He is Ahmad Ibn Muhammad, passed away in the year 295H. His biography is in *as-Siyar*, 14/70.

[432] In this context, Shaykhul-Islaam differentiates between two groups of the *Soofiyyah* with regards to experiencing or not experiencing such acts of *fanaa'*. A number of scholars have mentioned that the *Soofiyyah* in this regard and other matters are of varying degrees. As an example, refer to Aboo al-Faraj Ibn al-Jawzee's *Talbees Iblees*, chapter ten, on his discussion on the deceptions of Iblees on the *Soofiyyah*. [t]

[433] The following *aayaat* shows us how Allaah wants His slaves to observe creation, take heed from it and strengthen one's *eemaan* and action. Allaah says in Soorah Qaaf (50):6-11, **"Have they not looked at the heaven above them, how We have made it and adorned it, and there are no rifts in it? And the earth! We have spread it out, and set thereon mountains standing firm, and have produced therein every kind of lovely growth (plants). An insight and a Reminder for every slave turning to Allaah (i.e. the one who believes in Allaah and performs deeds of His obedience, and always begs His pardon). And we send down blessed water (rain) from the sky, then We produce therewith gardens and grain (every kind of harvests) that are reaped. And tall date palms, with ranged clusters; A provision for (Allaah's) slaves. And We give life therewith to a dead land. Thus will be the resurrection (of the dead)."** [t]

This is the reality that the Qur'aan invites to and which is upheld by the people who actualise *eemaan* and the complete from those who possess knowledge. Our Prophet (ﷺ) is the leader and most perfect of these people. As such, when he was taken up and ascended to the heavens and he saw with his own eyes the diverse *aayaat* that were there and all types of heavenly matters were revealed to him. The following morning, he was amongst them (i.e., the people) and his condition had not changed, nor did any effect of that experience manifest itself upon him in contrast to the haziness Moosa used to undergo, may Allaah extol and send peace upon them all.

As for the third type, which may be termed *fanaa'*:

It is to observe and witness that none exists but Allaah and that the presence of the Creator is the very presence of the creation. There being no difference between the Lord and the *'abd*.

This is the *fanaa'* of the people of deviation and *ilhaad*, those who commit *hulool* and *ittihaad*. This is a matter that the *shaykhs*[434] absolve themselves from, when one of them says, 'I do not see other than Allaah' or 'I do not look to other than Allaah' and such similar statements. Their intention behind this is, 'I do not see a lord besides Him, or a creator besides Him, or an arranger besides Him, or a deity for myself besides Him and I do not look at any besides Him with regards to love, fear or hope in Him', since the eye looks at what the heart is attached to.

Whoever loves, has hope or fears something, turns to it. If there is no love in the heart for that thing or hope, fear or hatred for it or any other matter which causes the heart to become attached to something,[435] the heart will therefore, not seek it in order to turn towards it and look at it. If it does look at it, incidentally, it will be similar to if he was to look at a wall or its like, which holds no attachment whatsoever in one's heart.

---

[434] In another transcript of this work it reads: "the *shaykhs* who are upright…"

175

The *shaykhs* who are righteous, may Allaah be pleased with them, discuss a certain amount on the purification of *tawheed* and actualising sincerity of the *Deen* in its entirety whereby the *'abd* does not turn to other than Allaah and he does not look to other than Allaah, not with love, fear or hope. Rather, the *'abd*'s heart is to be void and empty of all creation, not looking at it except with the light of Allaah. Thus, with al-Haqq he hears, with al-Haqq he sees, with al-Haqq he strikes and with al-Haqq he walks. He loves of the creation that which Allaah loves; hates of the creation that which Allaah hates; has *walaa'* for those of the creation to whom Allaah has afforded *walaa'* and holds animosity towards those of the creation whom Allaah has enmity for. He fears Allaah with regards His creation[436] and does not fear them for Allaah. He has hope in Allaah with regards His creation and does not have hope in creation for Allaah.

This is the heart that is clean and sound, that is *haneef* (upright), a professor of *tawheed*, a Muslim, a *Mu'min*, which is discerning and has knowledge of the knowledge of the Prophets and the Messengers and is aware of their reality and their *tawheed*.

As for this third category, which is a *fanaa'* of existence, this is the actualisation of the people of Fir'awn, and their knowledge and their *tawheed*; such as the Quraamitah[437] and their like.

---

[435] Whether it is an inclination for that thing or an aversion towards it. [t]

[436] i.e., in how he interacts and relates to them.

[437] They are a sect of the *Baatiniyyah* (heretical sects outside the fold of Islaam). They are affiliated to Hamdaan Ibn al-Ash'ath, who used to be known as Qurmut. "They used to adopt the method of (falsely) explaining away all the information and commands (found within the *Sharee'ah*) as it contradicted their intellect. These people are of those who have the greatest *kufr* and *ilhaad* within them." As said by the author in *Dar' Ta'aarud al-'Aql wa an-Naql*, 1/176. Refer to *al-Farq bayna al-Firaq*, pg. 281-291, *Maqaalaat al-Islaamiyyeen*, 1/98 and *al-Muntatham*, 5/110-119.

As for the type that the followers of the Prophets are upon it is the *fanaa'*[438] that is praiseworthy, whereby its maintainer is of those whom Allaah has praised from amongst His *awliyaa'*, the *muttaqoon*, His party, which are the successful; and His army, which are the victorious.

It is not the intention of the *shaykhs* or the righteous folk behind this statement that what I see with my eyes of the creation, that is the Lord of the earth and heavens. Since, such a thing is not uttered except by one who is extremely deviated and corrupt; either his intellect is corrupt or his belief is corrupt, so he wavers between insanity and *ilhaad*.[439]

All of the *shaykhs* who are emulated in the *Deen* are agreed upon that which the *salaf* of this *ummah* and its *imaams* are agreed upon, that the Creator (ﷻ) is separate from His creation; that nothing of His essence is within any of His creation; that nothing from his creation is within His essence; that it is an obligation to separate al-Qadeem[440] from everything novel (i.e., created) and to distinguish the Creator from creation. An account of their affirmation of this is too voluminous for us to relate it here.

---

[438] The labelling of it as *fanaa'* is done so from the context of comparing it to the other types. [s] As such, in general, one does not employ such terms because of their ambiguous nature. The position of the *Ahl as-Sunnah* is to not employ terms that are ambiguous, which may connote false meanings – as is the case with the word *fanaa'* - but to adhere to the terminology of the *Sharee'ah* as it has its own sanctity. As for the conduct applied when someone else uses such ambiguous terms, he is questioned further as to what his intention is. If he intends a false meaning, it is rejected. It he intends a true meaning it is accepted of him but he is advised of the obligation to abandon such terms and instead express himself using the terminology found within the *Sharee'ah*. [t]

[439] i.e., if his intellect is not sound then he is insane and if his belief is not sound then he is a heretic.

[440] i.e., Allaah. *Al-Qadeem* is derived from something old or age-old. It is not one of the names of Allaah and thus it is impermissible to employ it as if it is one of the names of Allaah. One should instead use a name of Allaah that has been established, which gives the same meaning: *al-Awwal* (the First). Shaykhul-Islaam here, is simply quoting the terminology of some of the *shaykhs* who have used this term, as his concentration here is to show that they did not uphold this heretical belief, which this third category alludes to. [t]

They also spoke about the diseases and misconceptions that befall the hearts. An instance of this, is that a person may witness the presence of creation and he then believes this presence to be the (very) creator of the earth and heavens because of a lack of differentiation and decisive criterion within his heart. He is equivalent to the one who sees the rays of the Sun and believes it to be the Sun itself, which is in the sky!

Further to this, they may even speak about *farq* (distinction) and *jam'* (unification). Such diverse terms enter into this discussion, which are similar to those that enter into the discussion on *fanaa'*.

If the *'abd* witnesses such division and multiplicity within the creation, his heart remains attached to them, dispelled and looking on at them.

This attachment he has for the creation, is either through love, fear or hope. If however, the *'abd* then turns to *jam'* (unification), his heart will unite on the *tawheed* of Allaah and worship of Him alone without any partner. Thus, his heart turns to Allaah after having turned to creation. Accordingly, his love turns towards his Lord, his fear becomes for Allaah, his hope now in Allaah and his seeking of assistance from Allaah. Whilst in this condition, his heart may not be able to accommodate looking at creation, whereby he is able to distinguish between the Creator and creation. As such, his heart may be gathered (totally) around al-Haqq and averse to the creation in both its knowledge and awareness and its intentions and deification. This is similar to the second category of *fanaa'*.

After this however, (comes) the second *farq* (distinction).[441] This is when the *'abd* witnesses that the creation is in existence by Allaah's

---

[441] The first distinction is to witness the difference between the Creator and creation with regard to *uloohiyyah* through love, fear, hope, etc. The second distinction is to witness the difference between the Creator and creation with regards to Lordship; to differentiate between the reality of the existence of the Creator and creation. [t]

command and subject to his arrangement and planning. He witnesses their multiplicity and that they were once non-existent (along) with the oneness of Allaah and that He is the Lord of all creation, their deity, creator and owner.

Thus, he becomes one who - along with the gathering of his heart around Allaah, with sincerity; love; fear; hope; recourse; *tawakkul* upon Allaah; having *walaa'* for Him; holding enmity for and so on - views the difference between the Creator and creation and differentiates between the former and the latter. He witnesses the diversity and multiplicity of the creation along with his witness and observation that Allaah is the Lord, King and Creator of everything and that He is Allaah, other than Whom none has the right to be worshipped.

This is a correct and upright attestation and it is an obligation as far as the knowledge, witness, mention and awareness of the heart is concerned. It is also an obligation with regards to the condition of the heart, its worship, desire, intention, love, *muwaalaah* and obedience.

This is the fulfilment of the witness and testification that none has the right to be worshipped but Allaah. Since, this testification negates from the heart an *uloohiyyah* for other than al-Haqq and it affirms in the heart the *uloohiyyah* for Allaah.

It negates *uloohiyyah* for all of creation and affirms the *uloohiyyah* for the Lord of the worlds, the Lord of the earth and heavens.

This comprises the gathering of the heart around Allaah and separating from all besides Him. Thus, the *'abd* differentiates between the Creator and creation in his knowledge, intent, witness, desire, his knowledge and love, whereby he is aware of Allaah, remembers Him and has knowledge of Him. Along with this, he is aware of Allaah's separation, isolation and singleness from His creation.

He remains loving Allaah, glorifying Him, worshipping Him, having hope in Him; being fearful of Him; having love and *walaa'* for Him; possessing animosity for Allaah's sake; seeking aid from Him and having *tawakkul* upon him. He refrains from worshipping other than Him, or to have *tawakkul*, seek aid, have fear, hope, *muwaalaah*, enmity or to obey other than Him, and other such matters, which are exclusive matters pertaining to the divinity of Allaah.

The *'abd*'s acknowledgement of the *Uloohiyyah* of Allaah exclusively, embodies his acknowledgement of Allaah's Lordship, which signifies that Allaah is the Lord, King, Owner, Creator and Disposer of every thing. Thereupon, he will be a *muwahhid*.

This is demonstrated by the fact that the best form of remembrance is (saying): الله إلا إله لا as related by at-Tirmidhee, Ibn Abee ad-Dunyaa and others from the Prophet (ﷺ) that he said: *"The best from of remembrance is:* الله إلا إله لا *'None has the right to be worshipped but Allaah' and the best supplication is:* الحمد لله *'All praise is for Allaah.'"*[442]

In *al-Muwatta'* and other sources, Talhah Ibn 'Ubaydillaah Ibn Kurayz relates that the Prophet (ﷺ) said: *"The best that I have said as well as the Prophets before me is:*

لا إله إلا الله وحده لا شريك له، له الملك وله الحمد، وهو على شيء قدير

'None has the right to be worshipped except Allaah, alone, without partner. To Him belong all praise and sovereignty and He is over all things omnipotent.'"[443]

---

[442] Related by at-Tirmidhee, 3383; an-Nasaaee in *'Amal al-Yawm wa al-Laylah*, 831; Ibn Maajah, 3800; al-Bayhaqee in *ad-Da'awaat*, 117; Ibn Abee ad-Dunyaa in *ash-Shukr*, pg. 37; al-Haakim, 1/498; al-Baghawee, 1269; Ibn Hibbaan, 846 and Ibn 'Abdil-Barr in *at-Tamheed*, 6/43 by way of Moosa Ibn Ibraaheem al-Ansaaree with a *sanad* that is *hasan*.

[443] Related by Maalik, 1/422/246 and al-Bayhaqee, 4/284 & 5/117 in *mursal* form. It was connected by at-Tabaraanee in his *Manaasik*…The *hadeeth* is *hasan*, Allaah willing. It has other chains, refer to *al-Futoohaat ar-Rabbaaniyyah*, 4/748; *Takhreej al-Ihyaa*, 1/253; *Ittihaaf as-Saadah al-Muttaqeen*, 4/373; *al-Bidaayah wa an-Nihaayah*, 5/174-176 and *as-Silsilah as-Saheehah*, 1503.

As for those who allege that this is the (form of) remembrance for the common folk and that the (form of) remembrance for the elite is the singular *ism*[444] and the (form of) remembrance for the cream of the elite is the implicit *ism*,[445] they are astray and erroneous. The utilisation of His saying:

قُلِ ٱللَّهُ ثُمَّ ذَرْهُمْ فِى خَوْضِهِمْ يَلْعَبُونَ ۝

"...Say, 'Allaah' then leave them to play in their vain discussions."[446]

by some of these people as evidence for this is one of their most evident blunders. The *ism* 'Allaah' (in this *aayah*) is mentioned within the context of the command to answer the question mentioned previously within the *aayah*. That (question) is:

قُلْ مَنْ أَنزَلَ ٱلْكِتَٰبَ ٱلَّذِى جَآءَ بِهِۦ مُوسَىٰ نُورًا وَهُدًى لِّلنَّاسِ تَجْعَلُونَهُۥ قَرَاطِيسَ تُبْدُونَهَا وَتُخْفُونَ كَثِيرًا وَعُلِّمْتُم مَّا لَمْ تَعْلَمُوٓا۟ أَنتُمْ وَلَآ ءَابَآؤُكُمْ قُلِ ٱللَّهُ

"Say (O Muhammad (ﷺ)), 'Who then sent down the Book which Moosa brought, a light and a guidance to mankind which you (i.e., the Jews) have made into (separate) paper-sheets, disclosing (some of it) and concealing (much)'. And you (i.e., believers in Allaah and His Messenger) were taught (through the Qur'aan) that which neither you nor your fathers knew. Say, 'Allaah'..."

---

[444] *Ism* (الاسم): one of the three parts of speech in the Arabic language. It is more general than the term *noun* in English grammar and as such I have left it transliterated so as not to cause confusion. English grammar categorises speech into eight parts. The categories *proper noun* and *pronoun* (and others) in English grammar, belong to the category of *ism* in Arabic grammar. The 'singular *ism*' referred to here is the word 'Allaah' by itself. [t]

[445] The 'implicit *ism*' referred to here is the pronoun (هو) 'He'.

[446] Soorah al-An'aam (6):91.

181

i.e., Allaah is the one who sent down the Book which Moosa brought. Thus, the *ism* 'Allaah' is the subject and its predicate is indicated by the question. This is synonymous to other expressions: one questions, 'Who is his neighbour?' and he is answered, 'Zayd'.[447]

As for the singular *ism*,[448] whether it is manifested[449] or implicit,[450] it is not a complete statement nor is it a sentence that provides benefit (to its sayer, listener, reader, etc.). It is not connected to *eemaan* or *kufr* nor command and prohibition.

This has not been maintained by a single one of the *Salaf* of this *ummah* and the Messenger of Allaah has not legislated such a thing. This (type of remembrance) does not by itself afford the heart any beneficial knowledge or useful condition. It instead imparts to the heart an absolute notion, which cannot be negated or affirmed.

If it does not by itself provide benefit with regards to knowledge and state of the heart it will be of no value. The *Sharee'ah* on the other hand, legislates words of remembrance that give benefit in themselves and it does not legislate words of remembrance whereby the benefit is attained with other than it.

Some of those who constantly practised this (form of) remembrance committed all sorts of *ilhaad* and *ittihaad*, as has been mentioned in detail in another place (i.e., in a different work).

---

[447] i.e., Zayd is his neighbour. The predicate 'is his neighbour' is not mentioned but indicated by the original question. As for why it is not mentioned, then that is because it is not necessary to do so, to avoid repetition and for purposes of brevity. This is a matter that is found in all languages. [t]

[448] In the book *al-Minhah al-Muhammadiyyah fee Bayaan al-'Aqaa'id as-Salafiyyah,* pg. 230, by ash-Shuqayree, is a chapter titled, *'Making remembrance with a singular ism is an innovation'*, so refer to it. Also refer to my book *al-Muntaqaa an-Nafees min Talbees Iblees,* pg. 431.

[449] As in the case of the proper noun 'Allaah'. [t]

[450] As in the case of the pronoun 'He'. [t]

As for what is related from some of these *shaykhs*, that they say: "I fear lest I die in between negation and affirmation," **one does not emulate the position of the person who maintains this**. This position contains such visible error, since if a person was to die in this state, he would only die upon that which he intended as actions are deemed by their intentions.[451]

Further, it has been established on the Prophet (ﷺ) that he ordered one to instruct the dying person to say: "لا إله إلا الله."[452] He also said: "*He whose last words are:* لا إله إلا الله *will enter Paradise.*"[453]

If what he mentioned was (truly) unsafe, the dying person would not have been instructed to utter such an expression, in which he fears of dying during its mention in a reprehensible way. Instead, he would be instructed to utter the singular *ism*, which he favours.

Engaging in remembrance with the implicit *ism* is even further away from the *Sunnah*, even more within (the realm of) innovations and nearer to the deviation of *Shaytaan*. One who says, '*Huwa Yaa Hu*' (He, O He) or '*Hu Hu*' (He, He) and utterances similar to that, the

---

[451] When it was said to one of the *shaykhs* of the *Soofiyyah*: "Why do you not say, لا إله إلا الله?" He replied: "I fear that if is say (لا إله) 'There is no deity', I might then die and I would have not yet arrived at (إلا الله) 'except Allaah'. I fear lest I die in between negation and affirmation and therefore become a *mushrik*, so I limit myself to (الله الله الله) 'Allaah, Allaah, Allaah'." Ibn Taymiyyah refutes them by saying that even if we assume that a person does die in that state, the decisive factor is his intention; if he is a *muwahhid*, it will do him no harm because he died without his own doing whilst being a *muwahhid* and actions are but by intentions. Hence, this is purely a false interpretation and untrue danger claimed by some of these *shaykhs*. [s]

[452] Related by Muslim in his *Saheeh*, 917.

[453] Related by Aboo Daawood, 3116; al-Haakim, 1/351; Ahmad, 5/233 & 247; at-Tabaraanee in *al-Kabeer*, 20/112/221 and in *ad-Du'aa*, 1471; al-Bayhaqee in *al-Asmaa wa as-Sifaat*, 99; al-Fasawee in his *at-Taareekh*, 2/312 and Ibn Mandah in *at-Tawheed*, no. 187 from Mu'aadh with a *sanad* that is *hasan*. A number of Companions have related this or similar *hadeeths*. There is a tremendous tale concerning this *hadeeth* and the instruction of the *shahaadah* to Aboo Zur'ah on his death-bed. Refer to *Taqdimah al-Jarh*, pg. 345 and *Fadl at-Tahleel*, pg. 81.

pronoun refers back to only that which the heart depicts and the heart may come upon guidance and it may deviate. The author of *al-Fuṣoos*[454] wrote a book, which he named *Kitaab al-Hu*.[455]

Some of them claim that His saying:

وَمَا يَعْـلَمُ تَأْوِيلَهُۥٓ إِلَّا ٱللَّهُ

"...but none knows its true interpretation except Allaah[456]**..."**[457]

means 'none knows the true interpretation of this *ism*, which is *al-Hu*.

This is something which the Muslims or rather the sane, agree to be of the most obvious falseness. Some of these people may truly believe this, until I once said to one who maintained something like this: "If it was as you said, the *aayah* would have been written ومـا يعلم تأويل هو, the words being separate from each other.[458]

A number of the *shaykhs* quite frequently contend that the saying of a person, 'Allaah' is based on His saying:

قُلِ ٱللَّهُ ثُمَّ ذَرْهُمْ فِى خَوْضِهِمْ يَلْعَبُونَ ﴿٩١﴾

"...Say, 'Allaah' then leave them to play in their vain discussions."

---

[454] He is Ibn 'Arabee –without the prefix (al)- referred to earlier on page 41. Ibn al-'Arabee – with the prefix (al)- is the well known Maalikee scholar. [t]

[455] Al-Ḥallaaj also did this, as mentioned in *as-Siyar*, 14/353.

[456] This is how the *aayah* reads, however, these deviant folk claim that the pronoun ه attached to the end of the word تأويل - which happens to be in the accusative case and translates 'its' as above - is intended in itself and it therefore reads – in their perverted view - 'None knows the true interpretation of *Hu* except Allaah'!!! [t]

[457] Soorah Aal-'Imraan (3):7.

[458] i.e., the pronoun would have to be in the nominative case and therefore unattached for it to give the meaning that their desires would like! [t]

They believe that Allaah commanded his Prophet to say the singular *ism* (as a form of remembrance). This is incorrect by agreement of the people of knowledge. His saying:

$$\text{قُلِ ٱللَّهُ}$$

"...Say, 'Allaah'..."

Its meaning is: Allaah is the one who sent down the Book which Moosa brought. This is a reply to His saying:

$$\text{قُلۡ مَنۡ أَنزَلَ ٱلۡكِتَٰبَ ٱلَّذِى جَآءَ بِهِۦ مُوسَىٰ نُورࣰا وَهُدࣰى لِّلنَّاسِۖ}$$
$$\text{تَجۡعَلُونَهُۥ قَرَاطِيسَ تُبۡدُونَهَا وَتُخۡفُونَ كَثِيرࣰاۖ وَعُلِّمۡتُم مَّا لَمۡ تَعۡلَمُوٓاۡ}$$
$$\text{أَنتُمۡ وَلَآ ءَابَآؤُكُمۡۖ قُلِ ٱللَّهُ}$$

Say (O Muḥammad (ﷺ)), 'Who then sent down the Book which Moosa brought, a light and a guidance to mankind which you (i.e., the Jews) have made into (separate) paper-sheets, disclosing (some of it) and concealing (much)'. And you (i.e., believers in Allaah and His Messenger) were taught (through the Qur'aan) that which neither you nor your fathers knew. Say, 'Allaah'..."

i.e., Allaah is the one who sent down the Book which Moosa brought. This is in refutation of the one who said:

$$\text{مَآ أَنزَلَ ٱللَّهُ عَلَىٰ بَشَرࣲ مِّن شَىۡءࣲ}$$

"...Nothing did Allaah send down to any human being (by inspiration)..."[459]

Thus, Allaah replied (with a question):

$$\text{مَنۡ أَنزَلَ ٱلۡكِتَٰبَ ٱلَّذِى جَآءَ بِهِۦ مُوسَىٰ}$$

"...Who then sent down the Book which Moosa brought..."

---

[459] Within the same *aayah*, no. 91, Soorah al-An'aam (6). [t]

Thereafter, Allaah replied:

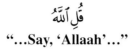

"…Say, 'Allaah'…"

i.e., (Allaah) revealed it, then leave these deniers to play in their vain discussions.

Another matter which clarifies what has already preceded is what Seebawayh[460] and other scholars of the Arabic grammar and language have said. They mention that the Arabs utter sentences after the word 'Say'[461] and that they do not utter after it what is not a sentence. Thus, only complete sentences are uttered after 'Say'; either a nominal sentence or a verbal sentence. This is why they place a *kasrah* on the word إِن if it comes after 'Say' (or any of its derivatives).[462] Hence an *ism* is not uttered (and intended by itself) after 'Say'. Allaah (ﷻ) does not order anyone to make remembrance (of Him) with a singular *ism* and nor has it been legislated for the Muslims.

Further, the singular *ism* provides no benefit whatsoever as far as *eemaan* is concerned by agreement of the people of knowledge. It is not commanded in any act of worship or any form of conversation.

A parallel of one who limits himself to a singular *ism* is what is mentioned about a Bedouin who passed by a person giving the *adhaan* for prayer. He recited: أشهد أن محمداً رسولَ الله in the accusative case.[463] The Bedouin remarked: "What is this person saying?

---

[460] One of the greatest scholars of the Arabic language. [t]

[461] or any of its derivatives, like: saying, said, etc. [t]

[462] Which is indicative of a complete beneficial statement. [t]

[463] i.e., instead of pronouncing the word (رسول) with a *dammah* at the end of it – which will rightfully make it into the nominative case and therefore turn into the predicate here - he pronounced it with a *fathah* –which has turned into an adjective of the word (محمداً). Hence, it now reads, 'I bear witness that Muhammad, the Messenger of Allaah.' instead of 'I bear witness that Muhammad *is* the Messenger of Allaah." [t]

This is (now turned into) an *ism* (as opposed to being a complete beneficial statement), so where is it's predicate, which will complete the statement?"

As for the *aayaat* that are in the Qur'aan, such as His saying:

وَٱذۡكُرِ ٱسۡمَ رَبِّكَ وَتَبَتَّلۡ إِلَيۡهِ تَبۡتِيلًا ٨

"And remember the Name of your Lord and devote yourself to Him with a complete devotion."[464]

His saying:

سَبِّحِ ٱسۡمَ رَبِّكَ ٱلۡأَعۡلَى ١

"Glorify the Name of your Lord, the Most High."[465]

His saying:

قَدۡ أَفۡلَحَ مَن تَزَكَّىٰ ١٤ وَذَكَرَ ٱسۡمَ رَبِّهِۦ فَصَلَّىٰ ١٥

"Indeed he shall achieve success: whosoever purifies himself (by avoiding *shirk* and accepting Islaamic Monotheism), remembers the Name of his Lord and prays."[466]

His saying:

فَسَبِّحۡ بِٱسۡمِ رَبِّكَ ٱلۡعَظِيمِ ٧٤

"Then glorify with praises the Name of your Lord, the Supreme."[467]

Along with other similar *aayaat*; these do not necessitate to remember Him in a singular fashion. In fact, it is recorded in the *Sunan*,[468] that when His saying:

---

[464] Soorah al-Muzammil (73):8.

[465] Soorah al-A'laa (87):1.

[466] Soorah al-A'laa (87) :14-15.

[467] Soorah al-Waaqi'ah (56):74.

[468] Related by Aboo Daawood, 869; Ibn Maajah, 887; Ahmad, 4/155; at- Tahaawee, 1/138; al-Haakim, 1/225 & 2/477; al-Bayhaqee, 2/86; at-Tayaalisee, 1000; Ibn Hibbaan, 1898; ad-Daarimee, 1/299; al-Fasawee in his *at-Taareekh*, /502; at-Tabaraanee, 17/889 and =

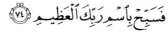

"Then glorify with praises the Name of your Lord, the Supreme."

was revealed, the Prophet (ﷺ) said: *"Place that in your rukoo' (bowing)"* and when His saying:

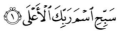

"So glorify the Name of your Lord, the Most High."

was revealed, he said: *"Place that in your sujood (prostration)."*

Hence, it was legislated for them to say in their *rukoo'*: سبحان ربي العظيم 'How perfect my Lord is, The Supreme' and in *sujood*: سبحان ربي الأعلى 'How Perfect my Lord is, The Most High'.

Moreover, it is recorded in the *Saheeh*[469] that he used to say in his *rukoo'*: سبحان ربي العظيم and in his *sujood*: سبحان ربي الأعلى."

This is the meaning of 'place that in your *rukoo'* and *sujood*' by consensus of the Muslims.

Therefore, 'glorifying the name of His Lord, the Most High' and 'remembering the name of His Lord' and other such expressions signify complete beneficial statements, just as in the *Saheeh*,[470] he said: *"The best discourse after the Qur'aan is four – and they are from the Qur'aan:*

= Ibn Khuzaymah, 600 & 670 from 'Uqbah Ibn 'Aamir. It contains a narrator whose condition is not known – Eeyaas Ibn 'Aamir, adh-Dhahabee said: "He is not known." None but a single narrator has related from him and he was declared *thiqah* by Ibn Hibbaan and al-'Ijlee! Al-Haafidh declared: "*Sadooq*." His (usual) methodology in such circumstances would make him say either: "*Maqbool*" or "*Majhool*".

[469] *Saheeh Muslim*, 772 from Hudhayfah.

[470] It is in *Saheeh Muslim*, 2137 in similar wording. al-Bukhaaree related it in *mu'allaq* form in his *Saheeh*, 11/566. It is also related by Ahmad, 5/10 &21; an-Nasaa'ee in *'Amal al-Yawm wa al-Laylah*, 845; al-Baghawee, 1276; at-Tabaraanee, 6791; Ibn Hibbaan, 835; at-Tayaalisee, 899 and Ibn Maajah, 3811 from Samrah Ibn Jundub. None of the quoted sources contain the phrase: *"and they are from the Qur'aan."*

سبحان الله، والحمد لله، ولا إله إلا الله، والله أكبر

'How perfect Allaah is, and all praise is for Allaah. None has the right to be worshipped except Allaah, and Allaah is the greatest.'"

Also in the _Saheeh_,[471] it is related that he (ﷺ) said: "(There are) two words, which are light on the tongue, heavy on the Scale and beloved to the Most Gracious:

سبحان الله وبحمده سبحان الله العظيم

'How perfect Allaah is and I praise Him. How perfect Allaah is, The Supreme.'"

It is related on the Prophet (ﷺ) in the _Saheehayn_, that he said: "Whoever says a hundred times during his day:

لا إله إلا الله وحده لا شريك له، له الملك وله الحمد، وهو على شيء قدير

'None has the right to be worshipped except Allaah, alone, without partner. To Him belong all sovereignty and praise and He is over all things omnipotent.' Allaah decrees for him protection from Shaytaan during that day until evening and none shall come with anything better except someone who has done the same or more."

Whoever says a hundred times during his day:

سبحان الله وبحمده سبحان الله العظيم

'How perfect Allaah is and I praise Him. How perfect Allaah is, The Supreme' his sins are diminished even if they were equivalent to the foam of the sea."

It is recorded in al-_Muwatta_ and other sources that the Prophet (ﷺ) said: "The best that I have said as well as the Prophets before me is:

---

[471] Related by al-Bukhaaree, 6406, 6682 & 7563; Muslim, 2694; at-Tirmidhee, 3468; Ibn Maajah, 3806; Ibn Abee Shaybah, 10/288; Ahmad, 2/232; Ibn Hibbaan, 831 & 841; an-Nasaa'ee in 'Amal al-Yawm wa al-Laylah, 830 and al-Bayhaqee in al-Asmaa wa as-Sifaat, 499 from Aboo Hurayrah.

لا إله إلا الله وحده لا شريك له، له الملك وله الحمد، وهو على شيء قدير

'None has the right to be worshipped except Allaah, alone, without partner. To Him belong all praise and sovereignty and He is over all things omnipotent.'"[472]

In *Sunan Ibn Maajah* and other sources, it is related that he (ﷺ) said: *"The best form of remembrance is:* لا إله إلا الله *'None has the right to be worshipped but Allaah' and the best supplication is:* الحمد لله *'All praise is for Allaah.'"*[473]

Such *hadeeths* on the diversity of what one says for remembrance and supplication are numerous.

Again, as for the *aayaat* in the Qur'aan, such as His (ﷻ) saying:

وَلَا تَأْكُلُوا مِمَّا لَمْ يُذْكَرِ اسْمُ اللَّهِ عَلَيْهِ

"Do not (O believers) eat of that (meat) which Allaah's Name has not been pronounced..."[474]

His (ﷻ) saying:

فَكُلُوا مِمَّا أَمْسَكْنَ عَلَيْكُمْ وَاذْكُرُوا اسْمَ اللَّهِ عَلَيْهِ

"...so eat of what they catch for you, but pronounce the Name of Allaah over it..."[475]

The meaning here is the expression, بِسْمِ اللَّه 'In the name of Allaah' and it is a complete statement;[476] either a nominal sentence[477] according to the most probable of the two opinions of the grammar-

---

[472] Its *takhreej* has already preceded.

[473] Its *takhreej* has already preceded.

[474] Soorah al-An'aam (6):121.

[475] Soorah al-Maa'idah (5):5.

[476] i.e., a complete statement is one that affords benefit to the listener. Not all parts of the statement have to be articulated as long as there exists surrounding factors that complete the parts that have not been articulated, such as a preceding discussion – like a question, as already shown - or the actual circumstances one is in. [t]

[477] A sentence that begins with an *ism*. [t]

190

ians or a verbal sentence.[478] The *taqdeer*[479] would be (concerning the previously quoted aayaat), 'My sacrifice is in the name of Allaah' or 'I am sacrificing by the name of Allaah'.

On similar terms is the saying of the reciter (of the Qur'aan): بِسْمِ اللَّهِ الرَّحْمَنِ الرَّحِيمِ 'In the name of Allaah, the Most Gracious, the Most Merciful'. Its *taqdeer* is, 'My recitation is by the name of Allaah' or 'I am reciting by the name of Allaah'.

In such a situation, some people have in their hearts (i.e., estimate it to be): My starting in the name of Allaah' or 'I am starting in the name of Allaah'. However, the first is better because the whole action is then undertaken in the name of Allaah and not just the beginning of the action. Allaah manifests the (usually) hidden part in His saying:

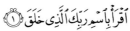

"Read, in the Name of your Lord, Who has created (all that exists)."[480]

This is also the case in His saying:

بِسْمِ اللَّهِ مَجْرَىٰهَا وَمُرْسَىٰهَا

"...in the Name of Allaah will be its moving course and its resting anchorage."[481]

Also, the Prophet (ﷺ) said: *"Whoever sacrificed before the prayer, should sacrifice another in its place and whoever has not yet sacrificed, should sacrifice in the name of Allaah."*[482]

---

[478] A sentence that begins with a *fi'l* (verb). [t]

[479] The estimation of this missing syntactical part. [t]

[480] Soorah al-'Alaq (96):1.

[481] Soorah Hood (11):41.

[482] Related by al-Bukhaaree, 10/17; Muslim, 1960; an-Nasaa'ee, 7/224; Ibn Maajah, 3152; al-Bayhaqee, 9/276; at-Tayaalisee, 936 and Ahmad, 4/312 & 313 from Jundub.

Another example of this, is the statement of the Prophet (ﷺ) - as in the *saheeh hadeeth* - to his step-son 'Umar Ibn Abee Salamah: *"O boy, mention the name of Allaah, eat with your right hand and eat from that which is near you."*[483]

The desired intention is that he should say, 'In the name of Allaah'[484] and the meaning is not that he should say the *ism* by itself (i.e., say 'Allaah' only).

Likewise, his statement - as in the *saheeh hadeeth* - to 'Adee Ibn Haatim: *"If you despatch your trained dog and mention the name of Allaah, then eat (your catch)."*[485]

Also, his (ﷺ) saying: *"If a person enters his house and mentions the name of Allaah whilst entering, leaving and eating, Shaytaan (to his other devils) says, 'There is no place to sleep tonight or dinner for you (here).'"*[486]

Examples of this sort are numerous.

---

[483] Related by al-Bukhaaree, 5376; Muslim, 2022; an-Nasaa'ee in *al-Kubraa* as mentioned in *at-Tuhfah*, 8/130; Ibn Maajah, 3267; ad-Daarimee, 2/100; al-Bayhaqee, 7/277; Ahmad, 4/26 & 27; Ibn as-Sunnee, 356 and at-Tirmidhee, 918 from 'Umar Ibn Abee Salamah from the Prophet (ﷺ).

[484] At-Tabaraanee relates the *hadeeth* in *al-Kabeer*, 8304, with the wording: *"O boy, if you eat, then say, 'In the name of Allaah'."* Its *sanad* is *saheeh* upon the stipulations of the two *shaykhs* (i.e., al-Bukhaaree and Muslim). Our shaykh says in *al-Irwaa'*, 7/31: "Thus, this contains an explanation of the absolute statement in the other narrations and that as regards the pronunciation to be made over food, the *Sunnah* is to say concisely, 'In the name of Allaah'. Remember this for it is important with those who value the *Sunnah* and do not see the permissibility to increase upon it."

[485] Related by al-Bukhaaree, 9/609; Muslim, 1929; Aboo Daawood, 2848; Ibn Maajah, 3208; Ahmad, 4/258; al-Bayhaqee, 9/ 236 & 237; an-Nasaa'ee, 7/83; at- Tayaalisee, 1030 and Ibn Maajah, 3213 from a number of ways from ash-Sha'bee from Jaabir.

[486] Related by Muslim, 2018; Aboo Daawood, 3765; Ibn Maajah, 3887; Ahmad, 3/436; al-Bukhaaree in *Adab al-Mufrad*, 1096 and al-Bayhaqee, 7/276 from Jaabir.

Moreover, the forms of remembrance of Allaah that has been legislated for the Muslims in their prayer, *adhaan*, *hajj* and *'eids* are all complete sentences, like the saying of the one who calls to prayer: 'Allaah is the greatest, Allaah is the greatest, I bear witness that none has the right to be worshipped except Allaah, I bear witness that Muhammad is the Messenger of Allaah.'

The statements of the praying person, 'Allaah is the greatest; How perfect my Lord is, the Supreme; How perfect my Lord is, the Most High; May Allaah answer those who praise Him; O our Lord, and for You is all praise; *at-Tahiyyaat*[487] is for Allaah'.

The statement of the one making *talbiyah*, 'Here I am O Allaah, (in response to Your call), here I am' and other examples.

Thus, concerning all that Allaah has legislated as being words of remembrance, they are complete statements, not a singular *ism* whether it be manifest or implicit.

This is what is termed in the language as '*Kalimah*',[488] like his saying: *"(There are) two words (kalimahs), which are light on the tongue, heavy on the Scale and beloved to The Most Gracious:*

سبحان الله وبحمده سبحان الله العظيم

'How perfect Allaah is and I praise Him. How perfect Allaah is, The Supreme.'"[489]

---

[487] i.e., all words which indicate the glorification of Allaah, His eternal existence, His perfection and His sovereignty. [t]

[488] Translated as 'word', but not meaning a single term – in Arabic - as the discussion is showing. [t]

[489] The *takhreej* for this *hadeeth* has already preceded.

Also, his saying: *"The best kalimah that a poet has ever said is the kalimah of Labeed,[490] 'Verily, everything besides Allaah is false.'"[491]*

A further example of this is His (ﷻ) saying:

كَبُرَتْ كَلِمَةً تَخْرُجُ مِنْ أَفْوَٰهِهِمْ

"...Mighty is the *kalimah* (word) that comes out of their mouths (i.e., that He begot sons and daughters)..."[492]

Also, His (ﷻ) saying:

وَتَمَّتْ كَلِمَتُ رَبِّكَ صِدْقًا وَعَدْلًا

"And the *kalimah* (Word) of your Lord has been fulfilled in truth and in justice..."[493]

There are many other examples in the Book, the *Sunnah* and discourse of the Arabs where the term *'kalimah'* is employed. In such instances, the desired meaning is none other than complete sentences. This is similar to their use of the term *'harf'* to mean *'ism'*; the Arabs would say, 'This *harf* is strange' i.e., the word of this *ism* is strange.

Seebawayh categorised speech[494] into: *ism, fi'l* (verb) and a *harf* that had a specific denotation (i.e., a particle), not being an *ism* or *fi'l*. In fact, all of these categories are termed *harf* but the specification of the third category, was that it was a *harf* that had a specific denotation, which was not an *ism* or *fi'l*.

---

[490] Adh-Dhahabee says in *Tajreed Asmaa as-Sahaabah*, 2/38: "Labeed Ibn Rabee'ah Ibn 'Aamir al-'Aamiree and then al-Ja'faree, Aboo 'Aqeel, the famous poet. He came as a part of the delegation of Banee Ja'far Ibn Kilaab and accepted Islaam and became a good Muslim. He never read poetry after embracing Islaam. He died in the year of the *Jamaa'ah* (i.e., 40H) in Koofah at the age of 150."

[491] Related by al-Bukhaaree, 3841; Muslim, 2256; at-Tirmidhee in his *Sunan*, 2853 and in *ash-Shamaa'il*, (207 – abridged version); Ibn Maajah, 3757 and Ahmad, 2/248, 391 & 442 from Aboo Hurayrah.

[492] Soorah al-Kahf (18):5.

[493] Soorah al-An'aam (6):115.

[494] As in his book *al-Kitaab*.

Each one of the letters of the alphabet was also titled by the name of that particular _harf_ (i.e., letter).[495] The term _harf_ covers these names as well as others, just as the Prophet (ﷺ): "_Whoever recites the Quraan, articulates it correctly, has for every harf, ten merits. I am not saying that that alif, laam, meem are one harf (letter) but rather alif is a (harf) letter, laam is a harf (letter) and meem is a harf (letter)._"[496]

Al-Khaleel Ibn Aḥmad[497] once asked his colleagues about the articulation of the _harf_ ز in the word زيد. They answered: "_Zaay_". He then said: "You have mentioned the name (of the _harf_), indeed the _harf_ itself is _Za_."

The grammarians later adopted the convention that what is referred to as _harf_ - in the language - be termed _kalimah_ and that the term _harf_ be specifically for that which has a specific denotation but is not an _ism_ or _fi'l_, like the _huroof_[498] _al-jarr_ (i.e., prepositions) and others like it.

As for the words of the alphabet, at times a letter is expressed by the very letter itself and at other times by the name of that letter.

When this convention prevailed, some of those who were accustomed to it thought that this is how it is in the language.

Some of them declared the term _kalimah_ in the language to be a term common to both an _ism_ for example, and to a sentence. However, in the pure language, the term _kalimah_ is not known to represent anything but a complete sentence.

---

[495] e.g., م is a _harf_ (letter) and it is named '_meem_', which is the name of the (_harf_) letter.

[496] The _hadeeth_ is _saheeh_ without the part 'articulates it correctly'. Refer to my commentary to _al-Waṣiyyah al-Kubraa_, pg. 58 by the same author, may Allaah have mercy upon him.

[497] Al-Faraaheedee, the founder of the science of prosody. He passed away in the year 170H. His biography is in _as-Siyar_, 7/429.

[498] Plural of _harf_. [t]

The intention here is (to show) that the remembrance of Allaah that has been legislated, is the remembrance via complete sentences and this is known as *kalaam*, the single of it being *kalimah*. This is what benefits the heart and causes it to gain reward and retribution. This is what attracts the heart to Allaah, knowledge of Him, love of Him, fear of Him and other such matters, which pertain to the lofty pursuits and sublime objectives.

As for limiting oneself to the singular *ism*, whether it is manifest or implicit, this has no basis, let alone for it to be the form of remembrance of the elite and knowledgeable!

Rather, it is a gateway to a diverse variety of innovations and deviations and it is a medium to corrupt and false perceptions and states of the people of *ilhaad* and *ittihaad*, as has been proficiently explained elsewhere.

The Epitome of the *Deen*

The epitome of the *Deen* is two fundamentals:

1. That we worship none but Allaah
2. That we do not worship Him except with what He has legislated: we do not worship Him through innovations.

Allaah (ﷻ) has said:

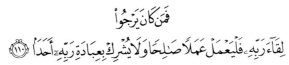

"So whoever hopes for the meeting with his Lord, let him do righteous deeds and associate none as partner in worship of his Lord."[499]

This is the actualisation of the *shahaadataan*: the declaration that none has the right to be worshipped except Allaah and the declaration that Muhammad is the Messenger of Allaah.

The first (declaration) denotes that we worship none but Him. The second (declaration) denotes that Muhammad is His Messenger, who conveys from Him and thus, it is upon us to believe the information he relates and to obey him.

He (i.e., the Prophet (ﷺ)) showed us what to worship Allaah with and prohibited us from (embarking upon) newly invented matters and explained that this was deviation.

Allaah (ﷻ) said:

بَلَىٰ مَنْ أَسْلَمَ وَجْهَهُۥ لِلَّهِ وَهُوَ مُحْسِنٌ
فَلَهُۥٓ أَجْرُهُۥ عِندَ رَبِّهِۦ وَلَا خَوْفٌ عَلَيْهِمْ وَلَا هُمْ يَحْزَنُونَ ﴿١١٢﴾

---

[499] Soorah al-Kahf (18):110.

"Yes, but whoever submits his face (himself) to Allaah and he is a *Muhsin* (i.e., doer of good) then his reward is with his Lord, on such shall be no fear, nor shall they grieve."[500]

Just as we are commanded to fear none but Allaah; have *tawakkul* on none but Him; to invoke none but Him; to seek assistance from Him alone and that our worship be for none but Allaah, likewise, we are also commanded to follow the Messenger, obey him and emulate him. The lawful is that which he made lawful, the unlawful is that which he made unlawful and the *Deen* is that which he legislated.[501]

Allaah (ﷻ) says:

$$وَلَوۡ أَنَّهُمۡ رَضُواْ مَآ ءَاتَىٰهُمُ ٱللَّهُ وَرَسُولُهُۥ وَقَالُواْ حَسۡبُنَا ٱللَّهُ سَيُؤۡتِينَا ٱللَّهُ مِن فَضۡلِهِۦ وَرَسُولُهُۥٓ إِنَّآ إِلَى ٱللَّهِ رَٰغِبُونَ ٥٩$$

"Would that they were contented with what Allaah and His Messenger gave them and had said, 'Allaah is Sufficient for us. Allaah will give us of His Bounty and (also) His Messenger (from alms, etc.). Indeed, it is Allaah we implore (to enrich us)'."[502]

Hence, Allaah made (the issue of) bestowal to (both) Allaah and the Messenger, just as He said (in another *aayah*):

$$وَمَآ ءَاتَىٰكُمُ ٱلرَّسُولُ فَخُذُوهُ وَمَا نَهَىٰكُمۡ عَنۡهُ فَٱنتَهُواْ$$

"...and whatsoever the Messenger gives you, take it, and whatsoever he forbids you from, abstain (from it)..."[503]

---

[500] Soorah al-Baqarah (2):112.

[501] Obviously, under the dictates of Allaah (ﷻ). [t]

[502] Soorah at-Tawbah (9):59.

[503] Soorah al-Hashr (59):7.

(In contrast), Allaah made (the issue of) *tawakkul* upon him Allaah alone, when He said:

$$\text{حَسۡبُنَا ٱللَّهُ}$$

"…Allaah is Sufficient for us…"

He did not say: "and His Messenger (is also sufficient)." Similarly, He said in description of the Companions, may Allaah be pleased with them, in another *aayah*:

$$\text{ٱلَّذِينَ قَالَ لَهُمُ ٱلنَّاسُ إِنَّ ٱلنَّاسَ قَدۡ جَمَعُواْ لَكُمۡ فَٱخۡشَوۡهُمۡ فَزَادَهُمۡ إِيمَٰنٗا وَقَالُواْ حَسۡبُنَا ٱللَّهُ وَنِعۡمَ ٱلۡوَكِيلُ ﴿١٧٣﴾}$$

"Those (i.e., believers) unto whom the people (i.e., the hypocrites) said, 'Verily, the people (i.e., the pagans) have gathered (a great army) against you, so fear them.' But this (only) increased them in *eemaan* and they (i.e., the believers) replied, 'Allaah (alone) is Sufficient for us, and He is the Best Disposer of affairs (for us).'"[504]

Similar to this is His saying:

$$\text{يَٰٓأَيُّهَا ٱلنَّبِيُّ حَسۡبُكَ ٱللَّهُ وَمَنِ ٱتَّبَعَكَ مِنَ ٱلۡمُؤۡمِنِينَ ﴿٦٤﴾}$$

"O Prophet! Your *Hasb* (i.e., one who suffices) as well as those who follow you of the believers, is Allaah."[505]

i.e., Allaah is the one who suffices you and the believers who follow you. Allaah says further:

$$\text{أَلَيۡسَ ٱللَّهُ بِكَافٍ عَبۡدَهُ}$$

"Is not Allaah sufficient for His 'abd?…"[506]

---

[504] Soorah Aal-'Imraan (3):173.
[505] Soorah al-Anfaal (8):64.
[506] Soorah az Zumar (39):36.

Allaah then said:[507]

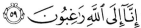

Allaah will give us of His Bounty and (also) His Messenger (from alms, etc.).

Thus, Allaah made the (issue of) bestowal for (both) Allaah and His Messenger. He first started with the mention that the Bounty is with Allaah. This is because bounty is in the hand of Allaah; He gives it to whom He chooses and Allaah is the possessor of great bounty. He has favour over the Messenger and the believers.

He (then) said (relating what the true believers should say):

إِنَّا إِلَى ٱللَّهِ رَٰغِبُونَ ۝

"...Indeed, it is Allaah we implore (to enrich us)."

Allaah made (the issue of) imploring, to Allaah alone, as in his (other) saying:

فَإِذَا فَرَغْتَ فَٱنصَبْ ۝ وَإِلَىٰ رَبِّكَ فَٱرْغَب ۝

"So when you have finished (from your occupation), stand up (for Allaah's worship, i.e., for prayer) and to your Lord (alone) turn your invocations."[508]

The Prophet (ﷺ) also said to Ibn 'Abbaas: *"If you ask, then ask Allaah and if you seek help, then seek help from Allaah."* [509]

The Qur'aan indicates to such a thing in many places.

Thus, Allaah made worship, reverence and *taqwaa* for Him (exclusively) and He made obedience and love for (both) Allaah and His Messenger, as in the saying of *Nooh*:

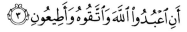

---

[507] i.e., continuing the discussion on the *aayah* 59, Soorah at-Tawbah (9). [t]

[508] Soorah al-Inshiraah (94):7-8.

[509] The *takhreej* for this *hadeeth* has already preceded.

"That you should worship Allaah (alone), have *taqwaa* of Him (alone) and obey me."[510]

Likewise, His saying:

وَمَن يُطِعِ ٱللَّهَ وَرَسُولَهُۥ وَيَخْشَ ٱللَّهَ وَيَتَّقْهِ فَأُوْلَٰٓئِكَ هُمُ ٱلْفَآئِزُونَ

"And whosoever obeys Allaah and His Messenger, fears Allaah, and has *taqwaa* of Him, such are the successful ones."[511]

There are other examples of this nature.

The Messengers were commanded with worship of Allaah alone; to implore Him; have *tawakkul* upon Him; be obedient to Him and to be obeyed. *Shaytaan* misguided the Christians and those similar to them; they committed *shirk* with Allah and disobeyed the Messenger. They took their priests, monks and 'Eesa Ibn Maryam as lords besides Allaah. They supplicated to them, had *tawakkul* upon them and would ask of them. At the same time, they disobeyed their (i.e., the Messengers) commands and opposed their example.

Allaah guided the believers, the sincere to Allaah, the people of the Straight Path, who knew the truth and followed it. They did not become of those who incurred the anger of Allaah nor the astray. They made their *Deen* sincerely for Allaah, submitted their faces to Allaah, turned in repentance to Him; loved Him; feared Him; sought from Him; implored Him; entrusted their affairs to Him and had *tawakkul* upon Him. They also obeyed His Messengers; exalted them; respected them; loved them; gave them *walaa'*; followed them; observed their legacy and took guidance by their landmarks.

This is the *Deen* of Islaam, with which Allaah sent the first and last of the Messengers. It is the only *Deen* that Allaah accepts from someone and it is the reality of worship of the Lord of the Worlds.

---

[510] Soorah Nooh (71):3.
[511] Soorah an-Noor (24):52.

We ask Allaah, the Majestic, to keep us firm upon it, to perfect it for us[512] and that He cause us and the rest of our Muslim brethren to die upon it.

All praise is for Allaah alone and may Allaah extol and send peace upon our leader, Muḥammad and his family.

---

[512] i.e., from the perspective of our adherence to it and obedience of Allaah with regards to it.

Glossary

'Aabid: Worshipper.

'Aarif: The one possessing knowledge. In *Soofiyyah* terminology: the one who knows Allaah and the true realities.

'Abd: Slave; worshipper.

'Eid: That which oft-returns; festivity, celebration, feast.

'Ibaad: Slaves; worshippers.

'Ibaadah: Worship. This term is discussed thoroughly within this essay.

'Irfaan: Esoteric knowledge

'Uboodiyyah: Slavery; servitude, worship.

Uloohiyyah: Divinity

Aayaat: Plural of *aayah.*

Aayah (pl. Aayaat): Sign; miracle; example, lesson… The *aayaat* of Allaah are of two types: (i) The *aayaat* that are heard, i.e., the verses of the Qur'aan. (ii) The *aayaat* that are observed/witnessed, i.e., Allaah's creation of the Sun, Moon, Stars, rivers, mountains, etc.

Ahl: Wife; relatives, family; People, members, followers, adherents, inhabitants.

Ahl al-Ma'rifah wa Ithbaat: People of *ma'rifah* (knowledge) and *ithbaat* (substantiation). Those who are endowed with the higher knowledge and verification amongst the *Soofiyyah.*

Ahl as-Sulook wa at-Tawajjuh: People of *sulook* (demeanor) and *tawajjuh* (orientation). Those who adopt a conduct and direct themselves towards a way pertaining to the *Soofiyyah.*

Ansaar: lit. helpers; the Muslims of Madeenah who supported and aided the Prophet (ﷺ) and Muslims who migrated from Makkah. Singular *'Ansaaree'.*

Adhaan: Call to prayer.

Awliyaa': See *walee.*

Bid'ah: Innovation. Any innovated practice introduced in the religion of Allaah.

Deen: Religion; the author discusses its meaning thoroughly within this essay.

Deenar: Dinar, a currency.

Dhaalim: One who commits *dhulm*: injustice, harm, wrongdoing or transgression either against Allaah, oneself or another creation.

Dirham: Pence; money; a currency

Du'aa: Supplication

Eemaan: Faith that also comprises a meaning of submission. It is in one's heart, upon one's tongue, acted out by one's limbs and it increases through obedience and decreases because of disobedience. The five points mentioned in the previous sentence describes the nature of *eemaan* and how it manifests itself, thus it is a definition of eemaan from the perspective of state and condition, as for the definition of the reality of *eemaan*, it is as the Messenger (ﷺ) answered Jibreel: to have eemaan in Allaah, His Angels, Books, Messengers, the Last Day and in *al-Qadar*, its good and bad.

Fanaa': Oblivion, absorption, annihilation, vanishing.

Fasaad: Corruption; decay, rottenness; invalidity.

Fiqh: Understanding, comprehension. Comprehension and application of the rulings and legislation of Islaam.

Fusooq: Plural of *fisq*. Immorality, transgression, wickedness, etc.

Ghayb: The 'Unseen'. Matters that are beyond our senses.

Hadeeth: A narration composed of the utterances of the Prophet (ﷺ), his actions, character, physical description or tacit approval.

Haqeeqah: Truth, reality; state of things as they are, etc.

Hijrah: migration; migration of the Prophet (ﷺ) and Companions from Madeenah to Makkah.

Hurooree: One who attributed to a place known as Hurooraa, which is a village on the outskirts of al-Koofah. This term refers to a follower of the *Khawaarij* (earliest sect in Islaam) as this was the village where they assembled after revolting against the Companions who subsequently fought them.

Ilaah: Deity.

Ilhaad: Deviation; Atheism; *Ilhaad* of Allaah's names and attributes is of many types.

Jabaree: An adherent of the doctrine of *al-Jabr* (Coercion)

Jabr: Compulsion, coercion; The belief that one has no personal will and is forced by Allaah to do the actions he does and as such, one cannot be held responsible for the crimes and sins he perpetrates.

Jahmiyyah: Adherents of Jahm Ibn Safwaan. This person is regarded to be one of the leaders of evils and deviations found within sects. The *jahmiyyah* have perverted beliefs about Allaah, His Names and Attributes, the Qur'aan, etc.

Janaazah: Funeral, funeral procession.

Jihaad: to strive; striving and fighting to make the word of Allaah supreme.

Jizyah: A tax imposed on non-Muslims who are under Muslim rule.

Kaafir: A rejecter of faith, disbeliever; One who covers up the truth and rejects Allaah, His Messengers and religion.

Kalaam: Speech, discourse; dialectics: scholastic theology.

Khameesah: A silk or woolen garment.

Khateeb: One who delivers a sermon, especially for Friday prayer.

Kufr: Disbelief.

Masaaneed: see *musnad*.

Mufsid: Spolier, corrupter, mischeif-maker.

Muhaajiroon: Plural of *Muhaajir*. One who performs *hijrah*. The Companions who migrated from Makkah to al-Madeenah.

Muhkam: Clear and definitive. An *aayah* of the Qur'aan that carries a conclusive and clear meaning.

Muhsin: (pl. Muhsinoon) One who does good; benevolent; who is in a state of *Ihsaan*.

Mukaashafah: In *Soofiyyah* terminology: a state of the heart that is beyond description in which one is exposed to matters that are beyond comprehension.

Mulhid: Doer of *Ilhaad*.

Murdaan: Naturally beardless males. Refer to *soorah*.

Mureed: One who wants, desires, aims for something; a devotee of a *Soofee shaykh*.

Murji: An individual who advocates *Irjaa'*: that *eemaan* does not consist of actions and as such, the believers (themselves, the Angels, the Prophets, etc) are of all the same degree in their *eemaan* and that sins do no harm one's *eemaan* as it does not increase or decrease.

Mushrik: One who commits *shirk*.

Musnad: (pl. *Masaaneed*) In the context of *hadeeth* literature it refers to a collection of *hadeeths* of the Prophet (ﷺ) that are arranged by the Companions who narrated the *hadeeths*, so all *hadeeths* narrated by a particular Companion are placed together and then the next Companion and so on.

Mutashaabih: Unclear and ambiguous. An *aayah* of the Qur'aan that is not clear and conclusive in meaning from the wording of the text itself.

Mu'tazilah: A deviant sect whose beliefs centre on five fundamentals: Negating Allaah's attributes, rejecting *al-Qadaa* and *al-Qadar*, the belief that one who commits a major sin is doomed to the Fire, that such a person in this world is not a believer or a disbeliever but in between the two and revolting against Muslim rulers.

Muwaalaah: Friendship; allegiance; loyalty. See *walaa'*.

Muwahhid: Professor of *tawheed*.

Qadaa: See *qadar*.

Qadar: *Al-Qadaa and Al-Qadar*: Allaah's decree of all matters in accordance with His prior knowledge and as dictated by His wisdom.

Qadaree: One who belongs to the *Qadariyyah*, who believe that Allaah has no knowledge of the actions of the slaves until they occur and that He has not universally decreed them.

Qateefah: A velvet garment.

Qiblah: Direction towards which all Muslims face when praying, i.e., toward the Ka'bah in Makkah.

Raafidah: One of the three main groupings of the *Shee'ah*. The *Raafidah* (or *Imaamiyyah*) split into sects such as the *Ithna 'Ashariyah* 'The twelvers'.

Ramadaan: The ninth month of the Islaamic calendar.

Riyaa': An act of worship undertaken by someone to be seen and praised by others and not purely for Allaah.

Ruqaa: Recitation used to cure an illness or a disease. There are permissible and impermissible types.

Saheeh: Healthy, sound; correct, authentic; A collection of authentic *hadeeths*; it is also used as has been done in this book to refer to *Saheeh al-Bukhaaree* or *Saheeh Muslim*.

Saheehayn: The 'two *Saheehs*' i.e., *Saheeh al-Bukhaaree* or *Saheeh Muslim*.

Salaf: Predecessors; more often employed to mean the Righteous Predecessors consisting of the Companions and the next two generations after them.

Shahaadah: Testimony, witness. The declaration that none has the right to be worshipped but Allaah and that Muhammad (ﷺ) is the Messenger of Allaah.

Sharee'ah: Divine Islaamic law as ordained by Allaah.

Shaykh: Old man; learned person, scholar.

Shaytaan: (plural Shayaateen) a devil; the devil, Iblees.

Shirk: A concise and precise definition is: to equate other than Allaah with Allaah in matters that are exclusive to Allaah .

Sihaah: Plural of *Saheeh*; *hadeeth* collections that contain only authentic *hadeeths*.

Sunan: Plural of *Sunnah*; A compilation of *Hadeeths*.

Sunnah: example or action of the Prophet (ﷺ); *hadeeth*; the other half of revelation i.e., the Qur'aan and *Sunnah*; in it's broadest sense it can mean the entire Religion.

Soofiyyah: Sufism.

Soorah: (plural: suwar) A chapter of the Noble Qur'aan.

Soorah: (plural: suwar) Image, form; face. The meaning here refers to attractive people. It is a perversion and love that certain people were -and are still- afflicted -especially during the era of Shaykhul-Islaam - with regards to women, youths and handsome beardless men! The attachment that developed in hearts of the lovers was an unhealthy and sick one which led to an *'Uboodiyyah* of the beloved. Some of the scholars relate a number of accounts of such people as well as the poetry they would chant about their beloved, which would contain great *shirk* and *kufr*.

Ta'leeq: As used within this book, commentary, slight commentary, marginal annotation.

Taabi': A follower; a student and follower of the companions in righteousness.

Tahqeeq: Actualization, fulfillment; inspection, examination; the correct position, the true state of the matter, etc.

Takhreej: Discussion on the sources, chains and grade of a particular *hadeeth*.

Takleef: Liability, obligation.

Taqwaa: Piety; to protect oneself from the punishment of Allaah by doing those things He has commanded and abstaining from those things He has prohibited.

Tawheed: To single out Allaah in areas exclusive to Him: Lordship, His names and attributes and worship.

Ummah: nation; the Muslim nation.

Walaa': Amity; allegiance; loyalty. *Walaa'* combines three principal matters: to assist, love and be in agreement.

Walee: (Pl. Awliyaa') One who offers or is offered *walaa'*. Allaah describes two main features of His *walee* in the Qur'aan as one who has *eemaan* and *taqwaa*.

Walaayah: In the context of this treatise, the state of *walaa'*.

Zakaah: One of the pillars of the religion; the tax levied on a Muslim's wealth that meets certain criteria.

Zindeeq: Heretic.